MW01164766

CELEBRATION WITH SURPRISES

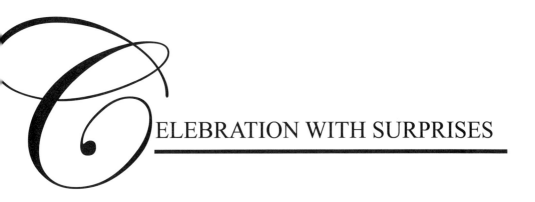

CELEBRATION WITH SURPRISES

Dominican Nuns Celebrate 800 Years

*Sr. Mary of the
Sacred Heart Sawicki, O.P.*

Outskirts Press, Inc.
Denver, Colorado

Scripture quotations marked (NIV®) are taken from the HOLY
BIBLE, NEW INTERNATIONAL VERSION ®. NIV®. Copyright
© 1973, 1978, 1984 by International Bible Society. Used by
permission. All rights reserved worldwide.

The "NIV" and "New International Version" are trademarks
registered in the United States Patent and Trademark Office by
International Bible Society®. Use of either trademark requires the
permission of International Bible Society®.

Scripture quotations marked (JB) are taken from the Jerusalem Bible.
Excerpt from The Jerusalem Bible, copyright © 1966 by Darton, Longman & Todd, Ltd. and Doubleday, a division
of Bantam Doubleday Dell Publishing Group, Inc. Reprinted by permission.

Scripture quotations marked (RSV) are taken from the *Revised Standard Version*.
The Scripture quotations contained herein are from the *Revised Standard Version Bible*, *Catholic Edition*, copyright
1965 and 1966 by the Division of Christian Education of the National Council of Churches of Christ in the USA.
Used by permission.

The opinions expressed in this manuscript are solely the opinions of the author and do not represent the opinions or
thoughts of the publisher. The author has represented and warranted full ownership and/or legal right to publish all
the materials in this book.

Celebration With Surprises
Dominican Nuns Celebrate 800 Years
All Rights Reserved.
Copyright © 2010 Sr. Mary of the Sacred Heart Sawicki, O.P.
v2.0 r1.0

Cover Photo © 2010 Sr. Mary of the Sacred Heart Sawicki, O.P..

This book may not be reproduced, transmitted, or stored in whole or in part by any means, including graphic,
electronic, or mechanical without the express written consent of the publisher except in the case of brief quotations
embodied in critical articles and reviews.

Outskirts Press, Inc.
http://www.outskirtspress.com

Paperback ISBN: 978-1-4327-4543-1
Hardback ISBN: 978-1-4327-5084-8

Library of Congress Control Number:2009942181

Outskirts Press and the "OP" logo are trademarks belonging to Outskirts Press, Inc.

PRINTED IN THE UNITED STATES OF AMERICA

This Book is dedicated to

Mary, the Mother of God and our Mother,

and

to my own mother,

Marie Theresa Lyons Sawicki

who fostered my love and devotion

for Our Lady

High on a hill overlooking the Connecticut River stands the Monastery of the Mother of God. Within the monastic walls, a community of cloistered Dominican Nuns lives out their quiet ministry of prayer, contemplation and good works.

Eight hundred years ago St. Dominic, a Spanish priest, established the Order of Friar Preachers. Through the centuries, Dominican priests and sisters have carried on the mission of their founding father. It was Dominic's intention that his spiritual sons and daughters would teach, preach and proclaim the gospel message by the word and witness of their lives.

We of Catholic and Christian heritage are inspired and enriched by Dominicans among us. Our faith is strengthened and increased by the fidelity and example of those who wear the shoes of their intelligent, humble and unpretentious Father in Christ. It is a privilege for me to acknowledge and congratulate Sister Mary of the Sacred Heart in her recollection of 800 eventful years.

Oh holy St. Dominic, you wanted nothing for yourself but only to be a friend and follower of Jesus, your Lord and Savior. May the memory of your good life encourage us, in the words of the Prophet Micah "to live justly, to love one another and to walk closely with our God."

The Most Reverend Joseph F. Maguire
Bishop Emeritus of Springfield

FRATRES ORDINIS PRÆDICATORUM
CURIA GENERALITIA

24 May 2009
Feast of the Translation of St. Dominic

Sister Mary of the Sacred Heart, O.P:
Monastery of the Mother of God
1430 Riverdale Street
West Springfield, MA 01089

Prot.n. 70/09/358 West Springfield - USA

Dear Sisters and Friends of the Dominican Nuns,

What a delight and joy it has been for me to read *Celebration with Surprises* by Sister Mary of the Sacred Heart! A few years ago I invited the Dominican Nuns to celebrate the 800th Anniversary of their foundation by St. Dominic. It was my intention that each Monastery both celebrate the grace of Dominican Monastic Life and renew their contemplative presence in such a way that it would be ever more fruitful for the Church and for the world. Even our Holy Father, Pope Benedict XVI, granted the extraordinary privilege of gaining a plenary indulgence to anyone who made a pilgrimage to a Dominican Monastery.

The Dominican Cloistered Nuns of the Monastery of the Mother of God in West Springfield, Massachusetts entered into this jubilee year in precisely this way. They shared the *fruits of their contemplation*, not by leaving their enclosure, but making their monastery a *light set on a lamp stand* inviting women, men, and children from all walks of life to offer thanks to God for the profound gift of this way of life for the Church. Policemen, firemen, and members of the armed services, doctors and nurses, the sick and the well, teachers and students, religious and lay, relatives and friends came month after month to pray the rosary, celebrate Benediction, enjoy a sacred concert and then join with the sisters for some moments of joyful and blessed recreation.

This book is the story of this experience and more. As one reads the creative monthly accounts, one comes to know some of the people involved and the manner in which they were touched by grace. Is this not the mystery of a monastery? Is this not an expression of the prayer of St. Dominic, day and night, for the Church and the world? One must answer with a resounding "yes". In addition to describing the celebrations, there is beautifully interwoven within the book an historical appreciation for the development of the Dominican nuns throughout their 800 year history. It is a story of particular monasteries, their growth, and inter-relationship one with another. It is a story of individuals called by God to live this expression of the charism of Dominic vibrantly as they have renewed their lives, founded new monasteries, formed the Association, improved the quality of formation, shared a unique moment of retreat, etc.

I wish to express my gratitude to all my Sisters of the Monastery of the Mother of God for taking the call for a jubilee celebration so seriously. I thank Sister Mary of the Sacred Heart for sharing this celebration with us. No doubt, in the course of the year, the nuns wondered what they had committed themselves to. However, as you now look back you must see how the Lord is never outdone in generosity and that the grace of contemplation is now even more vibrant among you precisely because of your apostolic outreach in calling the larger Church to prayer and adoration in your beautiful monastery.

Your brother in St. Dominic,

fr. Carlos A. Azpiroz Costa OP
Master of the Order

Contents

Introduction to *Surprises*
(A Surprise from the Master of the Order)

The community assembled, and our prioress, Sr. Mary of the Immaculate Conception, O.P., proceeded to inform us that she had a letter from Fr. Carlos Azpiroz Costa, O.P., the Master General of the Order of Preachers. Sister read that Fr. Carlos announced a Jubilee Year for the nuns in which to celebrate their 800th Anniversary of founding by St. Dominic! The jubilee celebration opened on December 3, 2006, the first Sunday of Advent, with nuns around the world ringing their bells for five minutes. Slated as a year long celebration, Fr. Carlos had obtained a special privilege from the Holy See, granting a plenary indulgence to those who piously visited one of the nuns' monasteries, during the Jubilee Year. This indulgence included the usual requirements for such an indulgence (sacramental confession, Eucharistic Communion and prayer for the intentions of the Holy Father). Each monastery of nuns celebrated the Jubilee in their own special way, choosing days and expressions for public celebrations. The Jubilee Year closed on the Feast of the Epiphany of the Lord, January 6, 2008.

The nuns of the Monastery of the Mother of God in West Springfield, MA decided upon a monthly prayerful celebration which invited the public to join in a Holy Hour, consisting of Vespers (Evening Liturgical Prayer), Benediction and the Rosary, with the added treat of a fifteen minute mini concert by the sisters. Special honored guests from all walks of life were invited to each celebration to lead the rosary, and after the celebration, encouraged to meet the nuns in their visiting area where each received a personal surprise gift.

The guests responded in an overwhelmingly positive manner. A good deal of planning went into the event, but many surprises came by unforeseen occurrences, such as the unexpected snowstorm the week after Easter with biting cold temperatures calling for hot chocolate relief!

God surprised us as well! These incidents combined proved to be beyond anything one could imagine, some too personal to mention — people coming back to the sacraments after 20, 40, or more years, a marriage saved, reconciliation between the estranged. These and other such stories are our joy to share within these pages.

This book would be incomplete without touching on the heritage of the nuns themselves: the unique circumstances which called them into being, the intrinsic character of their life, and the intensity with which they live out their vocations.

The format of the Holy Hour Celebration itself reflects the nuns' heritage. The rhythm of the monastic observance can be found in the **Liturgy of the Hours**; **Benediction** reminds us of the first American monastery of nuns founded in Newark, NJ, with the tradition of Eucharistic Adoration; the **Rosary** links to the first monastery of Perpetual Rosary Nuns, founded in Union City, NJ; and the **mini-concert** demonstrates the preaching the Word of God in song.

The US nuns produced a Jubilee Year calendar to demonstrate their **unity in diversity** among themselves. While the primary focus was the US monasteries, the calendar also included monasteries in other countries and exemplified the international scope of the nuns. We seek to some extent to do the same in this book.

This book would not have been possible without the encouragement and support of many friends. I am deeply grateful to Amy Gracey and Donna McCarthy for the many hours they spent editing my manuscript. Elizabeth Hanlon and Elizabeth Maloney provided me with valuable feedback on the manuscript; others who played a significant role by their support, encouragement and assistance include Patricia Broer, Helen D'Amour, Sr. Mary of the Sacred Heart Decuir, O.P. (Farmington Hills), Sr. Mary of the Sacred Heart Desmond, O.P. (Menlo Park),

Sr. Mary St. John Kinsella, O.P. (my prioress), Fr. Donald Lapointe, Sr. Mary Catharine, O.P. (Summit), Sr. Magdalen Ward, S.S.J. and Margaret "Peggy" Weber to whom I express my heartfelt gratitude. I would also like to thank Fr. Carlos and all the nuns for their interest and cooperation. Some of our honored guests have contributed to this story in various ways. All honored us with their presence. Many more who value our life of intercessory prayer were unable to attend. This jubilee year filled us with great joy and blessings, and so let me tarry no longer, but let the story of the surprises begin!

CHAPTER 1
A Shocking Surprise

Then you will know the truth, and the truth will set you free.
Jn. 8: 32 (NIV®)

In Fanjeaux, France in 1206, while Dominic prayed nine noble ladies came to him. They had heard him preach and were confused and struggled with the conflict between what they believed through the preaching of the Cathars and what Dominic preached. They saw Dominic was a holy man, but "The Perfect", the name given to the Cathar preachers, also seemed to live lives of holiness.

They told Dominic that if what he preached that day was true, then they were in error. Those whom the women called "good men", Dominic called heretics. With all their hearts they had adhered to the doctrine of the "good men," but Dominic's preaching left them uncertain. They asked Dominic to pray that God would make the true faith known to them.

After a few moments Dominic said, "Have patience and fear not. I believe that the Lord will show you what master you have served until the present," and invited them to pray with him. While praying, they saw a horrible and monstrous animal appear. It terrified them as it ran back and forth and from side to side. At the command of blessed Dominic, it disappeared into the belfry. Turning to the frightened women he said, "Behold, see the Master you have served!"[1]

The women were convinced and converted. They offered

themselves to Dominic as associates in his apostolate. Thus the seed of **new life** was planted, from which sprang forth the first nuns.

This Dominican life has continued for eight hundred years in which it has flourished, suffered persecutions, been forced into hiding, been suppressed in various countries, and still spread throughout the world. Its members strive for holiness of life, with a number of them beatified or canonized by the Church. Its counter cultural life challenges women to leave all and follow Christ in the way of Dominic. While the number of its members may be less in some countries, vocations are plentiful in others. While members are needed to carry on the life, the nuns first seek to hand on a quality of life that is fruitful in pursuing holiness and obtaining the salvation of souls.

(Endnotes)
1   *The Dominican Nuns in their Cloister,* trans. The Dominican Nuns of Corpus Christi Monastery (Philadelphia, PA: The Dolphin Press, 1936) 3-4.

CHAPTER 2

Surprising Graces

I have come that they may have life, and have it to the full.
Jn. 10: 10 (NIV®)

Surprises began from the very beginning, during the planning stages of
our first celebration. Telephone calls were made to invite individuals
to be among our honored guests, guests chosen to coincide with the
theme of "Life" for our December celebration. Dividing the theme
into four groups, each guest reflected an aspect of life. These groups
consisted of: the Sisters of Life; expectant parents and messengers of
Our Lady as patroness of the unborn; members of the military; and
law enforcement officers.

Sisters of Life

The words I have spoken to you are spirit and they are life.
Jn. 6:63 (NIV®)

Among the Sisters of Life, who joined us from New York were
Sr. Charlotte, S.V. and five of their postulants: Srs. Suzanne, Angela,
Bridget, Katie, and Mary. Sr. Angela has since become Sr. Maris
Stella. "Maris Stella" is a Latin term for one of Our Lady's titles: Star
of the Sea. The Sisters of Life are a contemplative / active religious
community of women. They were founded in 1991 by John Cardinal

O'Connor for the protection and enhancement of the sacredness of every human life.

**Knights
of Columbus**

Sisters of Life

**Sr. Angela
and her Dad**

**Sgt. Michael Cutone
Mass. State Police**

**Our Lady's Messengers
Mr. Bonfitto and Mr. Morrow**

**Lt. Steven Parentela
So. Hadley Police**

**Ofc. Michael Vezzola
W. Springfield Police**

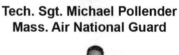

**Ofc. Robert Vogel, Jr.
W. Springfield Police**

**Tech. Sgt. Michael Pollender
Mass. Air National Guard**

**Andrea
and David
Broer**

**Petty Officer 1st Class
Sean C. Barry
US Coast Guard**

**Al, Jr. ("Bucky")
and Tammy
Sawicki**

New Life

Now choose life, so that you and your children may live.
Deut. 30: 19 (NIV®)

Another group was expectant parents. It certainly challenged us as cloistered nuns to know where to begin! I asked my brother, Al, if he knew of anyone we might invite for this group, but he was no help, at least not at that moment! A few days later he surprised me and asked if I had heard about his daughter-in–law, Tammy. It turned out that within those few days Al learned that Tammy and Bucky were expecting a baby! Tammy and Al, Jr. ("Bucky") came as honored guests to this opening celebration and on July 31ˢᵗ of the Jubilee Year, little Alexandra Marie was born!

My godson Christopher Broer and his wife Angela had lost 3 babies prematurely. Angela was pregnant again but, because they live in Idaho, were unable to make the long trip to join us. But Chris' brother Dave and his wife Andrea stood proxy for Chris and Angela. Chris and Angela were also blessed with the birth of a Jubilee baby and named him Benjamin!

CHRISTOPHER BROER:

We are very blessed to have Dave and Andrea as our brother and sister-in-law. They gave up going to a Patriots game in December, 2006 (and gave their tickets to others) so that they could serve as proxy for my wife Angela and me and my brother Steve and his wife Colleen at the monastery. Dave and Andrea also signed our names as well as Steve and Colleen on the prayer scroll at Our Lady's shrine. We know that it was through your prayers, theirs, and those of our many blessed friends and family that the birth of our baby Benjamin and another recent pregnancy was made possible. To show God's infinite generosity, He has also blessed Steve and Colleen with their child Aidan since that time, and I know He will greatly bless Dave and Andrea for their faith, perseverance, prayers for others, and their joyful disposition.

Mr. Robert Bonfitto and Mr. George Morrow joined the "Expectant Couples" group. They were listed as "Our Lady's Messengers" since Bob speaks on behalf of Our Lady of Guadalupe and George does a dramatization of Juan Diego. This was very fitting for our service because Our Lady of Guadalupe is patroness of the unborn as well as patroness of the Americas.

We were surprised when Mr. Bruce Smith offered to let us borrow his life-size framed picture of Our Lady of Guadalupe, which has traveled with "Right to Life" groups. Our Lady's image was placed within the sanctuary and we were pleased to have her join us.

Protecting the life of our country

The LORD will protect him and preserve his life; he will bless him in the land and not surrender him to the desire of his foes.
Ps. 41: 2 (NIV®)

Honored guests who protect the life of our country included members of the US Military. Bruce's son, SSgt Victor E. Smith, was among them. He represented the 103rd Fighter Wing, Connecticut Air National Guard, The Flying Yankees. CPT Madeline F. Yanford, a US Army JAG officer was home and being reassigned from South Korea. Other members of the military were recruited for the service through friends and through our guest Police Officers, who protect the life of the community. TSgt Michael Pollender and Petty Officer 1st Class Sean C. Barry were in this group.

Protecting the life of the Local Community

I will protect their lives. Jer. 49: 11 (NIV®)

I spoke with Regina Lourenco, a classmate of mine who is less than 5 feet tall and she asked if I would consider a State Trooper. She spoke highly of Tpr Michael Cutone, who frequently visited their religious goods store, Son Rises. Mike, who is over six feet tall, enjoys telling the story:

Tpr Michael Cutone:

I went to Son Rises and while there Regina told me that the Dominican Nuns were holding a once a month rosary for different vocations. In December they were doing it for the military and police. She was saying it in such a nice, sweet manner to entice me. And so Regina asked me: 'Well gee, Mike, would you know anyone who would be interested in going?' I responded, "What is it you want me to do, Regina? Tell me where, when, and I'll be there." She was very nice, sweet and kind. So how do you say "no" to Regina?! So I said, "Absolutely, I'd be more than happy to participate."

Mike stopped by the monastery to find out more details about the service. As a result, he recruited Tpr Sean C. Barry.

Lt. Steven Parentela of the South Hadley Police Dept., formerly a maintenance supervisor at the monastery, was among our honored guests. He recruited TSgt Michael Pollender, a South Hadley police officer, who represented the 104th Fighter Wing, Mass. Air National Guard. Our good friend Ofc. Robert Vogel, Jr. of the West Springfield Police Dept. suggested asking Ofc. Michael Vezzola.

We prayed for Mike Vezzola when he battled cancer. Because of his wonderful, hard-fought recovery backed by prayer, he was dubbed "The Miracle Man"! Mike was one of God's surprises at this celebration.

Ofc. Michael Vezzola:

When my friend and co-worker Bob Vogel invited me to the Dominican Nuns 800th year celebration I gladly accepted. My faith in God has always been an important part of my life. I started attending daily Mass at my church (Sacred Heart Springfield) around 1998. I felt a need in my life to be closer to God. I had always attended weekly Mass but felt something was missing. On December 16, 2006 I went to the Domincan's celebration with my friend Bob. There were other police officers there, some I knew and some I didn't. I met with Sister Mary of the Sacred Heart before the ceremony who gave us our instructions. We, as police officers, were being honored by the Dominican's for our work in the community. While I was reciting the Holy Rosary on the altar I was proud to be there not only as a police officer but as a Catholic, a servant to our Lord. As I left that afternoon and headed home, I made a decision to learn more about God's will for us, his graces and love for us. I purchased the Liturgy of the Hours and began to attend evening prayer at the Dominican's Chapel. I was thirsty for knowledge and enjoyed the daily readings and, though a challenge, I followed along in the book. Other people in the chapel helped me along the way. In the chapel I felt an overwhelming peace with the sisters singing and praising Our Lord. I have come to know the sisters well in the last few years and I thank the Lord for them and their work. In my mind, they are truly angels sent from heaven. I pray as much as the day's time allows me and feel it is important to give thanks for all we have in our short lifetime. We all have our own personal struggles each day but prayer always seems to make them easier to cope with them.

For Mike Vezzola, the celebration graces continued in abundance. Mike was drawn to visit our Chapel more and more. Then one day the intercom rang and our receptionist said that someone who was at our celebration wanted to know where he could get "one of those books". By that he meant the breviary. So I directed him to our friends at Son Rises[1], and now Mike frequently joined us for Vespers armed with his new breviary. Some of our Dominican Fraternity join us for Vespers too and they coached Mike in using the breviary, but at one point he asked for some in depth instruction.

Mike, a good practicing Catholic, attends Sacred Heart Church in

---

1   A religious goods store

Springfield regularly. That's also my brother's parish and Mike and Al got a bit more connected. Al began talking to Mike about the total consecration to Mary. This requires a 30 day preparation period. It is a wonderful undertaking to dedicate oneself totally to the Blessed Mother so that she may lead us closer to her divine Son.

My brother Al also participated in the celebration by being one of the acolytes along with Bruce Smith, Jr. It was nice to have father, son and daughter-in-law all participate in this first celebration of our Jubilee. It was also significant having Fr. Christopher Connelly, a long time friend of our community, serve as Emcee. Being the Bishop's secretary, he has a lot of experience and it set this cloistered nun's mind at ease, knowing that he would be guiding the action.

Special Honors

Ask and it will be given to you. Mt. 7:7 (NIV®)

In order to make this opening celebration a little extra special I contacted the Knights of Columbus, who have been long time friends of our community. But they already had commitments for veterans and for children's Christmas parties, etc. I was referred to other Chapters of Knights, but again previous commitments prevented their presence. Then one Knight mentioned a Dominican Fraternity member who might be able to accommodate us. Sir Knight Eugene Murphy would be attending the laity meeting that Sunday and he might be a possibility. So I followed through on that lead and Eugene was pleased to contact his superior officer to obtain permission for himself and Sir Knight Francis Gregory to provide us with an Honor Guard. It was a fitting Christmas surprise for us that at first seemed so impossible. A number of guests noted the presence of the Knights as being one of their favorite remembrances.

I was later surprised to learn that this was a special year for Sir Knight Eugene Murphy. He had been a Knight of Columbus for fifty years!

Life-giving Mini Concert

I will sing to the LORD all my life; I will sing praise to my God as long as I live. Ps. 104: 33 (NIV®)

Prior to the service we had a fifteen minute mini concert. Marian hymns were included as well as a few Christmas pieces. Our Sr. Theresa Marie, O.P. is especially gifted with a beautiful singing voice. The lights were dimmed in the Chapel and from our cloister choir she sang *O Holy Night*. Some people told us they had "goose bumps". Earlier in the concert, sister sang a verse of *Born Is Jesus* in French. The French Christmas Carol symbolizes the first monastery of Dominican nuns, founded in Prouilhe, France.

Surprise Prayer

In preparing the program for the event, there was a little bit of space available and my faithful helper, Sr. Mary of the Sorrowful Heart, told me that she had a soldier's prayer[1]. It was very appropriate given our military guests and we included it in the program. But there was still another surprise in store. It turned out that Tpr Michael Cutone was the author! He was the very person Regina Lourenco had directed our way! Small world!

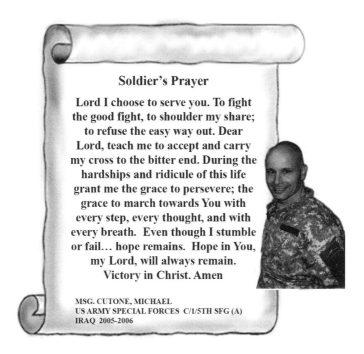

Soldier's Prayer

Lord I choose to serve you. To fight the good fight, to shoulder my share; to refuse the easy way out. Dear Lord, teach me to accept and carry my cross to the bitter end. During the hardships and ridicule of this life grant me the grace to persevere; the grace to march towards You with every step, every thought, and with every breath. Even though I stumble or fail... hope remains. Hope in You, my Lord, will always remain. Victory in Christ. Amen

MSG. CUTONE, MICHAEL
US ARMY SPECIAL FORCES C/1/5TH SFG (A)
IRAQ 2005-2006

A Closing Word

REV. MSGR. CHRISTOPHER D. CONNELLY

I am delighted to join my prayerful best wishes with all who celebrated this special anniversary of the Dominican Nuns. From their powerhouse of prayer -- a mighty fortress gracefully situated atop 1430 Riverdale Street and placed under the patronage of Mary, the Mother of God -- the Nuns are our Sisters by vocation, our steadfast friends by God's goodness. They assure us of the abiding presence of the Lord, and, ever faithful to the example of their founder St. Dominic, our Sisters continue to remind us that holiness and happiness are essential Catholic hallmarks.

(Endnotes)
1   MSG Cutone, Michael M., 280 Stafford Rd, Monson, MA. Used with permission.

CHAPTER 3

A Surprise for Dominic

The Lord himself will give you a sign… Is. 7: 14 (NIV®)

Now that Dominic had his nine noble women, as mentioned earlier, he needed to decide where to put them. As in all things, Dominic turned to the Lord in prayer. During the night of the 21st and 22nd of July that year, 1206, the feast of St. Mary Magdalen, he prayed at Fanjeaux on an elevated and solitary spot. From this vantage point he could see the vast plain below studded with hills stretching to the slopes of the Black Mountain. God's surprise came when he suddenly saw a ball of fire descend from heaven and come to rest above the little chapel of Our Lady of Prouilhe in the valley below. This same phenomenon occurred on the next two consecutive nights as well. Prompted by this sign from heaven, Dominic understood that the Chapel of Prouilhe must shelter his future monastery of nuns.

This event termed *Seignadou*, or the sign of God, is marked by a white marble cross where it is believed Dominic had his vision. Work on a monastery began in August and finished in November of 1206. On the 22nd of that month, the feast of St. Cecilia, the nuns took possession of it. The short time required for building the monastery suggests its modest size. Enclosure was established on December 27th, and thus the first foundation of Dominic's nuns was completed.

In addition to the nine noble ladies mentioned earlier, Dominic added Messane and Guillelmine of Fanjeaux, noble Catholic women, who were his first two spiritual daughters. He appointed Guillelmine prioress and he himself retained the spiritual and temporal administration of the Monastery.[1] So began one small humble monastery, a small candle lighting the dark world of their day. The daughters of Dominic, called *Light of the Church*, would radiate throughout the world, supporting the Holy Preaching with their prayers and preaching themselves by the example of their lives, living for God alone and interceding for all God's people.

(Endnotes)
1   Dominican Nuns in their Cloister 4-5.

CHAPTER 4

Surprises: Heroic and Lightsome

Welcome him in the Lord with great joy, and honor men like him…
Philippians 2: 29 (NIV®)

A blaze of guests marked our January Celebration with its theme of "**Light**". Leading the way was a contingent of Knights of Columbus providing us with an Honor Guard. Sir Knight Joseph Babineau was the Honor Guard Commander. Other members of the Honor Guard were Sir Knight Delfo Barabani, Sir Knight Robert Boulay, Sir Knight Ronald Brault, Sir Knight Francis Gregory, Sir Knight Roger Korell, Sir Knight Eugene Murphy and Sir Knight John Smus. These dignified Catholic men added to the solemnity of the occasion and so endeared themselves to us.

Firefighter Heroes

Snatch others from the fire and save them,… Jude 1:23 (NIV®)

Firefighters were among our honored guests, including Chief David Barkman from our West Springfield Fire Department, and Lt. Thomas Foley. Firefighter Robert "Bob" Germano wore badge No. 1 at the time. He had come to the monastery years before with a group of firefighters to instruct us on the different fire extinguishers and their use, as well as how to evacuate and carry sisters down the stairs in a chair should a fire occur. It is a blessing that we have not had to use these skills. Some of our monasteries have not been so fortunate.

Prouilhe, the first monastery of nuns, suffered from a number of fires. In 1715, fire destroyed the dormitories and 400 other rooms in that monastery. So extensive was the damage, that only 30 nuns could remain there until repairs could be made. The other nuns had to seek shelter at Fanjeaux or outside the monastery. In six month shifts the nuns took turns living in the monastery to preserve their monastic life.[1]

This same monastery was totally destroyed during the French Revolution. Not one stone was left upon another.[2] But in God's designs, the monastery was miraculously re-founded many years later, reviving monastic life there. In more recent years, another fire destroyed part of the monastery. Work continues on the monastery of Prouilhe and the daughters of St. Dominic continue their life of prayer and sacrifice.

Beginning with the month of January, we included historical tidbits in our program. These were in connection with the monthly theme. As a result, not only was mention made of Prouilhe and its fire experiences, but also of a monastery close to home.

Tragedy Strikes the North Guilford Monastery

Greater love has no one than this, that he lay down his life for his friends. John 15: 13 (NIV®)

In North Guilford, CT on Dec. 23, 1955, the nuns had finished night prayer and were preparing to retire when those at adoration heard the cry of "Fire!"[3] Immediate attempts were made to smother the blaze and to use extinguishers, but a short circuit in a wall plug had ignited the inside of the wall, spreading the flames with unbelievable rapidity. By the time the prioress came from the infirmary (about three minutes), the smoke had filled the chapel and made approach to the fire itself impossible. Mother started to telephone the fire department, then let another sister complete the call while she warned the rest of the community. Warning bells rang, the novitiate called, and sisters went from cell to cell sounding the alarm.

The floor was already hot under the novices' feet as their Mistress directed them to grab blankets and go. They came down the north fire-escape stairway in perfect order just before the flames burst into the novitiate building. The professed nuns, who were quartered in the old farmhouse, had a few more minutes' warning but experienced greater difficulties coming out. A door at the foot of the stairs acted like a barrier, keeping back the smoke from the second and third floors, but the thick, choking fumes beyond the door, perhaps from burning insulation, gave the impression that the most available exit was blocked. Despite this, most of the sisters took their chances and used the door, which brought them together outside the burning building. A sister suffering from thrombosis escaped with the help of Sister Infirmarian and another nun. Another sister escaped by a front window; and still another, who had gone through a second-floor window onto the low laundry roof, broke her foot in jumping to the ground. Sr. Mary Dolores, the youngest solemnly professed nun,[1] went promptly to the cell of a sister with a heart condition, put a blanket around her, and led her through the dark and smoke-filled corridors to safety.

A head count revealed one sister missing. Since the fire had not yet reached the part of the building where she was, Sr. Mary Dolores and Sr. Mary Constance of Jesus asked permission to return for her. Permission was granted because, in the few minutes which had elapsed, the fire had not reached the farmhouse. In any event, all of the front windows on the first or second floors could be used as exits.

The sister remaining inside, Sr. Mary Regina of the Rosary, must have been confused. She apparently climbed out of her cell window into an enclosed court rather than using a front window to escape to safety. The two sisters who returned to

---

1   Sister had made her solemn profession ten days before the fire.

find her apparently attempted to help her back up to her second-floor cell, but were themselves overcome with smoke. All three perished in the fire.

The remaining number of the nuns found themselves without stockings as they were wearing only flimsy slippers. The firemen, who were helpless against the blaze, took off their socks and jackets and gave them to the grateful nuns. The local Congregational Church, through their minister, promptly offered the evicted community clothing, food, and shelter in their parish hall. Doctors and nurses volunteered service. The Sisters of Mercy in Madison, Connecticut, hastily prepared food and lodging. A call to the Dominican Sisters at Albertus Magnus College in New Haven met a most generous response, and soon the thirty-nine surviving nuns with their chaplain, Fr. Reginald Craven, O.P., were aboard the bus of a near-by friend to go there. Fr. Craven had done his best to rescue the Blessed Sacrament, but was unsuccessful. Although he failed to reach the dying sisters, he none-the-less gave them absolution from where he stood.

At Albertus Magnus College a number of Dominican priests, including their former chaplain, Fr. Mulgrew, were waiting with the Dominican sisters for the arrival of the bus. All possible care, comfort, and kindness were offered to the weary nuns. Fr. McManus immediately gave them Communion (it was 12:15 A.M.) [2] so that they could have hot coffee and food to combat shock. All that night, and during the week that followed – Christmas week – the Dominican sisters at Albertus Magnus were untiring and completely self-sacrificing in caring for their homeless guests. The blending of the two communities into one produced a rich spiritual experience.

On December 24, by special permission, the sealed caskets containing the bodies of the three sisters who perished in the fire were brought to Rosary Hall, Albertus Magnus College, for the funeral Mass. The Very Reverend Vincent

---

2   At that time in order to receive Holy Communion one had to fast from midnight and the Sisters wanted to receive their Lord at such a traumatic time.

Firefighter's Prayer

When I am called to duty, God,
whenever flames may rage;
Give me strength to save some life,
whatever be its age.
Help me embrace a little child
before it is too late
Or save an older person
from the horror of that fate.
Enable me to be alert
and hear the weakest shout,
And quickly and efficiently
to put the fire out.
I want to fill my calling
and to give the best in me,
To guard my every neighbor
and protect his property.
And if, according to my fate,
I am to lose my life;
Please bless with your protecting
hand my children and my wife.
- Author unknown

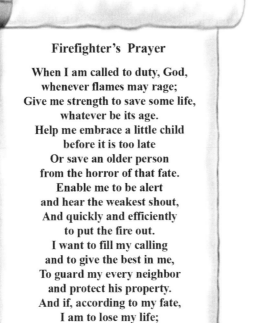

North Guilford Monastery

Burnell, O.P., P.G., Prior of Saint Mary's in New Haven, assumed financial responsibility for the funeral and made the arrangements, including permission for the sisters to be buried in the Dominican priests' section of Saint Lawrence Cemetery, until such time as they could be transferred to the monastery cemetery in North Guilford. Archbishop O'Brien gave the blessing both after Mass and at the cemetery.

Archbishop O'Brien and Bishop Hackett returned to Albertus Magnus and spent the afternoon with the stranded community. The fatherliness of the Archbishop, as he called the nuns together, consoled them. He promptly granted them a full dispensation from the obligation of Divine Office as well as all other necessary dispensations, and afforded them with a sense of care in a way that eased their stress and fear. Archbishop O'Brien made arrangements with the city and state officials so that the nuns might have the use of the Walter House, an unused County Home building at 1092 Campbell Avenue, West Haven, until they could rebuild at North Guilford. A few simple alterations provided the minimum requirements for cloistering, and the community returned to its customary life.[4]

More Heroes

Let your light so shine before men, that they may see your good
works and give glory to your Father who is in heaven.
Mt. 5:16 (RSV)

Two of our honored guests were AIC students who had themselves saved lives from a fire. Matthew Tourville and Christopher Bolognino had roused unsuspecting residents when they noticed part of a building on fire. Rounding out the crew of firefighters was Captain David Bourcier of the Wilbraham Fire Department. David had worked in maintenance at the monastery while waiting for an opening in the fire department. We promised to pray for his intentions but, unfortunately for us, our prayers were surprisingly answered all too soon! Our loss was Wilbraham's gain! It was a pleasure to have Fr. Gary Dailey with us as Emcee that month. It was very significant because Fr. Dailey was Chaplain of the Springfield Firefighters.

The Light of Learning – Religious Educators

Instruct a wise man and he will be wiser still;
teach a righteous man and he will add to his learning.
Proverbs 9:9 (NIV®)

Another "Light" represented among our guests was the "Light of Learning". White robed Dominicans inundated the day! Fr. Walter Wagner, O.P., Master of Novices for the St. Joseph Province, officiated. He brought along eight novices: Fr. Albert, Brothers Jordan, Michael, Bernard, Peter and Justin. Br. Augustine Reisenauer and Br. Matthew Carroll served as acolytes.

Sr. Ann Hyacinth, O.P., principal of St. Pius V School, Sr. Mary Rachel, O.P., Sr. Mary Sheila, O.P. and Sr. Mary Magdalen, O.P. came from Providence, RI. These Sisters of St. Cecilia are better known as the Nashville Dominicans, where their Motherhouse is located. Representing religious educators for the Sisters of St. Joseph were Sr. Magdalen Ward, S.S. J., Sr. Marie Martin, S.S.J. and Sr. Maureen Kervick, S.S.J., Campus Minister at Elms College. Sr. Magdalen Ward taught English at Cathedral High School when I was a student there. She provided very helpful proof reading of my monthly programs, and my English skills developed throughout the year, thus enabling me to attempt this book!

Sr. Marie Martin and her family have close ties to the community from its early days. Her mother, Connie, used to do card parties to help raise funds for the nuns. Sr. Marie was just a youngster at the time and her mother enlisted her services. She said it wasn't her favorite thing to have to get dressed up for such occasions!

Catholic Education

Let the word of Christ dwell in you richly as you teach
and admonish one another with all wisdom,… Col. 3: 16 (NIV®)

Saint Thomas' feast day falls on Jan. 28th and so it was appropriate that honored guests included teachers and students from Catholic High Schools and Colleges. Sr. Maureen Kervick, S.S.J., Campus Minister at Elms College in Chicopee, was among Honored Guests along with students Catherine Avery and Megan Brady. Elizabeth Weber, a student at PC, brought two students from RI, completing the Catholic college guests.

When I contacted principal Sr. Connie Roy, S.S.J., she said, "Don't you have someone from Holyoke Catholic that goes to your place?" Indeed we did! Mark Solatario served Mass for us quite regularly. He was scheduled to be Incense Bearer, so he encouraged classmates of his to attend. In the end, nine Holyoke Catholic students attended, including Maggie Kuntz.

Mr. Robert Lepage from the theology department at St. Mary's in Westfield rallied students from there. Martin Gaudrault was among the honored guests. And when I contacted my old alma mater, Cathedral High School, they referred me to Mr. Emanuel Vasconcelos, the Campus Minister. "Mr. V." is a graduate of PC and with that Dominican influence was quite pleased to get students to represent CHS at the Dominican Nuns celebration. It turned out that Scott Lozyniak was a senior who had previously made visits to the monastery Chapel.

Well, let me tell you the delightful surprise I enjoyed from such a positive response from the many young people, along with their faculty members. I felt so unsure of myself about recruiting guests of this kind, and had many questions as to the type of response I might get, etc. Who could imagine that such a goodly number of educators and students would honor us with their presence on a Sunday afternoon at a Holy Hour, and all that in addition to their regular Sunday obligation of Mass. If that isn't a surprise, I don't know what is! But we were able to reciprocate the surprise for them, because they got to meet the sisters who treated them with homemade cookies and beverages. The photos demonstrate their obvious delight! To see these photos and more, go to http://praedicare.com/Celebrations/2007JanPhoto.htm.

Remember the State Trooper, who came in December? Well he came again in January to take photos of our Honored Guests so that I could have pictures to put on my website. Some of the students also brought cameras, and Scott Lozyniak shared photos he had taken. All the photos were added to our collection.

Envisioners and Enlighteners

The eye is the lamp of the body. If your eyes are good, your whole body will be full of light. Mt. 6: 22 (NIV®)

Realizing how we need good eyesight as well as light itself to see, we invited envisioners who have served the community for many years --- Dr. Robert J. Donohue, M.D., an opthomologist and Dr. David C. Momnie, O.D., an optometrist as well as Paul Boucher, an optician. Dr. Momnie's father came to the monastery many years ago, equipped with optometrical glass frames for inserting lenses and turning dials to determine the vision of the sister (in those days we did not leave the enclosure for eye exams). When his son David followed his father's profession, he too offered his services to our community.

Our "Enlightener" representative came from WMECO. When I called the company, I was clueless as to what to expect or who to talk to. They referred me to Kate Agin, who worked as the Community Outreach Representative. She could not have been more de-**light**-ful and it gave us great joy to have her join our celebration!

KATE AGIN:

When we spoke, I mentioned to you that my Dad, Edmund J. Tate always ordered Mass Cards from the "Dominican Nuns". When I asked him one day why he only ordered from the Dominican Nuns, he said that he just had a strong connection.

Dad told me that he helped his Dad and Grandfather move the Dominican Nuns to West Springfield from Ingersoll Grove in Springfield. Dad would have been ten at the time. Dad was an altar boy at Sacred Heart Church in Springfield in the 1920's, and in my judgment felt the same strong connection; his faith was always strong. Dad was so pleased that I was asked to participate in the January, 2007, Celebration at the Chapel. His health had been failing and he wasn't able to attend, but I told him all about it. Dad passed away on December 21, 2007, and I am sure that he would have been so pleased that so many people sent Mass Cards for him from the Dominican Nuns.

Hearing Kate's story about her Dad's connection with our community, I couldn't help but realize how appropriate it was for her to be one of our honored guests. It also reminded me of the many times that, as one of the sister artists, I personally had inscribed cards for her dad. After his death, when his own name was inscribed on our cards, it felt like we were remembering a member of our family.

Luminous Mystery of the Rosary – The Wedding at Cana

There was a wedding at Cana in Galilee.
The mother of Jesus was there,
and Jesus and his disciples had also been invited. Jn. 2: 1 (JB)

With the theme of "light" we prayed the Luminous Mysteries of the Rosary that month. The second luminous mystery is the Wedding at Cana. So it seemed appropriate to have a couple of newlyweds with us. Calls were made to a few local pastors asking if they knew of any couples who might like to join us. We were delighted to have Mr. and Mrs. Michael McGill, who were married a few months before, join us for the occasion. My cousin David and his wife Andrea had been married in November and they too honored us with their presence.

Family Life Ministry

Sr. Mary Petisce, S.S.J., the diocesan Family Life Director, planned to come as an honored guest, since she is involved in the diocesan Pre-Cana Courses. An unforeseen illness prevented her from coming, so Sr. Frances White, S.S.J. came in proxy for Sister. That was a delightful surprise for me personally because I first met Sr. Frances when she taught at CHS as a PE instructor. At that time she was "Miss White" and we only had her for that one year. The following year we were surprised to learn that she had entered the Sisters of St. Joseph!

Sr. Frances White, S.S.J.

It was a delightful experience to be a participant in the Dominican Sisters' weekends of prayerful celebration. They reached out and touched so many people involved in community service. I especially enjoyed being in the procession with some police officers (my dad being one), firefighters and Knights of Columbus. A flood of memories brought me back to the early 50s when I remembered hearing about Sr. Mary John Dominic, the sister of police officers Dan and Bill Kelly. They spoke lovingly of their cloistered sister called to "a secluded prayerful lifestyle."

A former student of mine (in 1962), who was an outstanding athlete with boundless energy, invited me to this event; she too later entered the Dominican Order much to my surprise! Some 46 years later, after sharing such meaningful prayer, our paths met again as the sisters visited with all of us over coffee and refreshments. We truly are one in mind and heart, serving God in various ministries in action and contemplation together.

Student Brothers

Sisters of St. Joseph

Holyoke Catholic HS

Newly Weds & Family Life Ministry

St. Mary's HS - Westfield

Elms College

Knights of Columbus

Enlightener

Firefighters

Envisioner

Cathedral HS Springfield

Nashville Dominicans

St. Thomas Aquinas, who is patron of Catholic shools, outshone his teacher, St. Albert the Great.

Providence College

A Lightsome Mini-Concert

I will sing hymns to your name. Romans 15: 9 (NIV®)

Our musical mini concert included songs with the theme of light as well as the liturgical season and luminous mysteries. The last piece in the concert was an instrumental entitled *Sweet is the Name of Jesus*. Sr. Mary Regina played the organ and I accompanied with the soprano recorder.

Try to envision me greeting all our guests about one half hour before the service, cueing them in and giving them programs. This took place in a room about 9 ft. x 11 ft. (guest side area). All didn't come exactly at the same time, but they were packed in nevertheless. Then the challenge was to get to my place in choir in time to play the musical piece with a wind instrument. Breathless to say the least!

Devotions and the Infant of Prague

Having had Our Lady of Guadalupe with us in December, it seemed fitting to highlight a Catholic devotion each month. Many of these devotions seemed to have fallen by the wayside, but are still valuable and can be a source of strength to us today. In the January celebration we placed a statue of the Infant of Prague in the sanctuary and made mention of the history of the devotion in our program.

Tradition tells us that an old Spanish monk had a vision of the Christ Child, and made a statue of the Infant. In 1556, Maria Mauriquez de Lara brought the precious family heirloom statue of the Child Jesus to Bohemia, when she married a Czech nobleman. In 1628, Lady Polyxena presented the statue to the Carmelite friars, who enshrined it at Our Lady of Victory Church. Following the destructive invasion of the city and the Church by the Turks, Fr. Cyril, one of the shrine's friars, found the broken statue of the Infant Jesus in the ruins. While praying before it, Fr. Cyril heard a strange voice, "Have pity on Me and I will have pity on you. Give me my hands and I will give you peace. **The more you honor me, the more I will bless you.**" [5]

After its repair many miracles took place and great devotion once again restored..

The monastery of nuns in Farmington Hills, MI, was given a statue of the Infant of Prague. The sisters placed it in a niche in the reception area, quite lovely with marble and lights.

The Dominican Friars conduct five Solemn Novenas each year at the Shrine of the Infant of Prague in New Haven, CT. Also, Fr.

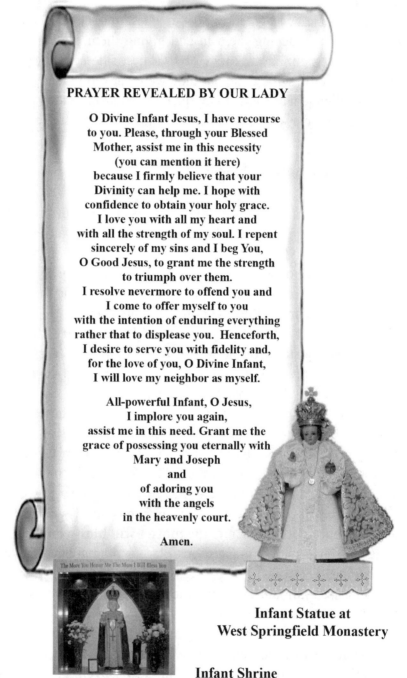

PRAYER REVEALED BY OUR LADY

O Divine Infant Jesus, I have recourse
to you. Please, through your Blessed
Mother, assist me in this necessity
(you can mention it here)
because I firmly believe that your
Divinity can help me. I hope with
confidence to obtain your holy grace.
I love you with all my heart and
with all the strength of my soul. I repent
sincerely of my sins and I beg You,
O Good Jesus, to grant me the strength
to triumph over them.
I resolve nevermore to offend you and
I come to offer myself to you
with the intention of enduring everything
rather that to displease you. Henceforth,
I desire to serve you with fidelity and,
for the love of you, O Divine Infant,
I will love my neighbor as myself.

All-powerful Infant, O Jesus,
I implore you again,
assist me in this need. Grant me the
grace of possessing you eternally with
Mary and Joseph
and
of adoring you
with the angels
in the heavenly court.

Amen.

**Infant Statue at
West Springfield Monastery**

**Infant Shrine
at the Farmington Hills, Monastery in Michigan**

Michael J. Mc Givney's remains are in New Haven. He is the founder of the Knights of Columbus and his cause is up for canonization.

Reflections

Sr. Magdalen Ward, S.S.J.:

Eight hundred year celebration of the Order of St. Dominic – Order of Preachers – Order of Teachers – eight hundred years of teaching faith, hope and charity!! What a tribute – what an honor.

What an awesome honor to have been chosen to participate in that celebration as one of the many educators being honored that day.

When I close my eyes and reflect upon that experience, I am filled with pride, joy and respect for all who were honored, for all who participated and for all who planned and organized it!

I recall the joyful chaos of so many educators gathering in the monastery foyer. A signal was given and we all obediently and reverently fell into step two by two. We followed the cross bearer down the steps, out into the bright chilly day, across the driveway to the main entrance to the Chapel.

There we ascended upward, upward to the very top step. A pause, then the doors opened wide --- Oh! oh! wow! There my breath was taken away, not by the chill of the day, but by the pageantry of what I was seeing and experiencing.

There stood on either side of the aisle the gloriously clad Knights of Columbus. The red and white satin lining of their black ceremonial capes glistened and reflected the lights of the stained glass windows. There stood the Knights of Columbus with plumed hats, holding high into an arch their ceremonial swords. Under the arch of honor the many educators of the diocese passed. I do believe it was one of my most honored moments.

I took a deep breath stood a little taller, focused my eyes on the golden altar toward which we processed to ceremonial music, entered our pew and in turn prayed the Rosary. The memory of that moment will long remain with me. At the conclusion of the ceremony, Rosary, Vespers, Benediction and concert, we exited again under the arch. I turned and thanked the Knights for their participation. They thanked me. We were thanking each other for the honor of being chosen to participate in this ceremony. It was an honor to be honored!

(Endnotes)

1   Religieuse du Meme Monastere, Histoire Du Monastere De Notre-Dame De Prouille (Grenoble: Baratier et Dardelet, 1898) 185.

2   Religieuse du Meme Monastere 301-302.

3   Monastery of Our Lady of Grace, "North Guilford Foundation," http://ourladyofgracemonastery.org/North-Guilford-Foundation.shtml (reference is made to the fire but previous data here is no longer displayed.) (accessed March 14, 2009).

4   Mother Mary Aloysius of Jesus, O.P., History of the Dominican Sisters of the Perpetual Rosary, (Patterson, N.J.: St. Anthony Guild Press, 1959) 192-196.

5   "Prayer to the Infant Jesus of Prague." http://www.institute-christ-king.org/latin-mass-resources/devotions/prayer-infant-prague/_(accessed August 20, 2009). Reprinted by permission of Institute of Christ the King Sovereign Priest, 6415 South Woodlawn Ave Chicago, IL 60657-3817. Used with permission.

CHAPTER 5
The Pope's Surprise

Freely you have received, freely give. Mt. 10: 8 (NIV®)

While Dominic was in Rome on Dec. 23, 1216, Pope Honorius III confirmed the Order, but with one stipulation: Dominic must bring together the various nuns scattered about the city, who lived either with their families or in monasteries where discipline was relaxed. Honorius had unsuccessfully tried to gather them together himself, but failed to unite them. He now charged Dominic to do so. Dominic accepted the task, requesting the assistance of capable co-operators. The Pope gave him Cardinals Ugolino, Bishop of Ostia, Stephen of Fossanova and Nicholas, Bishop of Tusculum.

Dominic went to the Monastery of Santa Maria in Trastevere, the principal monastery in question. Through his persuasion, the Abbess and all the sisters with one exception agreed to abide by the desires of the Holy Father. The nuns promised to move from their monastery to one of strict observance, that of St. Sixtus, where the Pope wished them to unite. They did make one condition, that their precious icon of Mary, painted by St. Luke, must accompany them to their new residence and **remain** there. On previous occasions when an attempt was made to move the icon it miraculously returned to its former place. The nuns knew this and knew that the same thing might happen again.

A grand procession with the icon took place on this auspicious occasion. Cardinals and bishops, too, accompanied the procession in all its solemnity. Moments earlier, Dominic had performed a miracle by raising the dead Napoleon back to life through prayer. He was killed in an accident, while Dominic was addressing the community before their departure. The young man was the nephew of one of the Cardinals present.

The icon remained and so did the nuns! Others joined the community, and by two weeks it surprisingly numbered one hundred and four nuns! St. Dominic bestowed much care and concern on this Monastery. For the next six months, he walked from the church of Santa Sabina on the Aventine down to the nuns' monastery every day to instruct and encourage them.[1]

St. Sixtus proved to be unhealthy because of the Marana stream which ran through the property. Three sisters caught the fever, making Dominic concerned for their health. He came one day and asked for news of Srs. Theodora, Thedramia and Nymphia. The portress, Sr. Constanza told him that the three still had fever. In his compassion he told her, "Go tell them that I order them to have no more fever." The three sisters immediately rose up, cured and Sr. Constanza quickly returned to announce the marvel to St. Dominic. Dominic left the monastery happy and praising God.[2]

(Endnotes)
1   <u>Dominican Nuns in their Cloister</u> 11-16.
2   <u>Dominican Nuns in their Cloister</u> 18.

CHAPTER 6

The Surprising Spectrum of Healing

*Jesus went throughout Galilee, teaching in their synagogues,
preaching the good news of the kingdom, and healing every disease
and sickness among the people. Mt. 4:23 (NIV®)*

Members of the Clergy

*Healing itself comes from the Most High, like a gift from a king.
Ecclus. 38: 2 (JB)*

There was a tremendous show of guests for the February celebration with its theme of healing. Three priests who work in the healing ministry attended, with Fr. William Hamilton, who had surgery on his hand, officiating at Vespers. His deep and resonating singing filled the Chapel. Fr. Gerald Brady is the Charismatic Coordinator of the Diocese of Springfield and Fr. Franklin Darling was Past Charismatic Coordinator of the Diocese. Fr. Darling heard confessions before the service and brought God's healing to those who approached the sacrament. Fr. Anthony Gramlich, M.I.C., Rector at the National Shrine of Divine Mercy, officiated at Benediction. Such ministries highlighted the greatest healing of all, that which comes to us from Divine Mercy.

Religious Women, Caring for the Sick

*Sometimes success is in their hands, since they in turn will beseech
the Lord to grant them the grace to relieve and to heal, that life may
be saved. Ecclus. 38: 13-14 (JB)*

These good priests were outnumbered by the three Congregations of
sisters serving in health care! The Sisters of Providence, well known to
all in the Springfield Diocese for the many and various health services
they provide, honored us with Sr. Joan Mullen, S.P., President, who
represented their community. Sr. Dorothy Young, S.P. accompanied
Sr. Joan. Many a Sister of Providence has cared for a Dominican nun,
even back in the days when the majority of these sisters were nurses at
Providence and Mercy Hospitals.

The Dominican Sisters of Hawthorne (Congregation of St. Rose
of Lima) came from New York. They were founded by the daughter
of Nathaniel Hawthorne the well known American novelist from
Massachusetts. Sr. Alma Marie, O.P., Novice Directress, came with
novice, Sr. Agnes Mary, O.P. and postulants Michelle and Marian.
The Hawthorne Dominican Sisters, who care for the poor, who are
terminally ill, describe their mission in this way:

*The Dominican mission is to preach God's love which we accomplish
through our apostolate of nursing incurable cancer patients who
cannot afford care. Our apostolate preaches the intrinsic value and
dignity of each human being in their last stage of life. We care for the
crucified and suffering Christ in each of our patients.[1]*

The Little Sisters of the Poor from Enfield, CT, rounded out the
group of religious women serving in health care. Sr. Marie Therese,
L.S.P., Sr. Gertrude, L.S.P. and Sr. Mary Gertrude, L.S.P. were a
welcomed trio. These sisters care for the sick poor and have been long
time friends of our community.

Knights of Columbus Honor Guard

Glory, honor and peace for everyone who does good....
Romans 2:10 (NIV®)

Sir Knight Donald Gladu – Honor Guard Commander
Sir Knight Roger Fontaine – Assistant Commander
Sir Knight Richard Beaudry – Past Faithful Navigator
Sir Knight Edward Beliveau - Past Faithful Navigator
Sir Knight Arnold Craven – Past Grand Knight
Sir Knight Edward LaFromboise – Navigator Fairview Assembly

Servers for Celebration

*Therefore I glory in Christ Jesus in my **service** to God.*
Romans 15:17 (NIV®)

Valmore Hebert, our faithful Mass server, was Cross Bearer in January and did so again in February. Another faithful server, Alexander Harshuk served as acolyte with great delight. Alex has since gone on to his eternal reward.

Do you not find it surprising that so many people would come on a Sunday afternoon for a service that lasted for an hour, not counting the cue time, mini concert and social? Well then, be surprised that many of them came back month after month. Scott Lozyniak, the CHS student, joined Alex in serving as an acolyte. Mark Solatario, our faithful server from Holyoke Catholic, was again present as Thurifer.

Our Lady of Lourdes

The Shrine of Our Lady of Lourdes in Southern France is the most visited pilgrimage site in the world. Many know the story about Our Lady appearing to Bernadette Soubiroux, the miraculous spring and the many miracles of healing that take place there. Since this feast is observed in February, it should be no surprise that "Healing" was the theme for our celebration that month. We had Our Lady of Lourdes statue in the sanctuary as well as some Lourdes water that friends had brought back from the shrine, and people were able to bless themselves with it. Richard "Dick" Butler had restored the statue for us, for which we were grateful.

Many Gifts

To one there is given through the Spirit the message of wisdom,...
to another gifts of healing by that one Spirit,
to another miraculous powers... 1Cor. 12: 8-10 (NIV®)

There are many levels of healing: physical, emotional, psychological and spiritual. Our honored guests exemplify all these various aspects in administering God's healing to us. Physical healing was represented by medical professionals from various fields.

Medical Professionals

Then let the doctor take over—the Lord created him too—and do not
let him leave you, for you need him. Ecclus. 38: 12 (JB)

We invited doctors who had served us for many years included Robert J. Donohue, M.D., an ophthalmologist, Joseph P. Keenan, M.D., in otolaryngology and Cyril Shea, M.D. in orthopedic surgery. Dr. Shea treated me when I broke two bones and dislocated my left ankle while tobogganing on the monastery hill out back 35 years ago. He's the reason I'm still on my feet and walking!

James P. Brown, D.D.S. provided dental services for us at the monastery. He can tell many a tale about his experience when another sister and I acted as his assistants. Sr. Mary of the Sorrowful Heart had some nursing education, and knew a bit more than I did, but we were at our best in developing x-rays and mixing amalgam. Doctor told us he could work better if we got a high speed drill. Eventually he convinced us that with technological developments, it would be better to go to his office. We finally did, and the two of us lost our jobs as assistants -– not a bad thing!

Dominican Fraternity Members

Spiritual Healing

in the Healing Ministry

Social

Representatives of Health Centers

Dominican Sisters of Hawthorme

Knights of Columbus

Representatives of Healing Services

Little Sisters of the Poor

Medical Professionals

Dr. James P. Brown:

I first began working at the Monastery in the spring of 1970. My intro was scary, to say the least. I waited in the lobby for the big oaken door (with no outside doorhandle) to open and was greeted by two smiling sisters who escorted me to the elevator and up to the dental clinic. They subsequently became my "dental assistants" (I use the term loosely).

My first impression of the clinic was a scary one. The dental unit was an antique Ritter tri-dent (which went out of use 10 years previously) and had no high speed attachment. We got help from Ryan Dental Supply and a high speed box was attached and worked well.

The x-ray unit was archaic and every time we used it I expected to see sparks flying across the room like in the old Dr. Frankenstein movies. It was still in use when I left.

The really worst news was that the sisters did not know how to make instant coffee, to which I was addicted. That was soon remedied.

These two who became dental assistants were a piece of work! I won't mention names but one was my age, the other a **few** years younger. I don't know who was more confused, but they learned together how to mix the materials and hand them to me. I remember saying to one of them, "No, Sister, you don't just wipe the instruments with a towel; they have to go in the sterilizer before re-use."

Honored guest Maggie Sullivan, a dental hygienist, also came to the monastery to provide services for us. Eventually the dental chair and equipment were removed (probably to some ancient antique dealer) and we went out for those services too.

Other medical professionals rounding out this group were Steven Forti, R.N., who worked in the Emergency Dept. at Greenwich Hospital in CT and my niece, Rebecca Sawicki, P.T., a physical therapist at Holyoke Hospital. Barbara Pappis, C.N.A. has served a number of our senior sisters needing care, which she provides at Mt. St. Vincent Nursing Home.

Representatives of Health Centers

Do not fail those who weep, but share the grief of the grief-stricken.
Do not shrink from visiting the sick; in this way you will make
yourself loved. Ecclus. 7: 34-36,39 (JB)

In addition to individual professionals we also had representatives of various health centers. Sr. Ramona, S.P., who serves as Chaplain, represented Mt. St. Vincent, where two of our sisters receive care. Paul Sanderson, the 3-11 Supervisor, represented Mont Marie Health Care. Paul was very helpful when some of our sisters received care at Mont Marie. And Jan Falkowski represented the Center for Mammography at the Mercy Medical Center.

Other Centers represented services for various types of health needs. Sr. Teresa Dube, S.A.S.V. represented Providence Behavioral Hospital; Spiritual Director, Barbara Gallagher Jarry, represented Brightside. Sr. Senga, S.P. was unable to attend our celebration but Cyndey Vadnais came and represented "Annie's House". Such a variety of gifts and all from the same Spirit. By inviting these dedicated people to our celebration, it was our way of acknowledging the good work that they do in bringing God's healing to others. It also allowed us the opportunity to express our thanks to God for them and ask his blessing upon them and all their endeavors. We pray too for all those they serve, who are so in need of healing.

The Luminous Mysteries

He sent them out to preach the kingdom of God and to heal the sick.
Lk. 9: 2 (NIV®)

We prayed the luminous mysteries of the rosary. That seemed fitting given the Proclamation of the Kingdom of God. We all know that Jesus and his disciples proclaimed the kingdom, and healing was very much a part of that. It touched people in their inmost depths.

Representatives of Healing Services

He (the Lord) revives the spirit and brightens the eyes,
he gives healing, life and blessing. Ecclus. 34: 17 (JB)

There are so many in need of healing today. It is a blessing to have a Sr. Maureen Griffin, S.S.J. in Pastoral Care at the Mont Marie Health Care Facility for those in need of support in their later days. Sr. Edie McAlice, S.S.J. is Pastoral Minister at St. Patrick's in Chicopee. She makes a big impact! I recall contacting the Knights of Columbus and telling them what the theme of the celebration was going to be and the various guests being honored. The Knight said, "Oh are you going to invite Sr. Edie?" Nobody wanted her to be overlooked! Indeed she is dearly loved by those who know her.

Sr. Edie McAlice, S.S.J.
Pastoral Minister — St. Patrick's — Chicopee

I was honored to be invited to participate in the significant anniversary of the Dominican Nuns' presence in our Church and in our world. They have been true daughters of St. Dominic throughout their 800 years, as they sought holiness for themselves and blessings for the world. I came away from the celebration with a renewed sense of their valued charism and contribution, and of my community's (Sisters of St. Joseph) partnership with them in the mission of keeping God's presence alive in our world. Their Monastery of the Mother of God is a beacon of faith and hope to all who pass by. May God's enduring love continue to shine upon her and all who live and serve within her.

Sr. Mary Petisce, S.S.J. is the Family Life Director for the Diocese of Springfield. She represented the ministry for those divorced and separated. Peggy Bradford was in Pastoral Ministry as Prayer Counselor at St. George's Parish. And then there was Jean Czajka, who represented Rachel's Vineyard. This is a relatively new ministry that provides healing retreats for women with regrets after having abortions.

Quite a few members of our Dominican Fraternity are in the healing ministry. Henry Sansouci is an Emergency Medical Technician and his wife Linda provides medical transport for some of the sisters. Marie Flynn does social services at the Soldier's Home in Holyoke

Mary Beth Dillon, B.S.N. has helped out at the monastery in various circumstances. Marie Laplante was a physical therapist aide. On the spiritual side Rose Marie Nathan is a Eucharistic Minister at Baystate Hospital Pastoral Care Department, and Linda Burr was an Occupational Therapist at the Department of Mental Retardation (Worcester County).

We also invited some guests who were struggling with cancer. Among these was Maureen Smith, a woman devoted to Our Lady and a woman of great faith. While this book was being written in October of 2008, Maureen was called home to the Lord to receive her eternal reward.

Cathy (O'Sullivan) Kelly was also invited to our celebration. We went to grammar school together at Our Lady of the Sacred Heart in Springfield, MA and became fast friends. We had kept in touch after I entered the monastery and Cathy sometimes wondered if she would ever meet the right man. Sr. Mary John Dominic had told her to pray to God's Mommy, Our Lady, and she would hear her prayer. Sister assured her that we nuns would also pray. It was not long after that that Cathy came to the monastery with Bob Kelly. She wanted us to meet this new acquaintance. He was surprised when a number of the nuns came in to visit and was awestruck. He was amazed that all these nuns had been praying for him!

It turned out that Cathy and Bob were unable to have a child and so prayers were requested once again. They were able to adopt a beautiful little baby boy. Christopher has grown up and become their pride and joy. He worked for us one summer before starting college. He proposed to his future bride and in August of 2008 the two were married.

Prayers were again requested for Cathy, when she was diagnosed with cancer of the breast. It spread to her lymph nodes, lungs, sternum and now her spine. After our celebration Cathy and a few selected individuals came to our small parlor where the charismatic priests prayed over them for God's healing. Fr. Brady told Bob to pray with Cathy every night, and he has. She is still being treated, still working somewhat and still alive. Our prayers continue to be with her.

My brother Al, better known as "MagicAl" came to the service too. He uses his gift of slight of hand magic to bring "Healing through Laughter". He has gone to entertain prisoners and those recovering from addictions and after the laughter part, gives them a short spiritual talk. He also has rosary beads on his magic stand and those present can take one if they so wish. At the jail, the officer in charge personally handed out the rosary beads to the inmates who came forward.

It was also significant that both Al and Fr. Darling should be present at this celebration. Al went through a spiritual conversion some years ago. At the time, I gave him a flyer about a charismatic retreat. He said he was not interested, but took the flier anyway. I was surprised to learn later that he actually went. At first he felt uncomfortable. This hand raising and "Praising the Lord" was not his cup of tea. As he sat among the crowd, he decided that at the break he was leaving! That was when Fr. Darling came and sat down beside him and began talking to him. Fr. Darling urged him to stay, at least until the healing part of the service was over. He did. When he saw people falling down as they were being prayed over, he again felt uneasy. When his turn came, he felt himself falling and hit the ground like a ton of bricks, bouncing off a chair! The pain in his chest was unbearable. He went to get it checked out later, but the doctors couldn't find anything wrong with him. Although this charismatic form of prayer is not attractive to Al, he has developed a spiritual friendship with Fr. Darling, which has helped him grow spiritually himself.

Lourdes and the Nuns

In the United States there were two branches of Dominican Nuns. The one branch first founded in Union City, N.J. (then called West Hoboken) has an interesting history. In April of 1876, Fr. Damien Marie Saintourens, O.P. made a trip to Lourdes to spend the night in prayer at the Grotto. During the night, he was inspired to found a new branch of the Order, the Dominican Sisters of the Perpetual Rosary.[2]

Mother Rose of St. Mary Wehrle, O.P. who became the co-foundress of the Dominican Sisters of the Perpetual Rosary, was a Second Order nun of the Mauleon monastery in France. The monastery "loaned" Sr. Rose to the new foundation, which was not intended to be Second Order, to assist Fr. Damien in building his dream community. Sr. Rose never returned to Mauleon.[3]

Fr. Potton acted as the spiritual director of the monastery of the nuns at Mauleon. He hoped to have a Dominican monastery at Lourdes. He found the appropriate site, the architect and proceeded to set it all up.

The nuns for the Lourdes foundation came from the monastery at Arles, which was founded by Mauleon. But things did not go well. Failing to get the land they desired, the nuns returned to Mauleon. In 1888 they joined forces with the new foundation at Lourdes.

Mini-Concert

> *...until he has ... made them rejoice in his mercy.*
> *Mercy is welcome in time of trouble,... Ecclus. 35: 25-26 JB*

Our mini concert offered a variety of songs and musical instruments. The Lourdes Hymn topped the list and was accompanied by Sr. Mary Regina at the organ. Sr. Mary of the Immaculate Heart and I played our guitars for the "Prayer of Peace". "The Master Came" reflected that much healing comes from forgiving others. One piece praised God who heals all our ills. The highlight of the concert was a solo by Sr. Theresa Marie, who sang "Pie Jesu" (Loving Jesus). The hymn

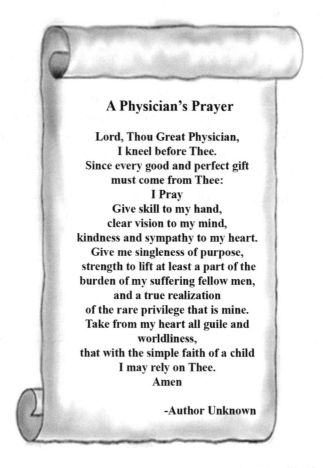

A Physician's Prayer

Lord, Thou Great Physician,
I kneel before Thee.
Since every good and perfect gift
must come from Thee:
I Pray
Give skill to my hand,
clear vision to my mind,
kindness and sympathy to my heart.
Give me singleness of purpose,
strength to lift at least a part of the
burden of my suffering fellow men,
and a true realization
of the rare privilege that is mine.
Take from my heart all guile and
worldliness,
that with the simple faith of a child
I may rely on Thee.
Amen

-Author Unknown

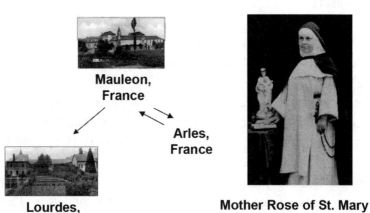

Mauleon,
France

Arles,
France

Lourdes,
France

Mother Rose of St. Mary
Wehrle, O.P.

calls out to "Pie Jesu", the "Agnus Dei" (Lamb of God), who takes away the sins of the world and who reconciles us with the Father and with one another. Words cannot describe the beauty and emotion with which it was sung by Sr. Theresa Marie. It touched the hearts of all who heard it!

(Endnotes)
1   Hawthrone Dominican Sisters. Used with permission.
2   Mother Mary Aloysius of Jesus, O.P. 19.
3   Mother Mary Aloysius of Jesus, O.P. 48, 80, 84.

CHAPTER 7

Communication Surprises for Nuns and Friars

Confident of your obedience, I write to you, knowing that you will do even more than I ask. Philemon 1: 21 (NIV®)

More Surprises

Men joined St. Dominic in his preaching, forming a community. Dominic was a man of prayer, ever open to the Holy Spirit. His band of preachers first focused their preaching in southern France. In 1217, Dominic's small band of friars gathered together as he announced that they would no longer live together in their present dwelling. He planned to disperse them throughout the whole world. Seven were sent to Paris, four to Spain, two remained at St. Romain in Toulouse, two remained at Prouilhe and Dominic reserved Stephen of Metz as his own companion on his return to Rome.[1]

Friar Pedro of Madrid and Friar Gomez composed one of the two groups that were sent to Spain. They ended up in Pedro's hometown of Madrid, an insignificant place at the time.[2]

The friars preached to the people with significant success and soon they began a convent. Catholic women wanted to become nuns, but there was no dwelling for them. When St. Dominic came to Madrid, he gave the habit to several of these women and attached them to the community of the brethren. They came together at the friars' small monastery for Mass and for praying the Office. Still, they remained scattered and could not live together.[3]

New surprises were unveiled in May of 1220 at the Chapter, which was held at Bologna. St. Dominic ordered that the Madrid house and the entire property be transferred to the sisters. The house became a monastery for the nuns. [4]

Enclosure was established and St. Dominic appointed his own brother, Mannes, who had followed him, as Director and Prior of the Nuns. Dominic gave the nuns the same rule as Prouilhe.[5]

Later St. Dominic wrote a letter to the nuns in Madrid. It remains the only written **communication** we have from him. It reads as follows:

Brother Dominic, Master of the Friars Preachers, to the Prioress and Sisters of the Convent of Madrid, health and increase in all virtue.

We rejoice greatly at the report we have received of your holy conversation, and give thanks to God that he has delivered you from the mire of the world. Continue, then, my daughters, to combat your ancient enemy, with prayer and watching, knowing that none shall be crowned save those who have fought valiantly. Hitherto you have had no house suitable for following your religious rule, but now you will have no such excuse for negligence, seeing that you are provided with a convent in which you can perfectly carry out every detail of religious life. I desire therefore that henceforth silence be better observed in the places of silence, such as the choir, the refectory, and the dormitory, and that you live in all other respects according to the Constitutions that have been given to you. Let no one go outside the enclosure, and let no one be admitted within it, unless it be some bishop or prelate who shall come to preach or to visit you. Do not neglect vigils and disciplines, and let all be obedient to the prioress. Let none waste time in idle conversation about unnecessary things. And inasmuch as we cannot help you in your temporal necessities, we desire not to be a burden to you, nor will we permit that any Brother should have authority to receive novices, but only the prioress with the council of her convent. We command our dearest Brother, who has labored so much for you and has gathered you together I this holy state, that he will dispose all things as seems best to him, to the end that your life may be ordered in a holy and religious manner. Therefore we give him full faculties and authority to visit and correct you, and if need be, to remove the prioress from her office, with the consent, however, of the majority of the community, and also to grant any dispensations that he may consider necessary. Farewell in Christ.[6]

(Endnotes)
1   Augusta Theodosia Drane, The History of St. Dominic (London & New York: Longmans, Green, and Co., 1891) 182-183.
2   M.-H. Vicaire, O.P., Saint Dominic and His Times trans. Kathleen Pond (New York Toronto London: McGraw-Hill Book Company, 1964) 252.
3   Drane 288.
4   Vicaire 252-253.
5   Dominican Nuns in their Cloister 28.
6   Drane 289-290.

CHAPTER 8

Surprises in Communication

I thank him that you have been enriched in so many ways,
especially in your teachers and preachers... 1Cor. 1: 4-5 (NIV®)

In our neck of the woods, the celebration of St. Patrick's Day is HUGE! The Holyoke St. Patrick's Day parade is one of the largest in the country. During the year of the jubilee, celebrations fell on March 18th, the third Sunday of the month, the same day as the huge parade. As all of our monthly celebrations took place on the third Sunday, we were not sure how this month's celebration would work out. The Knights of Columbus marched in the parade, making them unavailable for our event. But being Lent, all these things fit in with the idea of progressive solemnity.

Communicating in Prayerful Song

I will pray with my spirit, but I will also pray with my mind;
I will sing with my spirit, but I will also sing with my mind.
1 Cor. 14:15 (NIV®

Our theme for this month was "Communication". Heavenly Communication is by far the most important and was reflected in our first song of our mini-concert "Behold, Your Handmaid". Such was Mary's response when God invited her through the Angel Gabriel to become the mother of his Son. The hymn was accompanied by two sister guitarists and five sisters playing tone chimes. Two of these latter were from our Linden, VA, monastery, who were living with us at the time.

We did celebrate good St. Patrick by singing the "Prayer of St. Patrick", asking God's blessings upon us all. Certainly St. Patrick communicated the Good News to the people of Ireland! "Tell It Out" expressed the communication of the Gospel, the Good News, and was accompanied by our sister guitarists.

Communication is twofold: in prayer with God and with others. This prayer was reflected in the song "Jesus, Remember Me". It was the prayer of the Good Thief on Calvary and is our prayer in time of every need. It is a song that is very contemplative and filled with peace. "Were You There?", a Spiritual Song reflecting on the Passion of Christ, was sung by Sr. Theresa Marie, O.P. with Sr. Mary Regina accompanying her on the organ. Sr. Theresa Marie sang the hymn with all the emotion that is hidden in the song's depths.

Officiants

Remember your leaders, who spoke the word of God to you.
Consider the outcome of their way of life and imitate their faith.
Heb. 13:7 (NIV®)

We were pleased to have Fr. Franklin Darling as our Guest Officiant at Vespers. His family roots are English, but he has such a great sense of humor that one could mistake it for Irish wit! Fr. Michael Zielke, O.F.M.Conv., the Pastor of St. Stanislaus in Chicopee, officiated at Benediction. We have a special bond with Fr. Michael and the Franciscan Friars. They serve as our confessors and offer Holy Mass when our Chaplain is away.

Fr. Franklin Darling
All during my years in seminaries (Anglican and Catholic),

I played the organ for the ceremonies, including the Divine Office. I knew all the tones, the arsis and thesis[1], the qualisma[2], etc. However, never did I get to sing the Hours or never have I had the chance to preside; this was one of my dreams and you gave me the chance to do so at one of the 800th Anniversary celebrations. You asked me to preside. It was one of the happiest moments of my whole 50 years of priesthood --- to preside at sung Vespers. What a great gift. Thank you.

Servers Leading the Procession

*To this you were called, because Christ suffered for you, leaving you
an example, that you should follow in his steps.*
1 Peter 2:21 (NIV®)

The cross bearer for this service was my brother, Alexander J. Sawicki, Sr., better known as MagicAl. Officer Michael Vezzola served as acolyte together with Scott Lozyniak, a Cathedral High student. Holyoke Catholic senior Mark Solatario was incense bearer once again in our "liturgical parade".

The Printed Word

We will give our attention to prayer and the ministry of the word.
Acts 6: 4 (NIV®)

Among our honored guests were the Daughters of St. Paul from Eastern Massachusetts: Srs. Elizabeth Marie DeDomenico, D.S.P., Mary Paula Kolar, D.S.P., Mary Gabriella Tubick, D.S.P., Mary Louise Oddi, D.S.P. and Mary Frances Epplin, D.S.P. These religious women actively communicate the message of Jesus Christ and His message of love and salvation. In their work of evangelization, they strive to use

---

1   Rise and fall of the music
2   A formation of notes in Gregorian chant

the most rapid and effective means at hand.

For those associated with "publishing" we invited Marie Coburn Gill, T.O.P., the editor of the West Springfield Record. Marie was very helpful in announcing our celebrations in the <u>Record</u> and even gave us some good coverage on a few occasions with photographs included! Marie was a great resource person for me in making contacts. She knows many people and was so helpful. Mary Ellen Stroud, T.O.P. is responsible for the <u>Dominican Fraternity Newsletter</u>. These women are true Dominicans and women of the Word!

We were also pleased to invite two members of the Weber Family. Peggy Weber, a long time friend, is well known for her articles which appear in the diocesan newspaper, the <u>Catholic Observer</u>. Over the years she has written a number of articles on the Dominican Nuns for which we are grateful. Peggy's daughter Kerry followed in her mother's literary shoes. She has written for the <u>Catholic Digest</u> which we enjoy reading. It was great to have mother and daughter as honored guests.

Electronic and Digital Communications

> *Pray for us, too, that God may open a door for our message,*
> *so that we may proclaim the mystery of Christ.*
> *Col. 4: 3 (NIV®)*

Another group of honored guests of communication were representatives of TV, Radio, Web, Computer and Mailroom Systems. Heading off the list was Sr. Catherine Homrok, S.S.J., COO representing <u>Real to Reel</u>, a diocesan program shown each week on television. We are pleased we have been featured on this program a number of times.

Sr. Catherine Homrok, SSJ:

As I look back at the way the way the Dominican Nuns of the Monastery of the Mother of God in West Springfield spent

Representatives of TV, radio, web, computer, and mailroom systems

Artists, delivery services

and religious goods providers

Assisting in nuns' prayer card ministry

Publishing

Telephone Receptionists and Translators

Servers

Daughters of St. Paul

It has been said that God has three answers to prayer:

Yes

Not Yet

I have something better

the year 2007 celebrating their 800th anniversary, I am very impressed and inspired by their generosity. They looked out at the broader community around them and invited guests to join them each month of that year to pray and to celebrate the goodness of God with them.

I was fortunate to be among the group of communicators invited to participate in one of those special holy hours. It was a delight for me to look out at the diversity of the communicators assembled that particular Sunday. Some of us were there as media personalities and representatives while others were there as telephone operators, receptionists, and mail carriers or other occupations which help to link people together. I am very grateful to the Dominican Nuns for helping us to experience more deeply the link that we all share with each other and our loving God.

Ray Hershel, a well known reporter for WGGB, ABC-40, honored us with his presence. This was one of God's providential surprises. I had spoken with Ray on the telephone about our celebration and he expressed interest in coming. However, when I mentioned the actual date, he was sad to say that he had a commitment for the St. Patrick's Day Parade. Chanel 40 had participated in it every year for 39 years and he felt obligated to keep that commitment. A few days before the celebration, Ray called me and asked if the invitation was still open. I assured him that it was and he told me that circumstances had changed and that he was free to join us. We were delighted! His wife Maureen also came to the service. I was surprised to learn that his wife, Maureen, was a classmate of mine. It was a pleasure to see her after so many years.

Maureen (Pollard) Hershel
Wife of Ray Hershel

My husband has been reporting the news for channel 40 for over forty years and there are very few places in this area that he hasn't visited --- but the Monastery of the Mother of God was one of them! He was humbled by the sisters' request to visit and pray with them along with other members of the local media. After a beautiful service --- the singing was especially memorable, we both came away with a renewed sense of the power of prayer that is so badly needed in our troubled world today.

CHRIS BROER:

One of the names I saw mentioned was Ray Hershel of Channel 40. It brought back a story I remember from the late 70's. We were watching TV at 11pm on a Saturday or Sunday night, and at the time Channel 40 was a distant second to Channel 22 for viewers of the 11pm local news. We had Channel 40 on, and Ray was a brand new reporter. He read the news and they went to commercial. Then Ray did the weather and they went to commercial. Then Ray did the sports and they went to commercial. He did the entire half hour local news all by himself! I think he even wrote the scripts:) He's always been a nice, gentle figure in the news world, which I prefer to the loud style that some others have, so it was nice to see his Catholic faith mentioned. I'm sure his kindness, compassion, and interest in the story that comes through when he does the news is an example to those around him who know he's Catholic and that would inspire them to the Faith if they're not already Catholic.

Mrs. Rita Crocker of Crocker Communications was among our honored guests. Her company hosted my praedicare.com website. It was a pleasure to meet the person behind the name! Our guest Carol Pirog is a web developer. I was directed to her by a friend when I was trying to learn about websites and about how to create them. She explained the various elements needed and got me started in the right direction. She was the one who directed me to Crocker Communications.

Judith Deshaies came in proxy for Joseph Corigliano, Director of Microsoft. Joe, who lives in California, has been so good to us but was unable to come. Judith, his best friend's mother who lives in the area, filled his place by proxy. Gail Waterman, T.O.P. operates the Dominican Fraternity Web. She is quite active in communication and always ready to be of help. Stephen Tracy of WACE Radio Station in Chicopee represented the air waves; representing Mailroom Systems was Ron Motta. Ron was very helpful to me in understanding mail machines and any business connected with them!

Telecommunications and Translators

Always be prepared to give an answer to everyone
who asks you to give the reason for the hope that you have.
But do this with gentleness and respect… 1 Peter 3: 15 (NIV®)

Our next group of communications people included telephone receptionists and translators. Among our Monastery telephone receptionists were Monica Daly, Amy Gracey, Linda Stone and my aunt, Audrey Sawicki. Linda is one of our full time operators and we are grateful to the others who come part-time and as volunteers. Rosemarie Smith, telephone operator at the monastery, planned to be with us, pending travel. She lives in Holyoke on a street off route 5 (the route the parade takes) and got locked in due to the parade. She could not get out of her residence to attend. Cindi Laramee is the telephone receptionist at our local dentist's office and came with a big gift box of toothpaste! Eva Miner, T.O.P. is on the Telephone Prayer line for the Dominican Fraternity.

CINDI LARAMEE

While answering the phone for eleven plus years at work, and wanting to unplug it at the end of a very long day, I found myself wanting it to ring one day, one more time. While working in a dental office can be trying, when everyone wants an appointment on the same day, I couldn't help but think one day that I wanted the phone to ring again and with the

Dominican Nuns calling.

When asked to attend the 800th Anniversary Celebration to share in the Rosary, I was thrilled to be a part of this special event. After the service was concluded, I left the Monastery with the warmth of God in my heart, and I experience the same feeling when the phone rings at work and the nuns are calling. While I wish them no toothaches, I admit that I do hope to hear from them more often than they would like to call, I'm sure.

I have also found that a classmate from school, Deb Belisle, is now a Dominican Nun with the name of Sr. Mary Joseph. One of my most thankful blessings, Steven, has worked with these wonderful women for many years. Sr. Sorrowful Heart has blessed me with many warm words and comforting thoughts but I really rather her hugs.

Whether a classmate, or a close friend, or a Sister with a "HEART", I have found that we should always count our blessings and there is nothing wrong with saying a quick little prayer at work for the phone to ring "One more time"!

Sabine Charton-Long has done some translating for me from English into French for my praedicare web site. Araci Williams has done translating from English into Portuguese. She was unable to come due to a health issue but Laurence Carabine stood proxy for her. He was the one who enlisted Araci's services for me.

Professor Joseph Lake, T.O.P., retired Professor of Russian Language and Literature at UMass, has translated "Sr. Philomena's Journal". It is the account of a Dominican Community's experiences during the great persecution in Russia under the Communists. He never had the journal published, but shared the manuscript with us. One of our monastic customs is to have reading in the refectory during meals We had read Professor Lake's manuscript, and found it to be very interesting and moving. He has written an article based on the manuscript for the <u>Dominican Torch</u>. Professor Lake's translations are all connected with Mother Catherine Abrikosov and the Dominican Community which she founded in Moscow.

Prof. Joseph Lake, T.O.P.:

One day all of the translating and other work I will have done trying to make these Russian Catholic martyrs known will just be put on the web, to be there as these Dominicans hopefully move toward recognition as saints by the Universal Church.

Roles of Service

This service that you perform is not only supplying the needs of God's people but is also overflowing in many expressions of thanks to God. 2 Cor. 9: 12 (NIV®)

Elizabeth Newman represented Bassette Printing and Patricia Pasterczyk represented Springfield Label and Tape. Their services provide us with custom materials, which assist our postal needs for mailing spiritual prayer cards.

Another group of Honored Guests included four Dominican Fraternity members. Theresa Clark, T.O.P. came regularly to help with the preparation of our Spiritual Bouquet cards. Mary Hickson, T.O.P. did the same from home. Valmore and Shirley Hebert, T.O.P. came once a month with Shirley's sister Bea to assist with the phone and the front door. They also helped us give preliminary instructions for our services. Rounding out this group of volunteers was Josephine Gallant. In the program, I mistakenly put Gallagher and made her Irish in so doing! At the last minute something came up, which prevented her from attending. At this writing, she is a "young" ninety years old and proud of it! She is active in the community and could not come to the monastery during the "Big E" because she was helping out there!

Good News through Artists, Religious Goods Providers and Delivery Services

Pray for us that the message of the Lord may spread rapidly and be honored, just as it was with you. 2 Thess. 3:1 (NIV®)

God's Good News comes in all shapes and packages and we also wanted to honor those who bring good news through their delivery services. Patty Shea is our faithful Postal mail carrier and it was a delight to have her join us in the celebration. James Perkins, T.O.P. has a behind-the-scenes role as a Post Office Employee. My nephew, Alexander J. "Bucky" Sawicki, Jr. is employed by UPS and rounded out the delivery group.

God's Good News also comes through art. So we were pleased to have Lucille Roy, T.O.P. join us. Richard Butler does restoration of statues and has done a number of them for us. This began as a sort of hobby, and he learned as he went along. He has many requests to repair statues. A number of sisters in our various monasteries have artistic talents and this too is a way of preaching.

Last but certainly not least were Regina and Art Lourenco. Their religious goods store "Son Rises" brings many people across their path. Theirs is not just a place of business, but it reflects their faith and the desire to bring others closer to the Lord.

The Nuns and Communication

The nuns are no strangers to communication. Each of our vocations began with God communicating to us in our heart, drawing us toward the monastic life. He called each in various ways. Each heard that call and responded. Our constitutions read, "Let them (the nuns) earnestly seek the face of the Lord and never cease making intercession with the God of our salvation that all men and women might be saved..."[1]

Although the nuns are cloistered, nevertheless they communicate in sundry and various ways. On the international scene we have a publication named <u>Monialibus</u> through which we hear news of nuns throughout the world. On the home front, <u>Association Sharings</u> provides us with news from US nuns and Affiliates of the Association.

In order to benefit from one another, Nuns in Latin America use teleconferencing for inter-monastery formation classes. This need is important because they are geographically isolated from one another.

The Association of Nuns also provides for ongoing education by arranging for lectures at participating monasteries. The monasteries record the lectures and later make enough copies for all monasteries concerned. It is part of the Dominican spirit to give to others the fruits of contemplation. In this case the fruit of the nuns' study is published in a scholarly publication entitled <u>Dominican Monastic Search</u>. For our 800th anniversary a committee reviewed these articles, which had been published over a period of twenty-five years, and chose what they thought were the best for publishing a book entitled <u>Search For Living Waters.</u>

The book, <u>One Mind & Heart in God,</u> was the nuns' first joint publication and explains Dominican Monastic life. The most recent venture produced yet another book titled <u>Vocation In Black and White</u>. It is published by iUniverse and contains the vocation stories of nuns from various monasteries. Two West Springfield Nuns are included in the book, which can be obtained either from the publisher or from various monasteries.

The nuns in Langley, BC, Canada, are publishing a book of poetry called <u>Mercy Poured</u>. Most of the poems are on mercy. The monastery in Langley was founded by the monastery in Farmington Hills, MI, but the founding nuns themselves came from various monasteries. It was a joint venture by US nuns to found their first English-speaking monastery in Canada. They have had to relocate a few times and need to do so again, but have good vocations in their area, despite having no room to house them. This book was written as a fund raiser for the purchase of materials for a more permanent monastery. The author describes it as "a humble thing" but hopes it will help the foundation grow financially. The publisher, Frontlist, is based in Calgary, AB, Canada and their prices are in US dollars. These nuns prove very creative; not many a monastery would be built with books! The outcome of the tale is yet to be told!

Yours truly designed The *Commemorative Calendar* made to mark the 800ᵗʰ anniversary of the nuns. Each US Monastery was highlighted in a different month. Also included were smaller photos of foreign foundations made from the US Nuns. As many countries as possible were represented in some small way to show how world wide the nuns are. This could never have taken place without email technology! Help was also forthcoming from Fr. Manuel Merten, O.P., the promoter for the nuns around the world. I had the good fortune to meet him at the retreat given by the Master of the Order in 2006 at Adrian, MI.

More and more monasteries are developing websites. The Association has a web site too and provides links to many of the monasteries at http://usaopnuns.org/ They also have a link to my www.praedicare.com web site and mine to theirs. My praedicare site has three series of power point slide shows, touching on the life of St. Dominic, his nine ways of prayer and reflections on the nine ways. There are a few items of interest on the kids page. A Rosary page is being developed in which the visitor can join the nuns in praying the rosary. Each rosary decade depicts art works in and from the monasteries. There is a page for St. Dominic to honor him as "Preacher of "Grace". A theme is developed each month in a pictorial album format as well as in a calendar design (2009), which can be printed out by the viewer.

My technological talents have developed along the way even during the 800ᵗʰ anniversary. We started that year with posting pictures of our West Springfield celebrations. I learned how to make animated gifs[3] with some direction from the student brother, Bro. Dominic Bump, O.P. My next challenge was learning to successfully upload some of the music from our mini-concerts. By the end of the jubilee year I had even learned to use Windows Movie Maker.

The Dominican Order is revising and developing their web site and there are links to many monasteries of nuns around the world. Visit the Order's web site at (http://curia.op.org/en/). From "Links" on

---

3   Compressed file format used for making images appear to be animated

the menu bar select "Websites", and then "Nuns".

Our Summit, NJ monastery led the way with their blog and have won a number of awards for it. You might like to check it out at http://www.monialesop.blogspot.com/ Another monastery was quick to follow suit. So you can see that the nuns are keeping up with technology.

Dominicans have the initials "O.P." after their names. It stands for "Order of Preachers". The nuns preach by their lives and pray that the preaching of the friars may bear fruit, be it in the pulpit or in the classroom. "How beautiful are the feet of those who bring Good News!" – Is. 52:7

(Endnotes)
1   Book of Constitutions of the Nuns of the Order of Preachers, (Published by Direction of Brother Damian Byrne, Master of the Order: USA, 1987) 74:IV.

CHAPTER 9

Surprising Intensity

The Nuns Fight for Their Life

*We boast about your perseverance and faith in all the persecutions
and trials you are enduring. 2 Thess. 1:4 (NIV®)*

Throughout their history various calamities and persecutions have
assailed the nuns and their monasteries. Their spirit and fidelity has
weathered these storms of life and made the nuns flourish over the
waves of time.

The monastic observances are an integral part of the Nuns
contemplative life. For eight hundred years, the nuns have continued
the major observances of prayer, study, vows and common life, with
God as their focus. The minor observances of enclosure, silence, the
habit, work, the cell, table (meals in common with spiritual reading)
assist the major observances by providing the place and atmosphere.

The observances themselves may not surprise our readers but the
intensity with which nuns have lived them over 800 years may. We
would like to share some stories with you.

Common Life

"The first reason for which we are gathered together in community is to live in harmony, having one mind and heart in God." [1]

The life in common is directed to God. It is His face we seek and His Word that we ponder. In this common goal we have one another's example and support. One can well imagine how the lack of a common life would change the monastic atmosphere, and the hardship this would bring. Such was the case during the French Revolution when nuns were driven from their monasteries. During the Reformation the German nuns struggled with all their might against the ruling powers to preserve the life they held sacred and lived dedicated to serving God.

The Strasbourg Nuns Fight for Survival

Who shall separate us from the love of Christ?
Shall trouble or hardship or persecution… Romans 8:35 (NIV®)

In Strasbourg[1] in 1525 three magistrates, invested with the title of "Klosterherren", "The gentlemen of the Convent", went to St. Margaret's monastery. They informed the sisters of new decrees issued by the Senators of Strasbourg. "No more Masses; no more canonical hours. Confession is forbidden under the severest penalties. No more Sacred Hosts in the Tabernacle; no more administration of the Sacraments, even for the sick and dying. And lastly, no more enclosure and no more vows; the sisters are free of all obligations."[2] The nuns were unresponsive, even after imposed private interviews.

At the time, Mother Ursula de Bock was prioress over the 45 nuns in the monastery. When the magistrates brought apostate priests to preach to the nuns to lead them astray, Ursula forewarned and exhorted the nuns, "I beg you, dearly beloved Sisters, to persevere; to allow

1   At the time of this story Strasbourg was of the Alsace region of France, i.e., situated on the Franco-German border.

yourselves to be guided by me...Resist those who will come here with the avowed intention of seducing you." [3]

Mother Ursula de Bock had the young sisters make dummies and place them clothed in religious habits in the stalls behind the grille, who would thus represent the younger portion of the Community, while a few of the older and more prudent sisters would sit around them to break the rigidity of the dummies by their own movements. Martin Butzer, an apostate monk, who had renounced his habit and had married, had already perverted three convents of sisters at Strasbourg. He came and regularly gave his sermons but after a few sessions he discovered the trick. From that time on the nuns were constrained to leave the choir and to go to the nave of the Church to listen to him three times a week.

Seeing that he was making no headway, the "learned" Butzer had the sisters assemble in the refectory and a dialogue took place there, of which an account was recorded in the Chronicle. The following shortened excerpts give a sense of the intensity of the dialogue as well as the determination of the nuns.

MOTHER URSULA:

The example of 'Scholars' touches us very little, for knowledge is dangerous without humility and Our Lord has declared blessed the poor in spirit. We are determined to remain faithful to the teachings of our Holy Mother the Church, such as they have been handed down from generation to generation. It is therefore useless for you to preach any longer in this house.

BUTZER:

Blind nuns, beware of trusting in the words of this impertinent Bock. I will explode her powder; I have the power to do so.

MOTHER URSULA:

Your threats do not frighten me. We do not recognize your authority over us, for you are no longer a doctor of truth. You pervert convents, and instead of fulfilling the functions of a good shepherd, you behave as a hireling and thief, driving souls to their utter destruction. Alas! I cannot help weeping when I think of the doom which awaits you if you persevere in this path.

BUTZER:

Wicked she-devil, I have no need of your hypocritical pity. It is your perversity which prevents you from recognizing the good I wish to do you all, in setting you free from useless and heavy burdens.

MOTHER URSULA:

The vows which bind us to Jesus do not weigh on us at all. We know that if we persevere to the end we will have an eternal reward.

BUTZER:

You are deaf and mad. If you listened to my sermons, you would, know that the state of a nun is anything but a divine institution. I order all of you to come to St. Mark's tomorrow. A good dinner will be served to you; then I will explain the Holy Scriptures, and I will convince you, for the consolation of your souls, that the holy state of marriage was instituted by God for everybody. (Ursula made a quick glance to the sisters, who voiced their refusal to go.)

It is that Bock, that old witch, who gave you the signal of disobedience; I saw it perfectly well. But henceforth you will not have any Prioress; you will all be equal, and everyone will live as she pleases. I forbid you, besides, to speak to that wicked woman, who has ignored my exhortations and who is excommunicated.

MOTHER URSULA:

And who has pronounced the sentence?

BUTZER:

It is I. It is my right and my duty because you detest the word of God.

MOTHER URSULA:

Nothing is further from my thoughts. I esteem the Word of God and the tradition of the Church, as it is handed down in the writings of the Fathers and Doctors; but despise your words, your classes, and those of your colleagues, the apostates, because they are full of errors and lies.

.

Seeing the preacher choked with rage the nuns rallied around Mother Ursula to protect her and one sent word for help. Threatening Ursula with his fist Butzer continued.

BUTZER:

Wait, bold Nun, I will carry my complaints to the Senate. The magistrates, who hold me in high esteem and who do all that I ask of them, will punish your insolence and pride.

MOTHER URSULA:

Pardon me if I have offended you. I fulfill my duty in making you listen to hard truths. It is sad to see such an educated man as you, plunged in error and drawing others into it. It is obvious that your doctrine does not come from the Holy Spirit, for instead of urging souls toward perfection, it gives rein to the passions, and those who follow your counsels hasten to their ruin. If you were to recommend prayer, fasting, and mortifications, you would probably have fewer listeners and disciples.

.

Butzer's face was flaming and his mouth foaming. The sisters were frightened and hurriedly led the Prioress to a nearby room, where they barricaded themselves in. Departing in a rage he met the Prelate of St. John's and the cure of St. Pierre le Vieux, who had come to help the sisters.

.

BUTZER:

I wish I could beat that Bock down to the ground, that wicked witch, that brute, whose lips vomit error and blasphemy. She has dared hold discourses with me of the highest insolence, but I swear to make her regret it. These worthless nuns are going to leave their Convent, were the devil himself to make them go out of it.

Mother Ursula, overcome with emotion, had fainted. When she came to, she was comforted with words of encouragement by the two priests who had come to help. They warned the sisters to watch over their prioress carefully because Butzer was capable of throwing her into the stream in the garden if he could do so without being seen by anyone.

The sisters no longer had any enclosure. The Senate of Strasburg had constituted itself their only superior; its delegates entered when and how they pleased, taking possession of all the keys and watched to see if Mass was being said in some hiding place or some Office recited secretly by the choir. It was the regime of terror. The "Klosterherren" kept putting pressure on the nuns to free themselves from prioral guardianship and to return to their families, there to enjoy conjugal bliss, which they said "equaled the joys of Paradise". The sisters replied that they had no desire of making a trial of that Paradise.

It seems that the nuns were not outright expelled from their monastery because of decrees obtained at different times from the Emperor confirming their rights and privileges. Eventually the Senate managed to despoil their Church, pillage the sacristy and spread all kinds of rumors in hopes of turning the people against them. They hoped to force the nuns to return to their families and incite the people to lay siege to the monastery and leave it in ruins.

With the ruin of their Church the nuns put up portable altars in the Convent cellars. These could be easily removed in case of alarm. It was there that they prayed the Office and the rosary. The nuns' greatest sorrow was to be deprived of spiritual aid and they begged the Lord to send them a priest to hear their confessions and give them Holy Communion. Ursula de Bock secretly begged the Knights of St. John to render them this service, adding that there was at the end of the cellar a remote spot reached by a tunnel ignored by the persecutors. Thus a priest, dressed as a peasant, would go to the Convent before daybreak. An old, broken cask served as a confessional. After consoling and encouraging the nuns, the priest gave them Communion. It was a scene from the Catacombs!

The Senate, the Protestant ministers and the populace combined in their fury to terrorize or seduce the nuns. Butzer made continual efforts to spur the Senate to second his designs of vengeance by dispersing the sisters. To bypass the imperial protection the magistrates resorted to having the sisters claimed by their families. Thus, early on the morning of June 24th, 1529 a crowd led by the "gentleman of the Convent" rushed upon the Monastery. Ursula de Bock went forth alone to meet the invaders. "I protest with all my power against what takes place here. These things have happened against my will, and will not be charged to my conscience. The lord magistrates of Strasbourg will have to answer for them before God." Her voice was drowned out by the mockeries of the invaders; followed by a scene of confusion and disorder impossible to describe.

Thirty-three sisters were carried off by their relatives. Only the Prioress and eleven of the sisters, who were not of the country, remained. They were surrounded by some faithful friends who had slipped in and mingled with the crowd, and who sought to console the venerable Mother Ursula. But she was inconsolable. She and her eleven companions declared in a unanimous voice that they would suffer martyrdom rather than leave Saint Margaret's; and thus foiled the plans of the persecutors, who hoped to close up the house. They despoiled it completely. The magistrates even had the poor beds of these twelve heroic women taken away in the hope that the lack of the absolute necessities would force them to depart. But these courageous women slept on the floor and bore with their hunger.

With a daring that astonished the aldermen, Mother Ursula said, "I will not surrender this house to you. By making my Profession in it, I consecrated myself wholly to the service of God. I will fulfill my duty to the end, were it to cost me my life. But, know well, should anyone wish to do violence to my sisters and myself, I will lift my voice and have my complaints reach the imperial throne." At times she did write to the Emperor or set influential personages to work, at other times prostrate on the ground she would pour out her soul before God, begging for strength for all her daughters. Her indomitable energy won her cause. Charles V ordered the sisters to be reinstalled. The magistrates, finding it to their own interest to defer to him, resigned themselves a year later, to permit the sisters the freedom to return. They themselves stayed at a distance, determined to begin anew their annoyances at the earliest opportunity.

Of the forty-six nuns who lived at Saint Margaret's on June 24, 1529, only three failed to return, who had allowed their parents to marry them off. Mother Ursula herself was worn out and her days were numbered. On learning of her approaching death, the guardians of the house came and made new assaults on her faith. They hoped that her weakened condition would give them an occasion for victory. But to their surprise she responded, "Let the dead bury their dead; I will be faithful unto the end to the vows I have pronounced in making profession in this house; I have lived and I die in the Catholic, Apostolic and Roman Faith." Her agony was short, and her death peaceful. She breathed her last on November 12, 1532.

Those who succeeded her walked the same path. During Agnes Barr's term as prioress, the nuns almost died of hunger. The envoys of the Senate, vexed that their summons failed to make anyone leave, declared that they would take away all the provisions and furniture of the sisters. This declaration was at once put into execution by people bribed for this purpose. All the provisions without exception were carried off, even to the salt and oil, as well as the tables, chairs, benches and beds – the pillage was complete. Moreover, the steward imposed on the Monastery received orders to put padlocks on the granaries, bolt the doors, and put sentinels at the entrance so that none could bring anything whatsoever to these stubborn ones who insisted on being cloistered. Such was the fury against them that they had even removed the chains and buckets from their well in hope that they should suffer the torments of thirst and the horrors of hunger. Prisoners, without any hope of help (for their Catholic friends had gradually disappeared), without a mouthful of bread, without a word of consolation, the sisters of Saint Margaret's turned to the Lord and sent up their cries to Him. God answered them through a poor girl, a former servant, who had remained a Catholic. She made plans with several compassionate women of the neighborhood, and while some kept watch around the place, others threw pieces of bread over the walls. These pieces of bread, carried to the Prioress, were divided into as many small morsels as there were sisters. An old holy water pot fixed to the end of a rope served as a bucket to draw a little water from the well. After many days, a senator out taking a walk looked into the garden through a chink in a shutter. No sister was in sight, no sound was heard. Convinced that the nuns were all dead, he commanded the steward to open the main door so that he could enter the cloister. To his surprise he saw a young sister coming to meet him! "What has become of your companions?" he asked. "They are at dinner", she replied. The amazed old magistrate entered the refectory. A plank which had formerly been fastened to the wall, had been turned into a bench and table for the Community. The meal consisted of crusts of dry bread and a pitcher of water. As soon as he appeared, the Prioress gave a signal and the reader at the table stopped. An impressive and suggestive scene: thus did those poor starved nuns find strength to accomplish the smallest detail of their obligations, the one which prescribed reading during meals. Looking on such a spectacle, the senator was moved. God, who had sustained the sisters, touched this man's heart. "I recognize," he said in a trembling voice to the Prioress and her companions, "that God is with you and I promise to apply myself to obtain your liberty." He kept his word and Saint Margaret's once again enjoyed a moment of tranquility.

The conquest of Alsace by France brought them deliverance. The town of Strasbourg surrendered to Louis XIV on September 30, 1681. The Dominican Nuns, oppressed for a hundred and fifty years, joyfully raised their heads and as the Chronicle says, "sang in the joy of their hearts, 'Haec dies quam fecit Dominus, exultemus et laetemur in ea' (This is the day the Lord has made, let us rejoice and be glad in it.) Their bells, mute for so many years, rang out in joy at the restoration of the liberty of its faith.[4]

(Endnotes)
1   Book of Constitutions 2:I.
2   Dominican Nuns in their Cloister 77.
3   Dominican Nuns in their Cloister 79.
4   Dominican Nuns in their Cloister 80-89.

CHAPTER 10

Surprises: Historic and Heroic

Be on your guard; stand firm in the faith; be men of courage;
be strong. 1 Cor. 16:13 (NIV®)

In December of 2006 when I was preparing for our first celebration service, I called Fr. Jeffrey Ballou. As he is chaplain at Westover ARB, I thought he might be able to direct me to some military people I could invite. He suggested that I focus one celebration totally on the "full military". We discussed the appropriate month for this theme and decided on April. Fr. Jeff was unable to attend himself, but Fr. Eugene Honan honored us as our Guest Officiant. Fr. is a retired Lt. Col. Chaplain.

Fr. Ballou had hoped to secure a military Color Guard from Westover for the service, but our weekend celebration coincided with the National Guard weekend, making this impossible. You may not be aware that such Honor Guard/ Color Guard units consist totally upon volunteers. These good men and women offer this time to honor their comrades and their country. We wanted to recognize those who serve in the military by making them our Honored Guests, praying for all those serving near and far.

For a nun to make calls to the military in the first place took all the courage she could muster! This is not something a nun does every day! What to say? How to say it? Well, here goes… first get the phone number, dial the number,….

Unable to get a Color Guard from Westover, I was directed to Barnes ANG. What a delight to have MSgt Katie Fredette, MSgt Todd Mullane, SMSgt Joseph Delaney and SSgt Christine Willette[1] from the 104th Fighter Wing Base Honor Guard. After the program for the celebration had been printed, I received an email telling us that SMSgt Keith Buckhout would also be joining us. We learned that Keith works as a maintenance supervisor with the Post Office and is never too sure when he is able to participate until the last moment. Keith was a welcome addition!

An invitation was extended to Brig Gen Wade Farris of Westover Air Reserve Base. He had to travel to Washington, DC, so graciously offered to send a representative in his place, Col Michael J. Marten, Vice Commander! Also coming from Westover were MSgt Kimberly A. Babin, representing ICOIC and Family Support Center, and TSgt Louisa Gonzalez. MSgt Babin's husband also serves in the military. Fr. Ballou was delighted to hear the names of those representing Westover because he personally knew these dedicated men and women.

TSgt Michael Pollender also represented the 104th Fighter Wing. He is a member of the Massachusetts Air National Guard. Mike brought his lovely wife along but I'm not sure if it was for "support" or just for the joy of the occasion!

For the US Army MSG Michael Cutone, SOD-G represented the Rhode Island National Guard. Mike mustered a number of troops for the occasion. Among them were CPT Thomas Sarrouf and SFC Terry Schappert of A/2/19th SFG(A) (US Army Special Forces - Green Berets). They too had Guard weekend but managed to make it in time for the service.

Sgt Requilda N. Quintana, R.N. of the US Marine Corp. was all set to join us for the celebration. However, duty called her and like a good soldier always faithful ("Semper Fi") she responded to orders. She was with us in spirit and certainly in our prayers as were all military personnel, whom we were honoring that day.

My dad was in the US Navy and I knew I had to have someone representing that branch! Uncles Paul and Al (Dad's brothers) were

---

1   Staff Sgt. Willette was selected as the Honor Guard member of the year and was a finalist in national competition.

also in the Navy but we never got to meet Al, who was a Fireman 1c. He was on the USS Tasker H. Bliss, which was operating in dangerous waters on Nov. 12, 1942. It was torpedoed by a German submarine at Fedala Bay, Morocco during WWII. The ship burned all night long and then sank. My brother "Al", Alexander Joseph, was named after Uncle Al.[2]

So how did I get my sailor? I called the recruiting station and recruited one! After speaking with the recruiter, I emailed him a bulletin board brochure, which he could post or use to explain the celebration. Subsequent calls brought the good news that MASM Peter Noska would represent the Navy at our celebration. I was pleased to meet Peter's fiancé too. I hope that the jubilee brought many blessings to them and in the days that followed.

The only missing piece to the puzzle was the Coast Guard. That was probably one of the more challenging pieces for me. Again I called the recruiting station. I introduced myself and started explaining what I was looking for, only to hear, "This is the recruiting station." I said that I knew that and that I was looking for someone to represent the Coast Guard. I asked if I should speak to someone else and if so, could he connect me? He asked if I knew who he was. I responded that he was the Chief Petty Officer. Well, it turned out that he was CPO Ryan, the father of Trudi Ryan, who is a good friend of ours. I still hadn't made the connection and I wasn't sure if Chief Ryan thought this was a big joke or what, but we were pleased to have him honor us with his presence. I know his daughter, Trudi, influenced him to attend.

---

2   Uncle Paul's wife was expecting a baby at the same time as my mother and the family with the first boy to be born was going to have the honor or naming him after Al. And so my brother won the name, and we ended up with a cousin Glen, who is not related to the astronaut!

Veterans

*God will not forget your work and the love you have shown him
as you have helped his people and continue to help them.
Heb. 6:10 (NIV®)*

The next detail was to enlist the Veterans. That was a little easier because of Delfo Barabani. Delfo always holds a special place in my heart because he was the military person who came for my Dad's wake and funeral. He always honors his fallen comrades and I assure you that it is indeed a comfort to the family.

Although our celebration took place on April 15th, a week after Easter Sunday, the climate hardly seemed like Easter. The weather threatened snow or rain. Travel was not recommended. This did not hinder our indomitable forces of all ages and stations. Delfo recruited many and various veterans. Cecil Southerland wore a brown WWII army uniform and represented American Legion Post 452 in Chicopee, MA. In their light blue jackets Fred Browicz, Frank Pasternak, Jerry Roy and Kenneth Usher represented the Korean War Veterans Association, Western Mass. Chapter 2000. Leo Vance, Louis Brault and Paul Bradis, wearing red jackets, represented American Legion Post 275 in Chicopee Falls, MA. Manuel Gomes and Charles Kovitch represented American Legion Post 337 in Aldenville, MA, and Kenneth Doerpholz, Sr. represented American Legion Post 353 in Willimansett, MA.

One of the Korean War Vets walked with the aid of two canes or crutches. The weather did not keep him away and nothing would stop him from walking in the procession. I was told that he goes to all their events. At the reception one of the Korean Vets gave me a printout of the "Chosin Few". It describes a very special moment in these marine's history. It also explains the special logo of a star with the letters CF. The printout reads as follows:

The withdrawing marines encountered a major obstacle in the form of a destroyed section of a bridge at Changjin Power

Plant. Thick blinding snow began to fall at dusk. In order for the Air Force to air drop eight 2,000-pound bridge sections, the skies would need to clear up. They would need to see the drop zone at a makeshift airstrip at Koto-ri.

On Dec. 7 and 8, 1950 it snowed and the temperatures hovered around minus 40 degrees Fahrenheit with the windchill factor around minus 60 degrees. When dusk fell on Dec. 8 the storm had not abated. The situation for the marines was bleak. They needed the bridge sections, they needed close air support. They needed clear skies in order to get them. They needed the bridge so they could get out.

As evening wore on, the snow kept falling. Marines still looked to the skies in hope of seeing a break in the clouds. Just when it looked like all hope for the storm to subside was about to disappear, a faint, little white dot could be seen through the falling snowflakes around 2145. The small star provided a big beacon of hope for the Marines at Koto-ri.

A short time later, Col. Alpha L. Bowser, Jr. was taking a short walk around the camp when he heard noise coming from a tent. The Leathernecks inside the propped up frozen piece of canvas were singing the Marines Hymn and giving it their all. The music spread like a virus throughout the encampment. Singing could be heard from almost every tent.

That tiny star meant a lot to many of the Marines who saw it. To some it meant that God loved the Marine Corps and he wouldn't let a little thing like bad weather defeat them after fighting so valiantly against insurmountable odds. The Marines were fortunate to have good weather appear the next morning.[1]

When I was given the printout of the story, the marine told me that there was something else not found in the story. When I asked him what that was, he said it was the name of the marine who saw the star and began the singing. He was that marine.

Other Veterans present were Michael Franco, who represented

the Holyoke Veterans Service Office and James G. Berrelli, Jr., a US Army, Vietnam Veteran, who is Director and Service Officer of the Department of Veteran Services of West Springfield. George Kelly, a West Springfield City Councillor, is a US Army Vet and was also among our Honored Guests. Judy Rosenthal, S.S.J., MSgt., USAF, Ret. served with the 104th Fighter Wing at Barnes Air National Guard. It's not often that one hears of a Sister serving in the military.

In our local newspaper there were regular articles about SGT Mark Ecker II of the 2nd Infantry Division. Mark is from East Longmeadow and lost both his legs in Iraq. The people of Springfield and the surrounding area adopted Mark in a special way. Cards were sent to him in Washington at the Walter Reed Hospital through the Republican News. They reported on him regularly and everyone was eager for his recovery. I contacted his parents and in the end invited Mark's dad Mark to be cross bearer in proxy for his son SGT Ecker.

DEBRA ECKER (MOTHER OF SGT MARK ECKER):

Sr. Mary of the Sacred Heart and the Dominican Nuns were gracious enough to invite our son, SGT Mark Robert Ecker II, and our family to be honored guests at their lovely service. When our son's injury became publicized, the sisters reached out to him and our family in faith and in friendship. It is my belief that God saved our son's life when he was hit by the IED in Iraq. The sisters' welcome, support, and spirituality confirmed this faith. As my son and husband carried the cross on two separate occasions during the processions, it was with pride and gratitude that our family was able to participate in such meaningful and spiritual occasions. Our family will always appreciate the support, kindness, and faith that the Dominican Sisters have shown to us during our time of need. The Ecker Family

In Liturgical Service

Therefore I glory in Christ Jesus in my service to God.
Romans 15:17 (NIV®)

Our two acolytes for this month's celebration were Veterans. Alexander Harshuk served in the US Army and Valmore Hebert in the USAF. Incense bearer was another Alexander, who went to Bosnia to entertain the troops at Christmas of 1996 and into January of 1997… my brother MagicAl.

MagicAl was the only non professional who went to troops that other entertainers did not. His class act did not need a stage, making setup unnecessary. He loved to see the MP's shine their big flashlights on his hands to see if they could discover the secret to his sleight of hand magic, but they could never catch his movements. MagicAl suffered from the bitter cold, sleeping in tents, ready to move when told. At times he did not even have time to grab something to eat. He even entertained troops at the hospital, which was nicknamed the "Glue Factory". He heard that a Bosnian woman was there, who had had one of her legs blown off when she stepped on a mine. At the time of the explosion her mother was with her and was killed. Al asked if he could do a magic trick just for her, to put a smile on her face. Permission was granted. The smile was one he would never forget!

Color Guard

Guard what has been entrusted to your care.
1 Tim. 6:20 (NIV®)

When our celebration began, the Color Guard was the first to march down the Chapel aisle and present the colors. Delfo also introduced the presentation of the colors (flags) of each of the branches of the military. Their respective songs were played as each flag was posted.

Barnes ANG
Color Guard

Westover ARB

Procession with Vets

Staff Sgt.
Christine R.
Willette

Delfo
Barabani

Air National Guard

Army, Coast Guard and Navy

Korean Vets - WM Chapter 2000

American Legion Posts
337 - 353 - 337

Holyoke &West Springfield
Veterans Services Agents

Post 452

American Legion Post 275

Green Berets and the Sisters

Patriotism and Mini Concert

I give thanks to your name;
for you have been protector and support to me.
Ecclus. 51:2 (JB)

Our Sr. Theresa Marie Gaudet, O.P. sang the National Anthem
in her customary beautiful and moving way…full of emotion. I
later posted it on the praedicare website. (http://praedicare.com/
Celebrations/2007AprPhoto.htm) The Pledge of Allegiance followed
the National Anthem.

For our mini concert we had an array of joyful Easter songs. The
final song, "Jesus Christ, Yesterday, Today and Forever", was a solo
also sung by Sr. Theresa Marie, O.P. and accompanied on organ by Sr.
Mary Regina of the Angels Thomas, O.P. Being "Mercy Sunday" we
had a statue of Jesus, the Divine Mercy in the sanctuary with prayer
cards for those who wished to take one.

Boy Scouts Show Appreciation to Military

Give everyone what you owe him: … if respect, then respect;
if honor, then honor. Romans 13:7 (NIV®)

The weather was extremely cold that day with temperatures in the
20s or 30s, not counting wind chill, and snow and/or rain was predicted.
To display appreciation for our military, Boy Scouts from Troop 303
in South Hadley, under the leadership of Ron Boissonneault, and from
Troop 424 in Chicopee, led by Miclele Kappler, rallied to the cause.
After the service with flags in each of their hands Alex Parker, Robert
Embury, Matt and Jacques Lafleur as well as Josh Carpenter and Tyler
and Nick Kapper lined the monastery corridor leading to the reception
area. They also provided cover with umbrellas for guests returning to
their cars. It was a great opportunity for all to show their support and
appreciation for those who dedicate their lives to serving our country

and to keeping us safe.

Ofc. Michael Vezzola helped to coordinate the scouts' activities and suggested hot chocolate to be among the refreshments served at the reception. That provided a big hit along with our Dominican cookies, which always brought smiles to those who enjoyed them. Sr. Mary of the Immaculate Conception, O.P. was responsible for that aspect of the celebration. The refreshments were added beginning in January and were served at subsequent celebrations. I think that secretly it was a drawing card for Officer Mike!

Anchors Aweigh

...and immediately they left the boat and their father
and followed him. Mt. 4:22 (NIV®)

It may surprise you that there is a sister in our monastery in Syracuse, N.Y., who served in the military prior to her becoming a nun. It was on Feb. 19, 1943 during WWII that Pearl Worhach enlisted in the US Navy. She was among the first group of WAVES to serve our country. Her primary naval training involved international Morse code. On Nov. 9, 1945 she was honorably discharged with the rating of Radio Operator, 1st Class.

At the end of WWII she accepted an assignment with the US Army in a civilian capacity as a secretary and for four years worked with the European Command Intelligence School in Oberammergau, Germany.

During her time off she skied and climbed mountains in the Bavarian Alps as well as in Switzerland. She did extensive travelling. On one jeep drive, a group travelled to the Vatican in Rome. They had an interview with Pope Pius XII at his summer residence in Castle Gondolpho.

While she was on assignment at the EUCOM Intelligence School a small ad (about an inch in size) in the Army Stars and Stripes News Bulletin caught her eye. It announced a pilgrimage to Lourdes, France. She had sufficient leave time so she joined the pilgrimage. An Army Chaplain conducted the tour which left from Frankfurt, Germany.

Arriving at Lourdes, she and her travelling partner hurried down to the Grotto. It was late at night and they prayed there for a long time. Although Pearl had a deep love for the rosary, the thought of a religious vocation never entered her mind. When they left the Grotto, her partner asked her if she knew what he was praying for. He told her he felt a "calling" to the Priesthood. She gazed at him with amazement and wondered, "How does it feel to have a 'calling'"? She was not aware of the seed of a vocation which had been planted in her own heart until she returned to her place of work in the Bavarian Alps and found her life completely changed. The parties, skiing and traveling no longer held the same meaning for her. She was completely drawn to rise early in the morning so as to pray and to attend Mass. Her former activities became superficial.

She resigned from her employment and returned to the States. In time, Pearl was drawn to the monastic life and on April 25, 1956 she entered the Dominican Monastery in Syracuse, NY. In time, Sr. Mary Augustine, O.P. was elected prioress. She has been a nun for over 50 years and is still going strong! .

Our Lady of Victory

A great and wondrous sign appeared in heaven:
a woman clothed with the sun, with the moon under her feet and a
crown of twelve stars on her head.
Rev. 12:1 (NIV®)

Our Lady is patroness of America and the National Shrine of the Immaculate Conception is in Washington, DC, directly across from the Dominican House of Studies. People may not realize the powerful assistance Our Lady has given to troops and fleets. With rosary prayer backing the outnumbered Christian fleet at the Battle of Lepanto on October 7, 1571 had a miraculous victory. As a result the feast of Our Lady of Victories was established, later renamed Our Lady of the Rosary.

In 1683 King Jan Sobieski of Poland stopped at the shrine of Our Lady of Czefistochowa, (Czestochowa) where the troops prayed for a blessing on their arms before proceeding to the aid of Austria, which was being attacked by the Ottoman Empire. After the siege of Vienna and the glorious victory of Sobieski over the Turks on Sept. 12, 1683, the feast of the Holy Name of Mary (originally instituted in 1513) was extended to the universal Church.[2]

Hearing the Korean War Vet's story, I couldn't help but think of Mary, who is called Star of the Sea. Dec. 8th is the feast of her Immaculate Conception. Was she there watching over them?

MARY

Mary is a clear and shining star, twinkling with excellence, and resplendent with example, set to look down upon the surface of this great and wide sea

O you, whoever you are, that know yourself to be here not so much walking upon firm ground, as battered to and fro by the gales and storms of this life's ocean, if thou would not be overwhelmed by the tempest, keep your eyes fixed upon this star's clear shining. If the hurricanes of temptation rise against you, or you are running upon the rocks of trouble, look to the star, call on Mary. If the waves of pride, or ambition, or slander, or envy toss you, look to the star, call on Mary. If the billows of anger or avarice, or the enticements of the flesh beat against your soul's bark, look to Mary. If the enormity of your sins troubles you, if the foulness of your conscience confounds you, if the dread of judgment appalls you, if you begin to slip into the deep of despondency, into the pit of despair, think of Mary.

In danger, in difficulty, or in doubt, think on Mary, call on Mary. Let her not be away from your mouth or from your heart, and that you may not lack the help of her prayers, turn not aside from the example of her conversation. If you follow her, you will never go astray. If you pray to her, you will never have need to despair. If you keep her in mind, you will never fall. If she leads you, you will never be weary. If she helps you, you will reach home safe at the last. [3]

(Endnotes)

1   Sgt. Richard W. Holtgraver, Jr., "The Star of Koto-ri," Chosin Reservoir, http://www. chosinreservoir.com/kotoristar.htm (accessed March 14, 2009).
    The Star of Koto-Ri is the registered trademark of the Chosin Few. It is used with permission by The Chosin Few, Inc.

2   Holweck, Frederick. "Feast of the Holy Name of Mary." The Catholic Encyclopedia. Vol. 10. New York: Robert Appleton Company, 1911. 16 Mar. 2009 http://www.newadvent. org/cathen/10673b.htm . (accessed March 16, 2009). Used with permission.

3   [Breviary sept 12] "Devotion to the Most Holy Name of Mary: Mariae," The Most Holy Rosary.com, StGemma.com Web Productions Inc., http://www.themostholyrosary.com/ appendix8.htm. (accessed March 16, 2009).

CHAPTER 11
Our Blessed Mother's Surprises

*For to him who has will more be given,
and he will have abundance. Mt. 13:12 (RSV)*

Mary has given numerous surprises to the Order from the beginning, when the globe of fire was seen over her shrine in Prouilhe. (Chapter 3). But that is not the only gift the Order has received from her; she also gave us the habit.

St. Dominic was in Rome in 1218 when Reginald of Orleans arrived there. Reginald was a renowned professor who had taught canon law in Paris for five years and was a prominent public figure. While in Rome Reginald fell seriously ill with a fever. St. Dominic went to see him several times and urged him to join the Order.

As St. Dominic prayed intensely for this young man, Our Lady answered Dominic's prayer in an unexpected way. She appeared to Reginald and anointed his five senses. She also showed him the habit of the new Order, complete with its white scapular. Reginald was immediately cured and his whole body restored to perfect health. The doctors, who had given up hope for his recovery, were astonished. [1]

St. Dominic had worn the garb of a Canon of St. Augustine. But since that time, St. Dominic and all his followers adopted the habit Our Lady had given through this apparition to Reginald.[2] It is the habit we still wear today.

It should not be surprising that devotion to Mary is strong in the

Dominican Order. Once, Dominic had a vision of Our Lady. She was surrounded by members of various orders, all except for Dominicans. When Dominic saw this, he wept. Our Lady then opened her mantle, under which Dominic saw his spiritual children gathered there under her protective care.[3] She is patroness of the Order and each year on May 8th the Order renews its consecration to her.

The Habit

"The habit of the nuns, which is a sign of their consecration and a witness to poverty, consists of a white tunic, a belt with a rosary attached, a white scapular and a black veil and cappa." [4]

During the French Revolution nuns were expelled from their monasteries. There was little that they could take with them, being prevented from wearing their habits. And so the Dominican Order died out in France.

In 1843 a young Frenchman named Pere Lacordaire, established the first house of the restored Order at Nancy. In 1846 there lived a nun by the name of Sr. Marie Cecile Annion. She was the last survivor of the celebrated Alsacian Convent of St. Marguerite. Her only possession from her cloistered religious life was her monastic habit, which she had kept hidden as a relic. She heard a rumor of a Friar Preacher, who was a Frenchman, restoring the Order. He was to come to Strasbourg itself! She had her own surprise for him. She brought out her garments to show Lacordaire a Dominican Nun on French soil once again. She was 83 years old.[5]

Regular Observance

"To regular observance belong all the elements that constitute our Dominican life and order it through a common discipline. Outstanding among these elements are common life, the celebration of the liturgy and private prayer, the observance of the vows and the study of sacred truth. To fulfill these faithfully, we are helped by enclosure, silence, the habit, work and penitential practices." [6]

Study

"The blessed Dominic recommended some form of study to the first nuns as an authentic observance of the Order. It not only nourishes contemplation, but also removes the impediments which arise through ignorance and informs the practical judgment. In this way it fosters the fulfillment of the evangelical counsels with a more enlightened fidelity and encourages unanimity of mind.... "[7]

For the nun, study is not an end in itself but a means to an end. Blessed Margaret Ebner's study led her into the heights of contemplation, as it did for other Rhineland mystics.

Sisters in formation are instructed in Sacred Scripture, liturgy, church history, the history of spirituality and of the Order as well as dogmatic and moral theology.

In addition to the on-going formation program (see Chapter 15), individual sisters also pursue courses of study in other areas in varying degrees. My own studies included correspondence courses in Biblical Hebrew I, the language in which the Old Testament is written, as well as correspondence courses in Biblical Greek I and II and Biblical Greek exegesis. These studies help me better ponder the New Testament texts of scripture. Comparing the two, I realized that no translation can adequately convey the riches contained therein. Other sisters have done in depth studies on the Fathers of the Church and other related topics.

Silence

"Silence should be carefully kept by the nuns especially in places and at times appointed for prayer, study and rest. It is the guardian of all observance and a particular aid to peace and contemplation."[8]

During the night a stricter silence is observed in the monastery from the beginning of the night's rest until the office of Lauds on the following day, called Profound Silence. Thus it was just the norm for nuns of St. Margaret's in 1520 to keep Profound Silence when a big fire broke out near the Convent and threatened to consume it. The sisters hurriedly put tubs out in front of the entrance, filled them with water, procured buckets and formed a bucket chain. They set to work with extreme ardor, but, says the Chronicle, not one of them uttered a single word while the fire lasted. Such is the respect for our observance of silence.

(Endnotes)
1   Drane 250.
2   Drane 251.
3   Drane 240.
4   Book of Constitutions 59.
5   Dominican Nuns in their Cloister 60-61.
6   Book of Constitutions 35: II.
7   Book of Constitutions 100: II.
8   Book of Constitutions 46: II.

CHAPTER 12

More Surprises

Praise be to the God and Father of our Lord Jesus Christ, who has blessed us in the heavenly realms with every spiritual blessing in Christ. Eph. 1:3 (NIV®)

In our earliest celebration in December of 2006 Fr. Christopher Connelly joined with us in our 800th Anniversary Celebrations, acting as emcee. In May of 2007 he returned as our Guest Officiant, now a Monsignor! He is not one looking for honors, but we were honored to have him with us. He is a long time friend of our community.

Fr. Marek Stybor[1], O.F.M.Conv. stopped by one day and asked to see me. I was in the midst of planning our May Celebration but was able to take care of some prayer cards Fr. wanted done. The cards were for some children, who were to make their First Communion. After I did the cards, I surprised Father by what I felt they cost. I told him he needed to provide me with some First Communicants for our Celebration service. He later gave me the names of six children, who would join us for the celebration. One of the children had asked Fr. Marek if **he** were going too. Put on the spot, he answered "Yes"! So I too received a delightful surprise beyond what I expected.

---

1   Fr. Marek also brought his Morning Star Childrens' Prayer Group to the Monastery for a Mass, during our Jubilee Year.

In Service

There are different kinds of service, but the same Lord.
1 Cor. 12:5 (NIV®)

Mark Solitario acted as emcee that month. It was a new experience for him and he did a great job. Mark was a high school senior at Holyoke Catholic and frequently served Mass at our Chapel. Other faithful servers included Valmore Hebert as Incense Bearer and Henry Sansouci as Cross Bearer. Scott Lozyniak, the CHS senior, returned as acolyte and Ofc. Michael Vezzola assisted as the second acolyte.

Religious Women Educators

Our gifts differ according to the grace given us. If your gift is ...
teaching, then use it for teaching. Romans 12: 6,7 (JB) .

For our May Celebration we invited Religious Sisters involved in Catholic Elementary School education as honored guests. These were well represented. Sr. M. Andrea Ciszewski, F.S.S.J., Superintendent of Schools joined us. She was very helpful in sending information about the celebration to all the Catholic Schools in the diocese. Sr. Jacqueline Kazanowski, C.S.S.F., principal of St. Stanislaus Kostka School in Adams, MA., and Sr. Mary Amandine, C.S.S.F. honored us with their presence. Sr. Benilda, F.S.S.J. teaches at St. Stanislaus in Chicopee while Sr. Corinne Gurka, F.S.S.J., also from the Franciscan Sisters of St. Joseph, is principal at Mater Dolorosa in Holyoke. The Daughters of Mary of the Immaculate Conception came in full force from Ware. Sr. Mary Janice, D.M. is principal at St. Mary School. Sr. Mary Clare, D.M., Sr. Mary Philomena, D.M. and Sr. Mary Gloriosa, D.M. are all teachers there. Representing the Sisters of St. Joseph was Sr. Christine Lavoie, S.S.J., who is principal of St. Mary's in Westfield.

**Catholic Women's Club
and Guild**

**Catholic Elementary School
Educators**

Daughters of Mary

**Franciscan
Friar**

**First Communicants
and "Mothers"**

**Catholic Elementary School
Faculty and Students**

**Crowning
of
Our Lady**

**by
First Communicant**

Reception

**First Communicants
receive medals**

Volunteer Staff

**Our visitors
meet Sr. Pauline**

Mothers

"Honor your father and mother"—which is the first commandment
with a promise— Eph. 6:2 (NIV®)

Our celebration occurred on Mother's Day, so Sr. Christine brought her mother with her. We included First Communicants and their "Mothers" (Grandmothers, too) as one group of Honored Guests. They came from seven different parishes in five different cities. These wonderful "Mothers" were: Kimberlee Ayuyu, Mrs. Beliveau, Grazyna Bieniasz, Agnieszka Czarniecka and Grandmother Zofia, Mrs. Feltrin, Karen Ford, Julie M. Leonard (also a Teacher at St. Patrick's in Chicopee), Ewa Maziarz, Kara Mercier, Mrs. O'Neill, Keane O'Neill's Grandmother, Mrs. Paier, Debbie Poulton, Eileen Sullivan, the Grandmother of Sean Sullivan, and Mrs. Wright. Barbara Sypek, the Grandmother of two Catholic students, was also included in this group.

First Communicants

I am the living bread that came down from heaven.
If anyone eats of this bread, he will live forever. Jn. 6:51 (NIV®)

There were a number of First Communicants from Chicopee. Joshua Gilley-Murphy and Brianna Hundley were from St. Joan of Arc-St. George Parish and Brittany Beyette was from St. Patrick's. Those rallied by Fr. Marek, O.F.M. Conv. from St. Stanislaus were Keane O'Neill, Brayen Ayuyu, Carly Poulton, Paulina Maziarz, Alexandra Czarniecka and Victoria Bieniasz. From Mater Dolorosa in Holyoke came Molly Brainard and Jordyn Mercier. Elizabeth Ford came from Holy Name in Springfield, Sean Sullivan from St. Mary's in Westfield, and Lauren Beliveau, Nicole Feltrin, Keane O'Neill, Joseph Paier and Olivia Wright came from St. Thomas the Apostle School in West Springfield. The children wore their First Communion clothes and looked like angels.

Just before the rosary began we had two of the First Communicants do the honor of crowning the Blessed Mother. No one was chosen beforehand. We thought that we would ask the first girl and the first boy who arrived to do this honor. When writing this book I did not remember the name of those two children. However, I contacted a few schools and invited the children who came to write something of their experience and was surprised to discover that one of these happened to be one of the two who crowned Our Lady!

OLIVIA WRIGHT, ST. THOMAS SCHOOL, WEST SPRINGFIELD, MA:

The year I made my First Communion in May of 2007, I took part in a beautiful celebration. My Mother and I went to the Monastery of the Dominican Nuns to help them celebrate their 800th Anniversary on May 20, 2007. I was the first girl to arrive so I had the honor of crowning Mary. I felt so happy and very proud to be chosen to take part in this once in a lifetime service. It was awesome! I had been to the chapel before to light candles and pray with my Mom and my Grandma. I had seen the Nuns through the windows at the altar. They were singing and praying and I wanted to meet and speak to them. Then my wish came true on May 20, 2007! After the service my friend Lauren and I got to meet, speak to, and take pictures with some of the Nuns. Also what I thought was really cool was that one Nun had a puppet that was dressed like a Nun! This experience inspired me to love God even more than I did!

LAUREN BELIVEAU, ST. THOMAS SCHOOL, WEST SPRINGFIELD, MA:

When I went to the Dominican Nuns' Monastery it was a very special day to me. I went with my mom. We were one of the first ones there so we had to wait in a line. I remember we sat in the chapel and I smelled incense. Also there were two windows on the right and left side of the altar. That is where I could see the nuns singing and praying. When they were all together like that they sounded so beautiful. Especially the one who sang the Ave Maria. During the Holy Hour we said the rosary. The fifth decade, the coronation of Mary, was said for the first communion children and their moms. After the Holy Hour we went to a big room where the nuns were. We got to meet them and got to talk with them. I thought that was very special because they don't usually get to talk. They were all very nice. The one who sang the Ave Maria had a puppet that was funny. The nuns gave me a Mary medal and an envelope with a Mass card that said the nuns kept me in their prayers. My friend Olivia and I took pictures with the nuns so I would always remember them. I also remember talking about it the whole time I was home. This is a day I'll never forget.

Catholic Elementary School Education

You must teach what is in accord with sound doctrine.
Titus 2:1 (NIV®)

It was our pleasure to honor Catholic educators and their students, who have the privilege of such an education. Catholic education plays a very important role in forming the minds and hearts of the young. Our invited honored guests included: **St. Joan of Arc-St. George, Chicopee:** Susan Lemieux, Principal; Students: Danielle, Devin and Dylan; **St. Patrick's, Chicopee:** Anne T. Sweetman, Principal; Cathryn LaDuke, Teacher; **St. Stanislaus, Chicopee:** Mrs. Jean Wainwright, Teacher; **Mater Dolorosa, Holyoke:** Maryann Menard, Librarian; Emma Mercier, Student; **Our Lady of Mount Carmel School, Springfield:** Mrs. Carole Raffaele, Principal; Ann Di Mana Haines, Teacher; Emily Renaud, Trinnity Cruz, Chelsey Micole, Kristel Viera and Nyah Salsbury, Students; **St. Thomas the Apostle School, West Springfield:** Mrs. Sandra Hourihan, Teacher; and from **St. Mary's, Westfield:** Hanna Sullivan, Student. Many of us look back at our own Catholic education with grateful hearts and thank God for those who made it possible.

Religious Education

You yourselves are full of goodness, complete in knowledge and competent to instruct one another. Romans 15:14 (NIV®)

We did not want to overlook those, who dedicate themselves to giving religious instruction to the young, as this is an important part of forming the minds and character of the young. It prepares them to know and understand their faith, which will sustain them throughout their lives.

I made calls trying to contact people involved in religious education. It proved challenging because classes had already ended for the year. Fortunately we were able to have a few people represent this group of honored guests. Art and Regina Lourenco have taught religious education for many years and had previously brought a group of students to the monastery so that they could learn more about the contemplative way of life the nuns live. Listed in our program was teacher Nancy-Anne Duggan from **St. Mary's in East Springfield**, and student Emily Squires from **Holy Name in Springfield**. Also included in this group were Emily's mother and grandmother: Erin Squires and Ellen Ford. Intern Karen Cutone was listed with **Magnificat in Warren.**

Catholic Women

...those women who work hard in the Lord.
Romans 16:12 (NIV®)

Msgr. Connelly's mother was present as an Honored Guest for the Catholic Women's Club. Carol Hausamann, president of the Club, announced the mystery for their group. Other members listed on the program were: Claire Ashe, Mary Blais, Maureen and Sheila Collins, Ann Dryden, Elaine Foley, Suzanne Frennier, Anne Gibbons, Mary Hayes, Jeanne Joyal, Mary McCarthy, Alice Perry, Margaret

Scanlon, Janis Wise and Marcia Wright. The Catholic Women's Club has diocesan membership reaching far beyond a single parish. Club members have visited the monastery at various times. We have also been beneficiaries of their kindness and generosity.

Also included in the women's group of Honored Guests were Kathleen Guiheen and Audrey Sawicki of Our Lady of Hope Church Women's Guild in Springfield, MA. This group of Catholic women gathers together in a religious and social atmosphere in the lower level of Our Lady of Hope Church.

At their meetings, the women recite the Rosary and in May, crown the statue of Our Lady of Hope. They have an annual Silver Tea, a Fashion Show, a Communion Luncheon, a Christmas Party as well as guest speakers and bus outings. The Guild also serves as a means of financial support to the church and school by their various fund-raising activities.

In Service

...to prepare God's people for works of service, so that the body of Christ may be built up. Eph. 4:12 (NIV®)

Sarah Garrity and Cati Josefiak assisted me on a number of occasions with instructing our guests and answering their questions. Regina Lourenco also helped me out, especially with the children who would do the May crowning. Regina is a former classmate of mine and she and her husband, Art, own a religious goods store. They graciously provided "Hail Mary" coins for us to give each First Communicant and elementary school child.

Mini Concert Melodies

Sing to him a new song; play skillfully, and shout for joy.
Psalm 33:3 (NIV®)

Our mini concert had a number of Marian songs as was fitting for Mother's Day and for May being the month of Mary our Mother. We sang an Ascension Hymn, since we were still in Paschal time (Easter Season). One piece entitled "Now the Green Blade Rises" is a French Easter Carol from Languedoc, the area where the first nuns were founded. Some of the text reads, "Love (Christ) is come again, like wheat that springeth green." Our rendition was played with tone chimes. Sr. Mary Fidelis, O.P. and Sr. Angela, O.P. were the two Linden, VA chimers. Sr. Mary Joseph Belisle, O.P. and I played the chimes for West Springfield. Sr. Mary of the Immaculate Conception, O.P. was musical directress for this piece. We recorded it and posted the music on http://praedicare.com/Celebrations/2007mayphoto.htm The climax of the mini concert was a solo by Sr. Theresa Marie Gaudet, O.P. She sang the "Ave Maria" by Gounod. This too was posted on the page mentioned above so that those who were unable to attend might share the beauty and joy of the day.

Sister's Surprise

For you make me glad by your deeds, O Lord; I sing for joy at the
works of your hands. Ps. 92:4 (NIV®)

Sr. Theresa Marie has many talents, one being puppeteering. She has one puppet she named Sr. Pauline that she brings out for special occasions. She thought the children who joined us as honored guests would enjoy a surprise appearance at the reception, so she brought her out. Sr. Pauline proved a big hit and helped present the children with the "Hail Mary" coins. She attracted a lot of attention and even volunteer staff members (Sarah, Cati and Scott) enjoyed having their picture taken with her.

Blessed Imelda Lambertini – Patroness of First Communicants

Tradition says that Imelda Lambertini was born in Bologna in 1322. When she was nine years old, she asked to be allowed to go to the Dominicans at Val di Pietra. There is little information about her status in the convent, but we do know she wore the habit and followed the exercises as much as she was allowed to.

In those days the age for receiving Holy Communion was much older, making Imelda in-eligible. Imelda prayed earnestly for the grace of receiving Communion, and asked for the privilege on the Vigil of the Ascension. But when consulted on the matter, the chaplain flatly refused; she must wait until she was older. After Mass, Imelda remained in her place in choir, when a sound caused the sacristan to turn. She saw a brilliant light shining above Imelda's head and a host suspended in the light. The sacristan hurried off to get the chaplain.

He took the Host suspended in the air and gave it to the rapt child, who knelt like a shining statue, unconscious of all around her. Afterwards, when the prioress went to call her for breakfast, she found her still kneeling. There was a smile on her face and she was dead.[1]

Several miracles have been worked through her intercession and her cause for canonization has been under consideration for many years. In 1928 a major cure was reported of a Spanish sister who was dying of meningitis. Imelda has been declared the patroness of all First Communicants.

(Endnotes)
1   Sister Mary Jean Dorcy, O.P., Saint Dominic's Family, 2nd ed. (Rockford, IL: Tan Books and Publishers, Inc., 1983) 144-146.

CHAPTER 13

Surprising Growth and Expansion

In him we were also chosen, having been predestined according to the plan of him who works out everything in conformity with the purpose of his will, ... Eph. 1:11 (NIV®)

Eucharistic Adoration brings with it many blessings. That was evident to the husband of Countess de Villeneuve, the nuns of Chinon, France, Julia Crooks, a young woman in New York who became Mother Mary of Jesus, O.P. and Bishop Michael Corrigan of Newark, N.J. The great and small elements of this story show how God orders all things well. The Lord desires to give Himself to us, to bless us in so many ways, and indeed He has done so.

Surprise: A Monastery for Perpetual Adoration in France

It is not often that a man would bequeath his wife with money to build a monastery of perpetual adoration, but such was the case. In his last will and testament, a French gentleman, the husband of Countess de Villeneuve, bestowed on his wife a large sum of money for the erection of a monastery of Perpetual Adoration. After the monastery was built, the Countess offered it to Carmelite nuns. Initially they accepted, but later relinquished because their numbers made it impossible for them to maintain perpetual adoration. The Countess then offered it to the Dominican Nuns at Chinon and with the approval of Fr. Jandel, O.P.,

Master General, and the blessing of Pope Pius IX the nuns accepted the monastery in Oullins, France along with the privilege and obligation of Perpetual Adoration.[1]

Julia Crooks

God works in strange and sundry ways. Julia Crook's life testifies to this fact. She was born on September 22, 1838 in New York City, of a well to do family the last of nine children. Mr. Crooks was Scotch by birth, a non-Catholic. Julia's mother, Emilie, was a pious Catholic lady of French ancestry. As a young woman Julia became well acquainted with high society. After the death of her parents, she lived with her married sister, whose husband was a French gentleman. At times the family lived in New York City, and at other times in Lyons, France. Julia always went with them. While in France, Julia learned of the Dominican Nuns.[2] Just before returning to America, Julia's younger niece, Virginia, (born in New York City on Dec. 20, 1850) felt a sudden and unexplainable disinclination to board the steamer. It proved to be the work of Divine Providence: while crossing the Atlantic, the steamer sank. In time, this niece became one of God's instruments.

Upon the death of her sister, Julia returned to New York with her two young bereft nieces, whom she raised.[3] Years later after the older niece was married, Julia accepted an invitation to return to France, taking her younger niece, Virginia Noel, with her. It was on this trip that Julia determined to follow her vocation, and in 1873 at 34 years of age she entered the Monastery at Oullins. Her brother, over whose home she had presided in New York, opposed it strongly, but to no avail. It must be noted that before Julia departed from New York, her director Fr. Dold, a Redemptorist, told her that she was not to work for God in Europe, but was to come back to America. As a result, when Julia was received at Oullins, it was with the understanding that in due time she was to make a foundation in America.[4]

Oullins Monastery

Archbishop Michael Corrigan

Julia Crooks

Hunt's Point Monastery (Bronx)

Foundresses, standing (l. to r.), Sr. Mary of the Blessed Sacrament and Mother Mary of the Rosary; Seated (l. to r.) Mother Mary of Jesus and Mother Mary of Mercy; kneeling in front (l. to r.), Sr. Mary Antonius & Sr. Margaret Mary.

Newark Monastery

Corpus Christi Monastery Menlo Park, CA

Mother Mary Emmanuel

Mother Mary of the Trinity Menlo Park

Oullins Monastrance

Mother Mary of the Rosary

Eucharistic Adoration at Detroit Monastery

Lufkin, Texas

Mother Mary of the Eucharist

Los Angeles Monastery

Fr. Michael Corrigan

A certain remarkable priest from New York, named Fr. Michael Corrigan, had been confirmed by St. John Neumann when he was young. Neumann was then Bishop of Philadelphia. Fr. Corrigan studied in Rome and received his doctorate there, after which he was appointed director of the Seminary at Seton Hall, later serving as its President. In March of 1873 he received word of his appointment as the Second Bishop of the See of Newark. At 34, he became the youngest bishop in the country.[5] On the same day that he received his appointment to the Bishopric of Newark, New Jersey, Corrigan had written to Sr. Julia. He told her that in receiving this heavy cross, God had also given him news of her entrance at Oullins, which was a consolation to him, since he counted on her prayers. [6] Bishop Corrigan was consecrated as Second Bishop of Newark on May 4, 1873. In speaking of him, his predecessor, Bishop Bayley said that he "had learning enough for five bishops and sanctity enough for ten." [7] He would need all these gifts of mind and spirit because within five months of his taking office the Panic of 1873 would begin, with the recession lasting to March of 1879 and the "Long Depression" itself extending to as late as 1897.[8]

A New Beginning

Julia entered Oullins in June of 1873, Pentecost Monday, and received the habit on August 5th of that same year. She was given the name of Mother Mary of Jesus. She made her final profession a year later on August 16, 1874. That time frame would be surprising news for our day and age, but prior to the 1917 Code of Canon Law, there was no specification for the length of formation. The time frame was left to the discretion of the community/Order. There were no temporary vows as a rule and in some communities the novitiate began when the candidate entered.

In 1876, when Bishop Corrigan visited France on his *ad limina* visit to Rome, he saw Sr. Julia at Oullins and also visited with Mother

Marie Dominique, who was then Prioress. But when the matter of the foundation was mentioned, a long silence ensued. [9] It seems that Mother Mary of Jesus' niece, Virginia Noel, who was twenty-six years old at the time, had also entered Oullins in 1876. Her birthday being Dec. 20th she received the holy habit at midnight Mass on Christmas day and given the name Sr. Mary Emmanuel.[10]

The day finally came when Mother Marie Dominique believed mother Mary of Jesus could depart to the USA. She wrote Bishop Corrigan to inform him that the Community was in a condition to make the proposed foundation. Mother Marie Dominique also arranged for Mother Mary of Jesus to receive special guidance and instruction on a regular basis from the Very Rev. Antoninus Danzas, O.P., Provincial of the Province of Lyons. The instruction began a year prior to the foundation. The 74 year old Cardinal of Lyons, Louis-Marie-Joseph-Eusèbe Cardinal Caverot, came to the monastery to instruct them. Mother Mary of Jesus had three other sisters, who planned on traveling with her to the new foundation. The Cardinal recommended that they remain in New York for a few days to receive Cardinal McCloskey's blessing (he was Archbishop of New York).

And so in May of 1880, Mother Mary of Jesus sailed to New York, accompanied by her brother who had come to assist the nuns on their journey. On June 24th, Feast of St. John the Baptist, they departed from Oullins, went to Paris and attended Mass offered by Fr. Labore, O.P. at the shrine of Our Lady of Victories. They set sail for America on June 26, 1880. [11] Mother Mary of Jesus was accompanied by Mother Mary Dominica of the Rosary, who came as Sub-Prioress, Sr. Mary Emmanuel, who was destined to succeed Mother Mary of Jesus as Prioress at Newark, and Sr. Mary of Mercy, who was at the time only a novice, but who in later years succeeded Mother Mary of Jesus as Prioress in their foundation established in 1889 at Hunt's Point, New York. [12] They reached NY on July 6, 1880 and were directed to the Sisters of Charity of Seton Hall. The nuns stayed there for three weeks until their temporary dwelling in Newark was ready. On the Feast of St. Martha, the little house was blessed and Holy Mass offered by the Vicar General, Monsignor Doane, due to the absence of Bishop

Corrigan. The nuns at once began their monastic life. A Lay Sister[1] entered on the very day on which the nuns took possession of their house, and young women, who had made application upon the nuns' arrival soon followed as postulants. [13]

Another Lay Sister entered soon after, and on August 4, 1880, the feast of St. Dominic[2], Bishop Corrigan celebrated Mass in the temporary home of the nuns on Sussex Avenue, initiating exposition of the Blessed Sacrament. This was the official inauguration in the United States of perpetual adoration by a religious community. With the help of a few good lay people, the community kept Exposition of the Blessed Sacrament by day. [14]

On September 26, 1880, Bishop Corrigan was made coadjutor, with the right of succession, to Cardinal McCloskey, archbishop of New York. He left on November 9, 1880. Bishop Corrigan said his last Mass in Newark in the nuns' small Chapel. He blessed them and smilingly said, "Please God, you shall follow me." The community grew and in 1883 numbered twenty-one religious. A year had hardly passed before the new and permanent monastery was ready for occupancy. Bishop Corrigan had blessed the cornerstone; his successor, Bishop Wigger blessed the finished Monastery. It was on that occasion, April 14, 1884 that the nuns prayed the choral office in the new monastery for the first time. Archbishop Corrigan came to consecrate the altar, which was his gift, and afterwards turned the key to lock the enclosure. [15] On 10 October, 1885, Cardinal McCloskey died, and Archbishop Corrigan took over the metropolitan diocese of New York. As a result, he was the chief spiritual ruler of one of the most important dioceses in the world. He was not obliged to wait, according to the usual custom, for the pallium, in order to exercise his functions. He had so distinguished himself, that by an act of special courtesy, Rome permitted him to perform the duties of his office as soon as he ascended to the archbishopric.[16]

---

1   A lay sister was not obliged to the Latin Choral Office in Choir but said a certain number of Prayers (Our Fathers or Hail Marys). They were often uneducated and engaged in domestic work in the monastery and did not have active voice (voting rights). The lay sister class no longer exists in the monastery.

2   St. Dominic's feast is now observed on August 8th.

The Hunt's Point Monastery in New York

The Newark community grew rapidly, reaching forty-seven nuns within the enclosure and four extern sisters[3] in just nine years, 1889. The community felt able to begin a second US foundation, and looked toward "Hunt's Point", New York ("Hunt's Point is known today as the Bronx).[17] Archbishop Michael Corrigan had extended the invitation and asked expressly that in their prayer the nuns remember the seminarians and priests of his Archdiocese. Mother Mary of Jesus Crooks, O.P., who was the foundress of the first US monastery, was also foundress for this second American monastery in the Archdiocese of New York. On May 26th, 1889 she came with five other sisters, including Mother Mary of Mercy, who was born in France and was one of the original four who came to the first foundation. Her early studies included English, but she always retained her charming French accent. She served as Sub-Prioress in Hunt's Point and later as Prioress.[18] The depression was still in force and the sisters lived poorly. They often used old coffee grounds to make their coffee, grounds which the Extern Sisters had begged for and which were kept to be used several times over. Nevertheless, the foundation flourished. On May 30th Bishop Corrigan blessed their dwelling and established the enclosure. Three weeks later he blessed the cornerstone of the Chapel. On December 3rd of 1890 the nuns, now numbering twenty, had the joy of being enclosed in their permanent granite, Gothic style Monastery, appropriately named "Corpus Christi"[4].[19]

---

3   An extern sister professes perpetual vows and is not bound to enclosure. She is the contact person with the public. The extern sisters have their own Statutes from the Holy See.
4   Translated: "Body of Christ". It reflects their vocation of Eucharistic adoration of Christ present in the Eucharist.

Resurgence Abroad and Expansion at Home

During the French Revolution Dominican the Monasteries of Nuns were suppressed. The Monastery at Nay reopened in 1666, and it refounded Prouilhe in 1880,[20] the same year that the Newark foundation began. On the 700th Anniversary of Prouilhe, the Newark Monastery, having grown in stability and numbers, was able to make a new foundation in the central United States. Bishop Foley of Detroit welcomed Mother Mary Emmanuel Noel, O.P. and her six companions into his Archdiocese.[21] They came to Detroit on Passion Sunday, April 1, 1906 and the Monastery of the Blessed Sacrament was established. In 1966 the community relocated to their present location in Farmington Hills, MI. In 1915 two foundations were made. Mother Mary St. Peter and three other nuns began a foundation in Cincinnati, Ohio, while Mother Mary Emmanuel Noel, accompanied by five sisters, made one in Albany, New York. Both of these monasteries have since closed.[22]

A Surprising Offer Turned Down

Mother Mary of Jesus Crooks became blind toward the close of her life. Yet her inner vision remained sharp. When the Hunt's Point Community numbered sixty, she was offered a large amount of money if she would send sisters on a foundation. But the donor made one stipulation: it would have to be constructed in one of the Atlantic States, where the donors' interests were centered. Mother's inner vision was broader than that, as she had her sights on the Pacific coast. Fr. A. L. McMahon, O.P., the Dominican Provincial of the Fathers on the West Coast, had been making repeated requests for the sisters and keeping in touch with the Prioresses for some time.

An Earthshaking Delay

The nuns received word that Archbishop Riordan of the Archdiocese of San Francisco favored their coming. But then the great earthquake and fire in San Francisco, April 18, 1906 prevented the group from coming until the city could recover. In 1915 Fr. McMahon requested a new foundation from Archbishop Hanna, newly appointed to the See of San Francisco. On a trip East the Archbishop visited the nuns at Hunt's Point and extended a personal promise of welcome to the West. He informed them that Bertha d'Alte Welch, who was well known to the nuns for vestments she had purchased from them, had offered her former spacious residence as a temporary home for the sisters. After many obstacles were overcome Mother Mary of the Rosary, accompanied by seven sisters, left for San Francisco on May 29, 1921. Fr. McMahon, O.P. and several friars together with Mother Mary Louis, O.P., who was the Mother General of the Dominican Sisters of the Third Order of the Congregation of the Holy Name welcomed the nuns on their arrival. Mother Louis and her Congregation gave the nuns hospitality at their college for two months because a labor strike had prevented the necessary renovations to their temporary dwelling. On August 6th Archbishop Hanna said Mass at the temporary monastery and enclosure was established.

A suitable site could not be found in San Francisco for a permanent monastery, so land was purchased in Hillsborough, which was to the south. As the ground was being cleared, the residents rose up in opposition and in a few days, a public ordinance was passed forbidding religious construction in their precincts. The sisters suffered financial loss and spiritual gain when property was secured farther south at Menlo Park. This monastery is built in the Tudor Gothic style in a soft grey stone, and bears the name "Corpus Christi Monastery".[23] By April 9, 1928 the new monastery on Oak Grove Avenue was ready, and the sisters joyfully moved in. The community grew and flourished and strove to continue the apostolate of fostering love and devotion to Our Lord in the Blessed Sacrament.

Surprise in a Box

On January 5, 1977 the Menlo Park nuns were surprised to receive a box from France. Opening it they found that it contained the monstrance which had been used at Oullins, the first Dominican monastery of Perpetual Adoration and the founding monastery of the first American Monastery. The gift monstrance was sent from the Chalais, France Monastery. It had been crafted by Monsieur Armand Caillat of Lyon, France about 1885. The sisters at Chalais were the same community that had originally been in Oullins, prior to its closing. These nuns were no longer able to keep perpetual adoration, and so sent the precious gift to Menlo Park, who still kept up the tradition.

The monstrance also came as a gift given in gratitude for Menlo Park's assistance given to them during World War II, which forged a special bond of friendship. In 1976 when Mother Mary of the Trinity of Menlo Park worked with the Dominican Liturgical Commission in Rome she visited the nuns in Chalais, France on her way home. The gift of the Chalais nuns was a tribute to the unbroken line of descent from Oullins, France to Menlo Park, CA in the USA. The Menlo nuns continue to use the beautiful ornate jeweled monstrance with a warm realization of the unbroken connection to their roots.[24]

A Surprise for the "Stars"

The Newark Monastery would make one more foundation in 1924, and that was on the West Coast in Los Angeles, CA. The first foundation from Newark was in the financial metropolis of the country; the final one was in the entertainment capital. Standing on the curbside of the Los Angeles monastery, one can look up and see the famous "HOLLYWOOD" sign in the distance along the hillside. The Los Angeles nuns not only brought Eucharistic adoration to Los Angeles, they also brought the "stars" to the Eucharistic Lord too. Some among them were Irene Dunn, Jane Wyman, Jeanie Craine, Fred Mc Murray and his wife, and Bob and Dolores Hope. For a while movie star retreats were held annually at the monastery. Later this retreat was taken over by Dolores Hope at her residence.[25] At this point in our story, I cannot help but recall those words of St. Paul to the Philippians, "Shine like bright stars in the world; you are offering it the Word of Life…." (Phil. 2: 15).

Wherever monasteries are located, they continue to be a silent word pointing the way toward true values. Fame and fortune cannot make one truly happy. Money, though necessary for everyday living, cannot be an end in itself, for it too does not bring true happiness. True blessings come from putting the Lord at the center of our lives. Our Eucharistic Lord brings living peace and happiness. He is the strength and hope of all who turn to him. Many also find consolation in turning to his consecrated daughters who pray before him night and day.

Everythin's BIG in Texas — How 'Bout a Foundation?!

The last American foundation made from the Newark line was made by the Detroit Monastery in the diocese of Beaumont, Texas. Bishop Christopher Byrne welcomed Mother Mary Imelda, O.P., foundress, and about 10 sisters, who had joined her. When the sisters arrived, their temporary monastery was not ready for them, so the big hearted Dominican Sisters of Huston graciously gave the nuns the use of their convent, which was vacant for the summer. Later the priests made a BIG move - out of their rectory, so that the nuns could stay there temporarily. When the nuns attempted to build in Nacogdoches, the local opposition rivaled that of the battle of Alamo; such was the prejudice to a Catholic religious construction! The nuns, wanting to avoid the BIG guns relocated to Lufkin, TX. On November 9, 1945 enclosure was established and 24 hour adoration began immediately.[26]

Skeptics Beware!

When the first foundation was made in Newark many members of the clergy were skeptical as to the ability of the monastery to draw vocations from comfort seeking Americans. However, the skepticism dissolved as they saw how many American women responded to the grace of God with generous heart and an inner spiritual vision. Though the nuns are poor themselves, and unknown to the world, people from all stations of life know and believe in the value of their humble service to God and their dedication to prayer for all His people.

Perpetual Rosary Monasteries with Adoration

In 1922, when Mother Mary Hyacinth approached Bishop Thomas Mary O'Leary about making a foundation in the Springfield diocese, he requested that the nuns have perpetual adoration. An agreement was reached that as soon as enough nuns came to the monastery, adoration would start. When I first entered the Monastery, we had 24 hour adoration with at least two sisters in the chapel at any one time. Although we are no longer able to sustain the night adoration, we look forward to the day when new zealous vocations will permit us to resume this exalted calling.

The Monastery in **Summit, New Jersey** was established as a Perpetual Rosary Monastery in 1919. Approximately five years later, the nuns approached their bishop and requested permission to have perpetual adoration of the Blessed Sacrament. It was granted. There were many preparations which had to be arranged before it could begin. At that time, prescription required 14 candles to burn continuously before the Blessed Sacrament. Nuns desiring to have perpetual adoration had to have enough financial resources to sustain that amount of candles. On Feb. 11, 1926, the feast of Our Lady of Lourdes, Perpetual Adoration was added to the custom of perpetual rosary. The two customs being joined, it became known as the "Adoring Rosary". [27] When the Monastery of Our Lady of Grace in

North Guilford, CT was founded by Summit in 1947, the nuns' focus was more along the lines of Perpetual Adoration even though they pray a chaplet of the rosary in common each day.[28] The Monastery of St. Jude in **Marbury, AL** was founded in 1944 and when they had a sufficient number of sisters, permission was also granted them for Perpetual Adoration.[29]

All through the centuries, Monasteries have adapted to their circumstances. Since experiencing diminishing numbers, some monasteries have found it necessary to suspend their night adoration. However, nuns continue adoration from early morning till late evening in an effort to preserve the spirit of perpetual adoration. In some cases individual nuns rise during the night to spend time in prayer before Jesus in the Blessed Sacrament, asking for many blessings on souls. The nuns in Syracuse, NY keep two hour shifts through the night on the Easter Vigil. The monastery in Summit, NJ has night adoration three times a week, and hopes to increase it to four times a week. Each monastery strives to preserve this special tradition to the best of its ability. The monastery of Mary the Queen has adoration during the day at least one day a week with hopes to soon extend it to more.

(Endnotes)
1   Dominican Nuns in their Cloister 254-255.
2   Dominican Nuns in their Cloister 258-259.
3   Dominican Nuns in their Cloister 271.
4   Dominican Nuns in their Cloister 258-259.
5   **Archdiocese of Newark, "Archdiocese of Newark History and Archives,"** http://www.rcan.org/history/history-corrigan.htm (accessed March 16, 2009). Roman Catholic Archdiocese of Newark. Used with permission.
6   Dominican Nuns in their Cloister 259.
7   **Archdiocese of Newark, "Archdiocese of Newark History and Archives,"** http://www.rcan.org/history/history-corrigan.htm (accessed March 16, 2009). Roman Catholic Archdiocese of Newark. Used with permission.
8   VandeCreek, Ph.D., Drew. "1873-1876: The Panic of 1873." Illinois During the Gilded Age Digitization Project. 2002. *Northern Illinois University Libraries' digitization projects.* 23 Feb. 2009 http://dig.lib.niu.edu/gildedage/narr3.html .
9   Dominican Nuns in their Cloister 260.
10   Dominican Nuns in their Cloister 271.
11   Dominican Nuns in their Cloister 259-261.
12   Dominican Nuns in their Cloister 257-258.
13   Dominican Nuns in their Cloister 261-262.
14   Dominican Nuns in their Cloister 254.

15 Dominican Nuns in their Cloister 263.
16 Edited Appletons Encyclopedia, StanKlos.com "Virtual American Biographies: Michael Augustine Corrigan" http://www.famousamericans.net/michaelaugustinecorrigan (accessed March 17, 2009).
17 Dominican Nuns in their Cloister 263.
18 Dominican Nuns in their Cloister 268-269.
19 Dominican Nuns in their Cloister 275-276.
20 Dominican Nuns in their Cloister 181.
21 Dominican Nuns in their Cloister 276-277.
22 Dominican Nuns in their Cloister 278.
23 Dominican Nuns in their Cloister 279-283.
24 Information provided by a sister of the Menlo Park Monastery. March 2009.
25 Information provided by a sister of the Los Angeles, CA Monastery. February/March 2009.
26 Information provided by a sister of the Lufkin, TX Monastery. March 2009.
27 Information provided by Sr. Mary Martin, O.P. of the Summit, NJ Monastery. December 7, 2008.
28 Information provided by a sister of the North Guilford, CT Monastery. March 2009.
29 Information provided by a sister of the Marbury, AL Monastery. March 2009.

CHAPTER 14

Surprises: Paternal, Fraternal and Eucharistic

Jesus said to them, "I tell you the truth, it is not Moses who has given you the bread from heaven, but it is my Father who gives you the true bread from heaven. Jn. 6:32 (NIV®)

Our celebration in June fell on Father's Day, making it appropriate for us to invite fathers and fathers to be as our honored guests! Among those included were spiritual fathers, Dominican fathers, seminarians and deacons. The previous week we observed the Feast of Corpus Christi (the Body of Christ), present in the Eucharist under the species of bread and wine. We made these two themes central to our June celebration. Bishop Joseph F. Maguire, D.D. was our Guest Officiant. Bishop McDonnell was unable to be with us because of an out of town meeting with the US Bishops. When Bishop Maguire arrived early on the scene, he wondered where everybody was. It did not take long before priests, deacons and seminarians started pouring in after him!

The Knights of Columbus

They are representatives of the churches and an honor to Christ.
2 Cor. 8:23 (NIV®)

The Knights of Columbus were present in their full regalia with their wives who also came to the celebration. People may not realize that the Knights must arrive at least one half hour beforehand to prepare their uniform for the service. There were Knights who wore red, white or purple lined capes. Sir Knight Donald Gladdu, the Commander of the Honor Guard, had purple trim on his uniform. Three of the Knights wore white trim which indicates a "Faithful Navigator", either current or past, who have a one year term as head of the Assembly and takes charge of meetings. There were two additional Knights who wore red trim, which is symbolic of the "Honor Guard". A Knight must be of the fourth degree to serve on the Honor Guard. The Knights are practicing Catholics, and their membership is one of charity. Each group of Knights is called a Council. Each Council raises funds for various charities of their own choosing, such as, providing meals for the homeless or the lonely at Thanksgiving, providing scholarships or supporting seminarians. The Knights are pro-life, participate in civic affairs and Memorial services, and support monuments for the unborn. Their services are totally voluntary; no one ever gets paid.[1]

Priests and Seminarians

The elders who direct the affairs of the church well are worthy
of double honor, especially those whose work is preaching and
teaching. 1 Tim. 5:17 (NIV®)

We all know that without the priesthood, there would be no Eucharist. And so it was an honor for us to have so many priests join in our June celebration. Msgr. Christopher Connelly acted as our emcee once again. Our long time friends Fr. Franklin Darling, Fr. Vincent

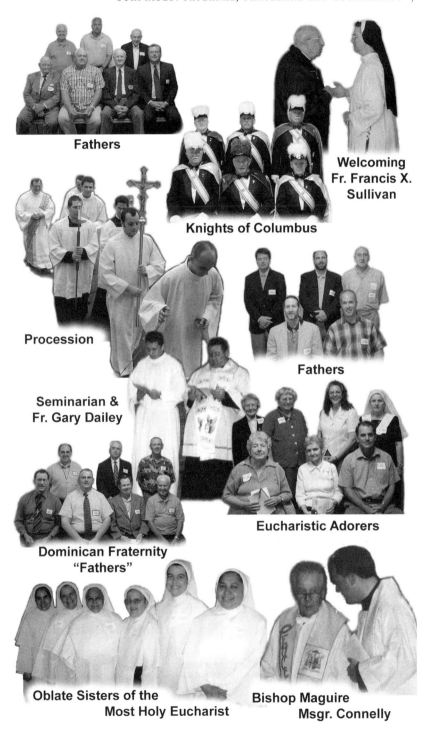

Fathers

Welcoming
Fr. Francis X.
Sullivan

Knights of Columbus

Procession

Fathers

Seminarian &
Fr. Gary Dailey

Eucharistic Adorers

Dominican Fraternity
"Fathers"

Oblate Sisters of the
Most Holy Eucharist

Bishop Maguire
Msgr. Connelly

O'Connor and Fr. Francis X. Sullivan joined us for this occasion, along with Fr. Gary Dailey. Fr. Dailey is responsible for the public Corpus Christi procession in the diocese. One year the procession began at Our Lady of Hope Parish, processed to Our Lady of the Rosary Parish, moved on to St. Francis' Chapel and culminated at St. Michael's Cathedral. Many priests and people participate in this demonstration of faith and love.[1] Many seminarians attended our celebration, including Fr. James Longe, a transitional deacon[2] who served as Incense Bearer (Thurifer), Seminarian Piotr Pawlus from Poland who served as Cross Bearer, and Salvatore Circosta and Charles Pawlowski, also seminarians, who served as Acolytes.

Fr. Gary Dailey

The participation of the seminarians for the 800th Anniversary celebrations at the Monastery of the Mother of God was truly a rewarding experience. It helped the seminarians to understand the monastic life and the need for solitude and silence in their own life as they discern their call to the diocesan priesthood. Participating in the various events made the seminarians very proud and thankful to have such a beautiful monastery with committed religious sisters living out their call to contemplative life. For some of the seminarians it was their first time at the monastery and from their beautiful experience, it won't be their last visit. They find in the Monastery of the Mother of God a place of refuge amidst the noise and hustle of life – a place where they can find Christ, present in the Eucharist, but also a place where others have answered the call to discipleship and now live a consecrated life. This assists them in their prayer of discernment. With gratitude to God for 800 years of dedicated service to the church, we rejoice in your joy and we hope and pray that the Dominican Nuns in West Springfield will flourish

---

1   Fr. Dailey is also spiritual guide and vocation director for the diocesan seminarians. Some years ago he suggested individual Sisters adopt one seminarian to pray for and encourage through their journey of becoming a priest. He has great faith in the nuns' prayers. Each year he sends us the list of seminarians' names and Sisters choose "their seminarian".
2   A man on the way to the priesthood as differing from the permanent deacon.

with vocations. May God continue to bless the Dominicans here and throughout the world.

Permanent Deacons

Deacons, likewise, are to be men worthy of respect…
1Tim. 3:8 (NIV®)

Not to be overlooked were the Permanent Deacons. Those included in our program were Rev. Mr. James Conroy, Rev. Mr. Paul Federici, Rev. Mr. Lincoln Rael and Rev. Mr. Theodore J. Tudryn.

The permanent deacon is a member of the hierarchy through the imposition of hands, which has come down through the apostles. The diaconate can be conferred on married men and the deacon brings to the diaconal ministry his own experience of integrating in his own life the obligations and commitments as husband, father and as one who has spent years in the workforce. He ministers in the Church's name be it in liturgical and pastoral life or through social and charitable works.

Sisters Dedicated to the Eucharist

Draw me after you, let us make haste…. We will exult and rejoice in you; we will extol your love more than wine; rightly do they love you.
Song of Solomon 1:4 (RSV)

Each month religious women were invited as honored guests. In June six Oblate Sisters of the Most Holy Eucharist joined us in the celebration: Sr. M. Victoria Garcia, O.SS.E., Sr. M. Inmaculada Chaires, O.SS.E., Sr. M Ines Hernandez, O.SS.E., Sr. M. del Sagrado Corazon Nava, O.SS.E., Sr. Josefina M. Sanchez, O.SS.E., and Sr. M. Luz Castro, O.SS.E.[3]

---

3   Sr. M. Luz has since returned to Mexico. She is assistant to their Mother General and

Sr. Luz, O.SS.E.:

Because of a special bond we have with the Dominican Nuns in West Springfield we responded to join in their 800th Anniversary Celebration. Like the West Springfield nuns, Perpetual Eucharistic adoration is part of our charism. The sisters relieve one another during 24 hours of prayer spent before Jesus exposed in the Blessed Sacrament.

In Mexico we teach Catechesis to children and adults. As a contemplative Congregation we do not go out, so we do this apostolic work inside our convents. In the United Sates we do this with Spanish speaking people. We also receive individuals and groups for retreats in our convents. We assist the priests with our prayers and work.

Eucharistic Adorers

Come, let us bow down in worship,
let us kneel before the Lord our Maker. Ps. 95:6 (NIV®)

Another group of honored guests were Eucharistic Adorers. There were twenty one guests: Mary Fernandez, Donald Golden, Pauline Gregory, Jane Hendrick, Mary Jane Kelley, Laura Landry, Barbara Lane, Mary Ann Magri, Frieda Mantha, Dorothy Mozden, Rose Marie Nathan, Donald Palmieri, Darrilyn Patterson, Deannette Pease, Alice Pisano, Barbara Quaglini, Linda Renaud, Ken Skowron, Mary Ellen Stroud, Elaine Trottier and Frances Vecchiarelli. During one period in our history, they had helped us with Eucharistic Adoration during certain hours of the day. Barbara Lane coordinated the scheduling.

The Dominican Fraternity

---

second in leadership. Their foundress, Sr. Maria Auxilia de la Cruz was a former Dominican Sister. They wear a white habit, white scapular and a cape with a symbol of the Eucharist emblazoned on it. A wine colored sash symbolizes the Precious Blood of Jesus. They have a strong devotion to the Eucharist.

"The word is near you; it is in your mouth and in your heart,"
that is, the word of faith we are proclaiming. Romans 10:8 (NIV®)

With Dominican Fraternity Members included as guests, representing Eucharistic Adoration as well as fathers of families, we asked the president of our local Chapter, Professor Joseph Lake, T.O.P., to provide us with a few words, so that our readers might better understand their relationship to the Monastery and to the Order.

Professor Joseph Lake, T.O.P.

The Mother of God Chapter of the Dominican Laity was formed some sixty years ago, and has long been one of the largest and most active Chapters in the country. Our community life as Dominicans has always been centered around the Monastery of the Mother of God and gained its inspiration from the support of the Nuns. At this time there are about sixty active members, with many others who mainly for reasons of health can no longer attend meetings. The Chapter continues to grow each year.

The Laity, like the other branches of the order, follow a Dominican way of life. We attend Mass and pray the liturgy of the hours daily, attend a monthly meeting at St. Dominic's Hall on the Monastery grounds, pursue a formation program, and organize a three-day annual retreat. Dominicans have a democratic form of government, and as such, professed members elect the local Chapter Council, which in turn selects its officers, i.e., president, etc. The Chapter Council reports to regional and provincial councils. At the head is the Master General of the Dominican Order.

Prayer and contemplation are at the center of our community life. From them flow our Chapter apostolates. There are many different types of ministry. We foster study and preaching as individuals and in groups. We are in the process of discerning our common Chapter Apostolate centered on preaching the message of Our Savior's Divine Mercy.

Dominican Fraternity "Fathers"

As a father has compassion on his children,
so the Lord has compassion on those who fear him.
Ps. 103:13 (NIV®)

Because of the abundance at hand, we separated our "Fathers" into two groups. One group consisted of Dominican Fraternity Fathers. Among them were Raymond Delisle, William Kelly, Kevin McClain, James Mitson and John Platanitis. Valmore Hebert and Henry Sansouci were fathers who have also served the monastery for many years as Mass servers. James Perkins rounded out this group of fathers. He is a very active father and serves as a Scout Master.

Other Honored Fathers

Respect your father in deed as well as word,
so that blessing may come on you from him. Ecclus. 3:8 (JB)

Other fathers included those whom we have come to know through their public service. These included Michael Cutone, Robert Germano, James Markowski, Robert Vogel, Sr. and Bob, Jr. Other fathers who have been long time friends were Joseph Amato, William "Bill" Bennett, Ronald Groleau, Edward Harris, Kevin Kervick and John Weber. Gerald Solitario is the father of Mark, who was one of our faithful altar servers. Steve Lozyniak is Scott's father and this celebration occasioned our first meeting with him. Relatives included cousin Michael Broer, my brother Al and my nephew Alexander, Jr. More recent friends included Sonny Roth, Timothy Weinandy and Greg Norflet.

TIMOTHY WEINANDY:

Last Father's Day I was asked to participate in a special Rosary, to honor all types of Fathers. I happen to be a Father by adoption and Father's Day is very special to me. Taking part in this Rosary was a special honor because my Father had passed away the year before and I was given his Rosary beads. While praying the Rosary, I happened to notice that the Cross on the Rosary was engraved with my Dad's initials and a date. It was the date on which he was confirmed. The Holy Spirit graced me that day, just as the Holy Spirit had blessed my Dad on his Confirmation Day.

We met William Raffaele through his wife Carole, who was related to our deceased Sr. Mary John Dominic. Paul Swierzewski worked at the monastery during his school years before he was a Dad.[4] When I called Paul to ask him if he would like to write something for this book, he told me how he had been gazing at the beautiful Mother of God plaque encased in the Rose Window, which he was facing at the time of the service and which he had never noticed before. Then suddenly it was his turn to lead a Hail Mary. He began it and then his mind went blank. He was so embarrassed. Paul has a great family and he is greatly loved by his children.

PAUL SWIERZEWSKI:
The truth is I was embarrassed when I forgot the second phrase of the Hail Mary. I say it all the time, but this time I drew a blank in front of the crowd, my parents and my children. I couldn't believe it. I didn't even go out to dinner afterwards because I was so upset and didn't feel like eating. The good that came out of it was when I got home my daughters, Kaitlyn and Kristine, sang to me "Nobody is perfect". Later that night my son Brian said "Dad nobody is perfect except God, I think? No he is". So, they seem to be on the right track, which is a big blessing these days.

---

4   He was innovative in removing a huge hornet's nest from one of the trees. First he drove the truck up near the branch of said tree, rolled down the window a crack and shot it with bee spray and quickly rolled up the window again. He later returned to remove the nest for all the sisters to view up close, relieved that the menacing occupants were no more.

Eucharistic Monastery

And we know that in all things God works for the good of those who love him, who have been called according to his purpose. Romans 8:28 (NIV®)

In our program we included in the "History Tidbits" the story about the Dominican Monastery of Nuns in Bamberg Germany, which had close links to the Eucharist from its very foundation. Today it bears the name Monastery of Heilig Grab (Holy Sepulchre). In 1314 a small Corpus Christi Chapel was built in expiation of a sacrilege when a young boy had stolen a ciborium from the old St. Martin's Church, and deposited the sacred hosts in a corn field outside the city walls. It was the Dominican Bishop Wulfing V. Stubenberg (1304-1318) who elevated the sacred hosts and, barefooted, carried them back into the city in an expiatory procession, accompanied by a large number of clergy and common folk. This is the very spot where the Dominican Monastery of the Holy Sepulchre now stands. The monastery was founded on May 1, 1356 by six Dominican nuns from St. Mary's Monastery, Frauenaurach/Bavaria. This monastery in Bamberg, Germany has always been a place of adoration and veneration of the Blessed Sacrament. Through secularization (the takeover by the government) the monastery was declared closed in 1803. The brave nuns stayed till they were thrown out in 1806. Church and convent buildings were given over to military purposes. In 1926 the monastery was refounded and again Dominican cloistered life renewed itself at this desecrated yet still holy place. The Church was re-consecrated on October 17, 1926.[2] In Macerata, Italy the Dominican Monastery "Corpus Domini" (Body of the Lord) was founded in 1692 by the venerable Mother Giacinta Bossi, O.P. This monastery was the first to establish perpetual adoration in Italy.[3]

Mini Concert

It is good to praise the Lord and make music to your name, O Most High. Ps. 92:1 (NIV®)

We had a number of Eucharistic pieces in our Mini concert. These included Latin classics "O Sacrum Convivium" (O Sacred Banquet) and "Ave Verum". The sisters' singing of "Ave Verum" is posted on the June photo web page. http://praedicare.com/Celebrations/2007junphoto.htm The "Panis Angelicus" (Bread of Angels) was done as an instrumental solo with flute and organ. Sr. Mary of the Sacred Heart, O.P. was the flautist and Sr. Mary Regina of the Angels Thomas, O.P. played the organ. Sister is quite a proficient organist and her organ prelude can also be heard from the above web page.

"See How the Father Has Loved Us" was sung with fathers in mind as we recalled our heavenly Father's love for us all and asked his blessing on all in attendance. Some years ago one of our sisters put together a Litany of the Father. The invocations were taken from Sacred Scripture and from the writings of St. Catherine of Siena, a Doctor of the Church.

St. Joseph, foster father of Jesus, is patron of fathers and his statue was placed in the sanctuary. In this way we continue to bring to the attention of the faithful devotions which have been a part of our Catholic heritage for centuries.

May our Lord Jesus Christ himself, and God our Father who has given us his love and , through his grace, such inexhaustible comfort and such sure hope, comfort you and strengthen you in everything good that you do or say. – 2 Thess. 2:1

(Endnotes)

1   Information provided by a Knight of Columbus as well as the pamphlet "Knights of Columbus INSURANCE: Making a difference for life. 4602 2/08.

2   Sr. Maria Berthilla Heil, O.P., "2006 – A Year of Jubilee for *Heilig Grab* in Bamberg, Bavaria", Monialibus. (Nuns of the Order of Preachers International Bulletin, Number 15. December 2006: 13-14 Used with permission and Franz Machilek, /Das Dominikanerinnenkloster zum Heiligen Grab in Bamberg, /Kunstverlag Peda, Passau 2006.

3   Sr. Bernadetta Giordano, O.P., Oasi Domenicane: Monasteri Domenicani Italiani, (Cortona, Italy: Calosci. 1987). Information provided in English by Sr. Mary Jeremiah, O.P. of the Lufkin, TX Monastery.

CHAPTER 15

Discipleship: Surprising Developments

Calling the Twelve to him, he sent them out two by two…
Mk. 6:7 (NIV®)

Jesus called his disciples together, and later sent them out in twos to preach the Good News. They worked together as a team. At various times the nuns have been called together. One such instance took place here at our Monastery of the Mother of God in West Springfield.

First Assembly held at a Nuns' Monastery

I will give you thanks in the great assembly;
among throngs of people I will praise you. Ps. 35:18 (NIV®)

In June of 1982 a grand convergence of nuns from all over the United States took place at our Monastery of the Mother of God. It was an historic event because it was the first time US nuns ever met together for an assembly at one of the nuns' monasteries. It consisted for the most part of the prioress and at least one delegate from each monastery, although some monasteries had four nuns in attendance. Here in West Springfield, we all pitched together to make preparations. Sr. Maria and Sr. Mary Immaculata did the lions' share, while the rest of the community carried on the regular duties of the monastery. Many sisters gave up their cells[1] for the use of our guest sisters. Friends lent us cots for setting up temporary quarters for the interim. These included the "dentist room" in the infirmary, the sewing room, a workroom, etc. Our community ate in the refectory and special arrangements were made for our guests in another area. There was excitement in the air and a great spirit of unity. Our West Springfield sisters who were not "delegates" had the joy of meeting our guests during free and recreational moments. It was a wonderful occasion for strengthening the bonds that unite us.

Fr. Vincent de Couesnongle, O.P., Master General at the time, came to our West Springfield monastery to address the nuns and dialogue with them. Fr. Master proved a very vibrant and animated speaker, as energy permeated the room as he spoke about the importance of our monastic values, the crisis of vocations, and the principles of formation. I can still hear his voice echoing in my ears as he spoke about teaching the young "to know St. Dominic, to know the psalms…."

One day during the meeting, a number of our Dominican brethren came to join us in our monastery courtyard for a reception, which was followed by Compline[2] in the nuns' Choir. It was a rare moment when the successor of St. Dominic blessed all present with holy water during the "Salve"[3]. It was like having St. Dominic himself with us.

Sr. Mary Martin, O.P. of the Summit, N.J. Monastery had compiled, edited and printed the *Calendar of the Saints and Blesseds of the Dominican Order*. This book was dedicated to Fr. de Couesnongle.

---

1   The personal room a nun uses for prayer, study and rest.
2   Liturgical night prayer
3   Traditional sung antiphon to Our Lady at the end of Compline.

Master meets Bishop Maguire

Mass

Bishop O'Neil meets Father Master

Fr. Magonigle

The Liturgy

Fr. Sheridan & Fr. O'Donnell

The Prioress & Father Master

Compline Blessing

Master's session with the nuns

Sr. Mary Catherine and Father Master

Fr. R. Daley Provincial

1982 Assembly

West Springfield

Sing along

Sr. Mary of God Fr. Augustine DiNoia

Eager to hear

Panel

Farewell Recreation

Postings

Conference Established

"Behold, I make all things new." Rev. 21:5 (RSV)

As a result of this Assembly, the nuns established a "Conference of Nuns of the Order of Preachers of the United States of America". Sr. Mary Catherine, O.P. of the Lufkin, Texas monastery was elected as its first president. Fr. Gabriel O'Donnell, O.P. was elected as first "Priest Consultant" to the Conference. Two publications were founded at this time: *Dominican Monastic Search*, a forum for sharing insights gained through prayer and study, and *Conference Communications*, the official newsletter of the Conference. The editorial boards of the two publications were composed of volunteers from different monasteries.

Follow Up

In the aftermath of the West Springfield meeting, it was decided that a seminar and workshop should be held at Saugerties, N.Y., which was attended by novice mistresses. Two focal points emerged from this meeting: the initial and permanent formation of the nuns and the preparation of novice mistresses for the competent fulfillment of their office. In time, programs were developed for each of these. [1]

First "Official" General Assembly of the Conference

In June of 1984 the first "official" General Assembly of the Conference of Nuns took place in Farmington, CT. Fr. Damian Byrne, O.P. was the Master General at the time, and made himself available to the nuns. Sr. Mary of God, O.P. of the North Guilford, CT Monastery was elected president.

On-Going Formation

As a result of the Farmington assembly Sr. Mary Magdalen, O.P. of the Newark, N.J. Monastery was appointed coordinator for Study Programs and On-Going Formation. A Study Commission was formed from volunteers, and an annual program was devised. It was decided that guest speakers would give lectures to the nuns in member monasteries on a given topic for their on-going formation. Recordings done of the lectures would then be duplicated and distributed to the various monasteries.

The Prioresses' Meeting and Retreat

Another fruit of this Assembly was the decision to have a Prioresses' retreat and workshop. This gives prioresses ample opportunity for a time of spiritual renewal, apart from the demanding circumstances at home. It also provides for instruction and sharing among the participants. Such meetings are often held midway between Assemblies.[2]

Theological Formation Program

At the 1988 General Assembly in Mc Lean, VA a proposal was made for a program of theological studies for sisters in temporary vows. Sr. Maura of Menlo Park considers this to be "the most significant accomplishment of the Assembly".[3]

The proposal went into action with a committee of nuns and friars meeting at the Monastery of Mary the Queen in Elmira, New York in February of 1989. Fr. Augustine Di Noia, O.P. and Fr. Gabriel O'Donnell, O.P. were the friars in attendance. The nuns on the committee were: Sr. Mary Ann, O.P. of North Guilford, CT, Mother Mary of Mercy, O.P. of Farmington Hills, MI and Sr. Mary Paul, O.P. of Washington, DC., who later withdrew from the committee.[4]

In 1990, the Theological Formation Program (TFP) was inaugurated. It took place at the Dominican House of Studies in Washington,

DC. The program consists of two weeks of formal classes, assigned readings and seminars. The student nuns return to their monasteries with packets of lessons to study. They are assigned tutors, who both receive the nuns written assignments and give them feedback. It began as a three year program. An additional year was recently added, making it a four year program. The studies give the sisters a firm grounding in theology and discipline them in regular study habits. The process assists them for future personal study pursuits.

Novice Directresses' Program

The Program to help our Novice Mistresses began at the Dominican House of Studies in Washington, DC at the same time (June 1990) as the TFP. It was an annual two week program and continued until 2008. It was originally decided upon at a meeting open to all the Mistresses at the House of Studies during the Christmas-Break in January 1990. There was no permanent committee; each year one or two mistresses volunteered to be responsible for the following year's Program.

The annual Program consisted of lectures on some aspect of the Initial Formation of Novices, given by speakers invited by the Novice Mistresses. The Mistresses then collaborated in deciding on headings or titles for lectures (20 to 40 - depending on the topic) for their own presentation of this aspect of formation. Next, individual mistresses volunteered to draw up the outline for a lecture under each of these headings and to provide a list of bibliographical material the mistress might use for it. This they did during the course of the following year. At the next year's meeting the outlines were presented for the group's critique and then put in final form on a computer disk for each mistress.

This procedure happened each year until the various aspects of initial formation had been covered. Fr. Gabriel O'Donnell, O.P. acted as the advisor and resource friar for the mistresses during their work in deciding on the headings or titles for the lecture outlines. He also joined in their group-critiquing of the outlines' final form, which he personally approved before they were put on disks. [5]

Infirmarians' Workshop

In August of 1991 there was a meeting of Infirmarians. Morning lectures were devoted to the theoretical aspects of the office of infirmarian: theological and monastic principles given by Fr. Gabriel O'Donnell, O.P., the infirmarian as person and caregiver by Bro. Ignatius Perkins, O.P. and virtue and medical ethics by Fr. Benedict Ashley, O.P. On the last day Dr. Mary Scheimann spoke on emergency medical situations in the monastery. Jackie Lampasona, RN also gave a presentation to the sisters. Afternoon lectures, questions and discussions dealt with concrete applications. With the principles of our tradition articulated, the sisters were enriched and prepared to respond medically, ethically and practically to situations as they came up in their monastery infirmaries.[6]

Source Book

The nuns' source book, <u>One Mind and Heart in God</u>, was published in June of 1989. Sisters from various monasteries wrote articles for it and Sr. Mary Catherine, O.P. of the Monastery in Elmira, was the General Editor with Fr. Boniface Ramsey, O.P. as editorial consultant. The title reflects the Rule of St. Augustine, which we follow, as well as our Constitutions. Fr. Master Damian Byrne made mention of this theme of being of "one mind and heart in God" in his introductory letter to our revised Constitutions of 1987.[7]

Moving Ahead

Circumstances, originating from Rome, have initiated the transition of the "Conference" to the status of an "Association". It was a process that the nuns labored over intensely. This change brings the organization more in accord with what is acceptable to the Church by allowing for the normal programs mentioned above to operate on a regular basis with the approval of the Church regarding enclosure. Permission does not have to be sought for each meeting. It is built into the structure, which is approved by Rome.

As with the Conference, each monastery's autonomy is safeguarded. Membership in the Association is sought by individual monasteries with a two thirds vote of the local monastery's chapter[4]. The purpose of the Conference and Association is basically the same: to foster the monastic, contemplative life of the member Monasteries in the spirit of St. Dominic. At the same time, it supports and strengthens the spirit of cooperation and communion among them through sisterly sharing and intercommunication, which facilitate the spiritual, intellectual, human and cultural development of the sisters. [8]

Time and space does not permit a complete record of all that has been accomplished in and through the nuns with the assistance of our Dominican brethren. It is our hope that this overview will give some idea as to the fruitfulness that has come about by the nuns working together to foster our Dominican Contemplative life as well as deepen our sisterly bonds.

(Endnotes)

1   Sr. Mary of God, O.P., "Some On-Going Plans/Committees Formed at the Meeting", *Conference Commuications*. Special Issue: 57. Used with permission.

2   Sr. Mary of God, O.P., "The President's Message: Report of Term 1984-1988", *Conference Commuications*. 8.4 December 1988: 1-3. Used with permission.

3   Sr. Maura, O.P., "Menlo Park", *Conference Commuications*. 8.4 December 1988: 22. Used with permission.

4   Information provided by Sr. Mary of Mercy, O.P. of the Farmington Hills Monastery. Feb./March 2009.

5   Information provided by Sr. Mary Magdalen Braun, O.P. of the Farmington Hills Monastery. Feb./March 2009.

6   "Report on Meeting of Infirmarians", *Conference Commuications*. 11.2 October 1991: 12-13. Used with permission.

7   Sr. Mary of God, O.P., "Report on Term 1988 - 1992", *Conference Commuications*. 12.2 Fall 1992: 34-35. Used with permission.

8   "Minutes of the First Meeting of the Conference Council January 22 – 26, 2001," Conference Communications. Vol. 21 2001: 3-4.

---

4   The Monastery Chapter is composed of those nuns enjoying active voice, under the presidency of the prioress.

CHAPTER 16

Surprising Variety of Guests

We have different gifts, according to the grace given us.
Romans 12:6 (NIV®)

Our July Celebration's theme was Discipleship, which brought a great variety of honored guests. These included Scouts, Athletes, Catholic Youth, the Ecker Support Group and the Daughters of the Heart of Mary.

In Liturgical Service

Be dressed ready for service and keep your lamps burning…
Lk. 12:35 (NIV®)

Fr. Jeffrey Ballou, whom we had known since he was a seminarian, was our Guest Officiant. He has long been a friend of our community. It was fitting to have Fr. Jeff with us during the month when we celebrate the Fourth of July because he is Chaplain at Westover Air Reserve Base.

We were honored to have SGT Mark Ecker II with us leading the procession as our cross bearer. SGT Ecker had led his men in Iraq, risking his life for the good of others. In the process Mark lost both his legs. We supported SGT Ecker with our prayers through his recovery, as did many other people. Mark came home from Walter Reed Hospital for a stay and actually marched in the 4th of July parade. We were thrilled to have SGT Mark Ecker as our cross bearer, as he had shared in the sufferings of Christ and was an example of Christian leadership to all.

SGT Ecker's Dad followed close behind him serving as an acolyte. Michael Vezzola, who hadn't missed a celebration since the first one, served as the other acolyte, and Scott Lozyniak served as Incense Bearer. Henry Sansouci, who has acted as server for our community Mass on frequent occasions and who is a member of the Dominican Fraternity, did a great job serving as Emcee for the first time.

HENRY SANSOUCI

When I was first approached by Sr. Mary of the Sacred Heart O.P. to be the Emcee for the July celebration for the 800th Anniversary Jubilee, I can only say that I was stunned and overwhelmed. My first reaction was "I cannot possibly do this"! However, there was a theme constantly coming back to me that said "respond to the Grace of God" and see what marvels He will do! Well, I finally said "YES". All the Grace I needed and more was there for me. I was so blessed in many ways in what I was asked to do. The greatest gift was the sense of being connected to the entire Dominican Order. This is an experience I will always be grateful for.

LINDA SANSOUCI
WIFE OF HENRY SANSOUCI

It was a bewildering experience for me in seeing the Holy Spirit's Power at work throughout the entire year of celebration! I was particularly struck by the way He worked in Henry as He emceed the service. It was for me a true testament of God's Love and action in our simple lives.

Daughters of the Heart of Mary

They all joined together constantly in prayer, along with the women
and Mary the mother of Jesus, and with his brothers.
Acts 1:14 (NIV®)

The Daughters of the Heart of Mary were the religious women among our honored guests. They included Harriet Brezinski, Kathy Devine, Paula Gaudet, Martha Keen, Barbara McKenzie, Mable Menendez, Marianna Mercurio, Joan Sweeney and Virginia Towner. You will read about Blandina Adjou and Itsu Tada in another chapter, where they participated with their foreign language skills.

The Daughters of the Heart of Mary were founded in times of religious persecution. Because of that they have never adopted a habit. In the early days they provided a place for priests to say Mass in secret and have also provided a place where people could come to encounter the Lord in an atmosphere of prayerful quiet. It was at the Marian Retreat center that I discerned my own vocation to the contemplative life.

The Ecker Support Group

Therefore encourage one another and build each other up,
just as in fact you are doing. 1 Thess. 5:11 (NIV®)

We invited SGT Ecker's family and friends and designated them as the "Ecker Support Group". Those listed in our program were Debbie and Kyle Ecker, Tina, Sue, Connie and Sandy Fielding, Jacqui Hebert, Phyllis McLane, Jean St. Pierre, Andrea Walsh and Arianna and Matthew. They reflected Christian discipleship in extending their Christ-like love and caring during this time of great trial for this brave soldier. It is love such as this, which can transform our world one person at a time. Only God can bring good out of evil and His love has indeed been manifest. So many people took Sgt. Mark Ecker II into their hearts as family. We are all one family in God. St. Paul encourages us, "We must never get tired of doing good because if we don't give up the struggle we shall get our harvest at the proper time. While we have the chance, we must do good to all, and especially to our brothers in the faith." (Gal. 6: 9-10)

Scouts

Be prepared in season and out of season.
2 Tim. 4:2 (NIV®)

Scouts reflect discipleship in their motto, "Be Prepared". We must "be prepared" for whatever or whomever the Lord puts in our path. "Be prepared" for whatever challenge or circumstance we encounter. "Be prepared" to live our faith and be Catholic leaders in our world. The scouts were indeed prepared for our Celebration and provided us with a Scout Honor Guard. Christopher James was from Troop 550. Alex and John Henle, Andrew and Matthew Laverdiere, Jeremy James and Joshua Perkins were from Troop 32 of Longmeadow.

The timing of our celebration gave quite a challenge to our invited scouts, as it came between summer camp comings and goings! Nevertheless we saw an excellent showing. Mr. Robert Mashia, the Lay Chairman for the Catholic Committee on Scouting for the Diocese of Springfield honored us with his presence and had a surprise for us later in the day. Alison Wells, Paul Lizak, Pamela Kosnicki and Denis St. Laurent were Committee Members who also attended.

ROBERT MASHIA, LAY CHAIRMAN OF SCOUTING FOR THE DIOCESE OF SPRINGFIELD

In the spring of 2007, I was invited by Sr. Mary of the Sacred Heart to join the sisters in West Springfield, MA for a Sunday afternoon celebration to honor the diocesan scouting family and to bring a delegation of scouts. Being curious, I inquired as to how she had reached me, the Lay Chairman

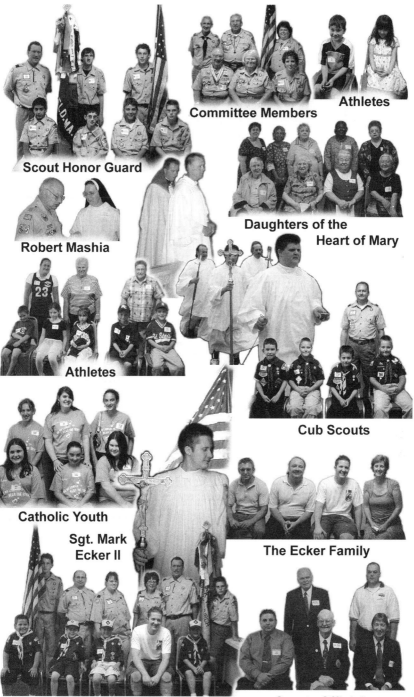

Scout Honor Guard

Committee Members

Athletes

Robert Mashia

Daughters of the
Heart of Mary

Athletes

Cub Scouts

Catholic Youth

Sgt. Mark
Ecker II

The Ecker Family

Scouts with Sgt. Mark Ecker II

Sports Officials

of Scouting (Boy scouts and Girl scouts) for the Diocese of Springfield. I cautiously agreed to accept her invitation and try to secure a delegation for a July 15 program. I knew I would be hard-pressed to get a decent delegation with summer vacations, scout camp time, typical family commitments and the usual excuses from many that I would call. I called sister a few days before the event and told her that my numbers were very slim, so she went to work on her own and contacted a Cub Scout leader she knew.

On July 15 we had a very respectable representation of boy scouts, cub scouts and leaders that I think numbered thirty or so. Each of our units was graciously welcomed, photographed, and then piously participated in the rosary and afternoon program. At the conclusion of the celebration the scouting family recognized the sister's devotion to the rosary with a framed collection of scout patches for each of the four chaplets (themes) of the rosary, presented by the National Catholic Committee on Scouting, and a patch to symbolize that "Scouting is Youth Ministry". To conclude the afternoon, the scouts were graciously received for a social with all the sisters and were presented an anniversary remembrance. In departing, the diocesan scouting family promised their continued prayers and best wishes to the Dominican Community for many more successful years.

During the preliminary preparations photos of the various groups were taken. The Boy Scouts and Cub Scouts along with their leaders wanted their picture taken with SGT Mark Ecker II. This hero was "surrounded" and enjoyed being so.

Jean Bussolari, Committee Chairman for Cub Scouts was present. Cub Scout Pack 303 of South Hadley really "packed" them in! Cub Scout Leader Bill Hoefler was present with Tanya, also a Scout Leader, plus scouts Luke, Matthew and John. Scout Leader Cheryl Lak was present with Robbie; Blake and Pierce Curtis completing the Pack.

Pack 15 of Springfield was represented by Larry and Trish Pion,

WolfPack Den Leaders, together with Ethan. James Perkins, Assistant Cub Master, was present with his son, Benjamin. Vincent Bussolari and Daniel James completed this Pack. Jim Perkins proved a great contact person and helped me immensely with recruiting the Scouts.

JAMES PERKINS O.P.
ASSISTANT CUB MASTER

It was on the month for Scouting that the forecast of the day was for rain. I wondered if the processional and recessional wouldn't be the cause of people getting drenched. The rain held off for the processional but you could tell that the skies were ready to flood the earth. During the ceremony the skies did open up and it poured. I asked myself what would happen if the rain didn't stop for the recessional. I thought it would be appropriate to let everyone know that there was a way to see the nuns without getting wet. Nearing the end of the ceremony I started to wonder if the rain would let up. When we were at the end of the service Father and the others in the procession began moving down the aisle and proceeded outside. I said to myself, "They're going to get wet". Yes, a moment of dry faith! I stood up and began to inform everyone that if they didn't want to get wet, they could go through the vestment room, down the hall and meet with some of the nuns. Well, wouldn't you know it – I was standing, opening my big mouth and giving instructions, when an altar server from outside signaled to me to send the people outside. Wouldn't you know it; the rain had just stopped enough for everyone to go out! There was no place for me to hide. Yes, and after everyone reentered the monastery, it started to rain once again. So my advice is: Let God's Divine Providence prevail and trust in the Lord to provide or you might just get stuck in a dry moment, getting all wet! I like to say, "Let go, let God!"

Athletes

I press on toward the goal to win the prize
for which God has called me heavenward in Christ Jesus.
Philippians 3:14 (NIV®)

Athletes too reflect the message of discipleship. St. Paul used the image of athletes to convey how we must strive to live our faith. When speaking of **how** to win spiritually he says, "Take an athlete – he cannot win any crown unless he has kept all the rules of the contest." (2Tim. 2:5) And speaking on the **intensity** of the spiritual life he says, "All the runners at the stadium are trying to win but only one of them gets the prize. You must run in the same way, meaning to win." (1Cor. 9:24)

During this jubilee year, the nuns worked on a book. Vocation in Black and White included vocation stories of US Dominican Nuns. My own vocation story is included, entitled "Making the Call." Before entering the monastery, I was very much involved in athletics. I was the catcher for "Ma Manning's Cadalettes," the 1963 Women's Softball State Champions in Massachusetts. My story told how it was not the "catcher" making the call, but the Lord. The call was not one to "shake off" either, despite questions from behind the plate. The book is now available and can be obtained either from most monasteries or from Amazon.com.

Our dear friend Mary Hickson surprised me when she told me that her husband Walter was a Western Mass Basketball Official serving as Secretary/Treasurer of Board 31. Walter joined us as an "Honored Guest" and was instrumental in having "Billy" Collamore, Vice President of the Volleyball Hall of Fame, join us as well as two basketball coaches, Robert "Bobby" Prattico of Holyoke Catholic High School and Bill Rigali of Holyoke High School. Through Walter's assistance we were also pleased to have Dave Hager, who was the Coordinator of CYO in Holyoke.

MARY HICKSON:

When, on behalf of Sr. Mary of the Sacred Heart, I asked Walter if he would be one of the sisters' honored guests, there was an expression of complete surprise on his face. He had quite a few questions. He and the other gentlemen he influenced in attending knew it was an honor and it made them think more of the Dominicans. Seeing Walter there, I was very proud of him. I knew it was a great blessing he had been given. I will always be grateful for Walter's part in the celebration in such a profound way.

BILL COLLAMORE
VICE PRESIDENT VOLLEYBALL HALL OF FAME

I was pleased and humbled to be chosen to participate in the celebration of the 800th Anniversary of the Order of Dominican Nuns of West Springfield, Mass. The event itself at the monastery was heartwarming and stirring. I felt inspired by the loveliness of the habited women and their aura of commitment to God. I enjoyed very much the service and the choral harmony.

At my pleasure in receiving the scroll from the Dominican Nuns, I sent a copy of the scroll to Fr. Kevin Lixey, L.C., an acquaintance of mine at the Vatican, to share my joy.

"Honored Guest" Sarah Garrity had graduated from Cathedral High School the previous month. She played lacrosse and soccer for Cathedral. Sarah was able to contact the school and obtain permission to wear her former "23" purple and white uniform for the service. Two of my former softball teammates joined us for the celebration. Pat McNeal was team captain for Ma Manning's Cadalettes. Joan Valentino was a superb shortstop. Younger athletes included uniformed Jacob Broer, who played baseball for St. Stan's in Chicopee. Christina Ransom had her Holy Cross softball uniform. Her Sr. Hannah and Benjamin Henle were soccer players. Theresa Henle and Rebecca James represented dance, while Matthew Ransom was the Taekwondo athlete. They were a vibrant and colorful group.

Catholic Youth

*Don't let anyone look down on you because you are young,
but set an example for the believers in speech, in life, in love,
in faith and in purity. 1 Tim. 4:12 (NIV®)*

Catholic Youth are called to discipleship in whatever state of life they embrace. Pope John Paul II challenged them to "say 'Yes' to Christ," to be lights for our world. They are called to be followers of Christ and leaders in our world. Catholic Youth were represented by "The Challenge Group." Carol, Lora and Mary Hill as well as Emma Maciaszek and Katrina Perkins are all members. They and Claire, Mary and Rachel Seaver were decked out in their colorful pink jerseys and were outstanding in more ways than one!

LEADERSHIP

L = **LEAD BY EXAMPLE**
E = **EDUCATION**
A = **ATTITUDE & ACCOUNTABILITY**
D = **DISCIPLINE**
E = **EMPOWER**
R = **RECEIVE & RESPECT INPUT**
S = **SACRIFICES**
H = **HUMILITY**
I = **INITIATIVE**
P = **PLAN**
(prayer, patience, prepare, & practice)

Leadership

They chose Judas (called Barsabbas) and Silas,
two men who were leaders among the brothers. Acts 15:22 (NIV®)

Special Forces/State Tpr Michael Cutone, who was in our first celebration, had his own subsequent surprises. A priest asked Michael to come to Rome with him regarding some works that he had developed. Mike Cutone felt particularly blessed to visit the holy places. He returned with a new assignment: to develop the "Leadership Principles" he had spoken about. The work was developed using the letters of the word LEADERSHIP. With Mike's permission I included this outline in our program. This seemed to fit in with our celebration that month.

St. Dominic

St. Dominic's statue was placed in the sanctuary for this July celebration. St. Dominic is a true spiritual leader. He is called Champion of the Lord and Light of the Church. We selected "Sound the Mighty Champion's Praises" as one of the pieces to be included in our Mini Concert. St. Dominic is known as the Lord's true champion in his zeal for souls.

Mini Concert Messages

You welcomed the message with the joy given by the Holy Spirit.
1 Thess. 1:6 (NIV®)

The message of the disciple "being prepared" for the Lord was reflected in the "Alleluia" with its verse. "Be watchful and ready; you know not when the Son of Man is coming." The song "Quietly Await," written by a Sr. of St. Joseph of Boston, was accompanied by Sr. Mary of the Immaculate Heart, O.P. and Sr. Mary of the Sacred Heart, O.P.

on guitars. The disciple waits for the Lord, ready to respond to his call and be a healing presence to all he/she meets. "The Prayer of St. Richard" was indeed a sung prayer asking the Lord for the grace to follow him more nearly. Sr. Theresa Marie Gaudette, O.P. did another superb job singing this as a solo. "Living Waters" was sung by the whole choir beginning in unison and breaking into parts. It was gloriously accompanied by Sr. Mary Regina, O.P. on the organ, who makes the organ resonate in full vigor. All disciples are called to intimacy with God. When we encounter him we cannot help but yearn for a greater friendship and a deeper intimacy. This piece conveys the longing of the soul as the music itself reaches heavenward and then comes to repose with a sense of having encountered him in the very longing.

May he give you the power
through his Spirit for your hidden self to grow strong,
*so that **Christ** may live in your hearts though faith....*
Glory be to him whose power, working in us,
can do infinitely more than we can ask or imagine...
- Eph. 3: 16-17, 20 (JB)

CHAPTER 17

A Surprising Contrast: Action and Contemplation

The "Mary and Martha" Element

A woman named Martha opened her home to him. She had a sister
called Mary, who sat at the Lord's feet listening to what he said. But
Martha was distracted by all the preparations that had to be made.
Lk. 10:38-40 (NIV®)

Our sisters in Washington, DC were in the process of relocating and building a new monastery in Linden, VA. Since they had to sell their temporary monastery in Washington, DC in order to have the funds to begin building the new one, they were basically homeless. We invited them to stay at our monastery in West Springfield during this interim time, which lasted for about two years. So it happened that they were with us for the Jubilee Year.

Every monastery has an annual retreat and the Linden Sisters had theirs scheduled for August of that year. Their conferences were held in our large parlor. It was decided we would not have our monthly public celebrations this month, but instead we would let the month better reflect the "Mary" element of our lives, which is prayer and contemplation. That gave me a "vacation" from the "Martha" element (busyness). It was a respite from planning for another monthly celebration, with its many facets. The reader may wonder just what that involved.

"Martha" Busy about many things

'Martha, Martha,' he said 'you worry and fret about so many things,... Lk. 10: 41 (JB)

First there was the headwork of choosing a theme and determining what guests might fit in with that theme. I had a general idea in the back of my head. Then came the "nitty- gritty" of making telephone calls to invite people to be among our honored guests. Often I had to leave a message or wait for the individual to get back to me with an answer. So it was quite commonplace during that year for me to be working at a computer and to have my beeper go off indicating a phone call on hold. Sometimes I was like a Jack-in-the-Box, springing up from my chair to go to the phone. I kept a list in my pocket with phone numbers and categories of guests and it was rewarding to see each group as it got finalized.

Thank God for computers, especially when they are working! When things go wrong, they say it's the operator and not the computer, but that's not always true! At any rate, I could not have pulled this off without one! My computer experience allowed me to set up the program for the service and, when complete, print it out. Oh, yes, and for the most part the printer was working! But do you ever have those times when the ink jet printer streaks? That means one has to do a "head cleaning." Not mine, the printer's! Eventually the program masters got printed out on two legal size sheets of paper. Then they were taken down to one of our printing machines. Sometimes colored paper was used for various months. Time had to be allowed in printing the reverse side so as to avoid smudging. Usually that meant an overnight wait. However, there were a few months, when I was pressed for time and took the stack of papers to a warm place in the kitchen to speed up the drying process! Then the programs had to be folded. Fortunately, we had been given a folding machine by our friend Mr. Wilfrid Jubinville. I fixed the settings to make an initial 3" fold on the legal size paper. Then the sisters took it from there. Sr. Mary Immaculata and Sr. Mary Mannis and Sr. Mary of the Sorrowful Heart were always ready to help with the second fold. The finished program was 5 ½ " x 8 ½ ". There was so much that I wanted to get on the program that I used every available inch! One month I needed an additional half sheet as an insert and that small 3" flap did just the trick to hold it all together. Only in a monastery can you find things like that!

Since we were obviously in our cloister, it was important to have things organized in the hope of having as little confusion as possible, although at times there was "mass confusion," at least on my part! In order to help dispel some confusion, I also made a color coded Chapel seating plan printout to hand out to the guests with their programs. Computerized signs were made to hang on the pews to designate the various groups. A few months down the road I began making name tags. It made it easier for the sisters at the reception rather than having to ask each person their name. We learned as we went along and tried to improve.

Oh, and then it was real teamwork for the prayer booklet. Sr. Mary of the Immaculate Conception did the master layout and passed it on to me. Again I was off to our printing machine for the multiple pages. Then the sheets had to be collated and folded. With multiple folded pages the booklets' protruding edges also had to be trimmed, so Sr. Mary of the Sorrowful Heart and I took care of that with our large cutter. These were then placed in a colored cover, suitable for the season, and tied with colored yarn. Again the sisters pitched in to help with this.

After our very first celebration, Sr. Magdalen Ward, S.S.J. suggested having cookies and beverages for the guests at the reception. Sr. Mary of the Sorrowful Heart and I moved two tables into the parlor and Sr. Mary of the Immaculate Conception decoratively arranged colorful paper plates and dishes laden with our homemade cookies. At each month's reception we had a unique surprise for each of our guests, and each month presented them with a personalized prayer card and a jubilee calendar.

The Lord sent me a few two legged angels with big hearts and cameras in hand! Because of them we had photos of the celebration and these were posted on a web site I developed. The photos can be accessed through a link at http://www.praedicare.com/pgshom/HomeEnglish.htm. Tpr Michael Cutone was our very first photographer. He had come as an honored guest for the opening celebration service and returned the following month to help out in any way he could. He did a "lineup" of each group and photographed them with their giant sized smiles. One of the individuals in the lineup was Scott Lozyniak, who was a high school senior at the time. He brought his camera and took some photos at the reception. Scott shared his photos with us too, returning in various capacities for subsequent celebrations, always bringing his camera with him. My cousin, David Broer, and his wife Andrea supplied some photos, as did Bruce Smith. All these added to a wonderful collection of remembrances captured in living color and enabled others to share in those wonderful days of grace.

We tried to foresee as much as we could and prepare accordingly. Adjustments and improvements were made along the way and more "angels" recruited! For the first service, I greeted our guests in our small parlor and cued them in so that they would feel comfortable with the order of events and their part in it. It became obvious that the room was too small and the guests too many to accomplish the task at hand. Our prioress gave me permission to go out to our monastery reception area, and that helped very much. Angels also helped me with the cueing in. These angels had to come even earlier to be cued in themselves. This allowed us to direct our honored guests into their distinctive groups with an assigned angel to guide them. It certainly helped me immensely in coordinating the whole celebration and answering questions from guest officiants, emcees and other participants.

As you can well imagine, there was much activity behind the scenes. We are most grateful to all those who assisted us in making things go so well. Each person played a part to make this a prayerful, peaceful and joyful experience. Many thanks also to all our guests who were so patient and kind in the time prior to the service, coming in advance and sometimes from quite a distance. May God continue to bless you and your loved ones!

CHAPTER 18

Mary, the Contemplative

A Surprise Retreat

> *"Come away by yourselves ... and rest a while."*
> *Mk. 6:31 (RSV)*

Yes, even the contemplative nun needs a time of more interior silence and withdrawal from her duties in the monastery. This usually comes during a time of retreat. The nuns have one annually but, in 2006 we experienced a most unusual one. It came about in a surprising way.

Sr. Mary Rose Figura, O.P. of the Farmington Hills, MI, Monastery had invited the Mater General of the Dominican Order to give their community a retreat in honor of their 100th Anniversary. On that occasion a sister for a Vietnamese foundation of nuns was to make her solemn vows. Fr. Carlos replied and suggested that the retreat include nuns from all the US monasteries

Sr. Mary Rose was on the Council for the Conference/Association of the US nuns and asked the councillors to approve the retreat as a "Conference Project for the 800th Anniversary." Upon approval sister was given the charge to proceed and make all the arrangements. She sent invitations to all the monasteries with no limit as to how many nuns could come from each monastery because the Adrian Sisters had given the nuns the use of their whole Weber Center for the retreat. A total of 81 nuns participated!

Sr. Mary Rose also invited the four Provincials to the last day of the retreat. The friar, who was the provincial from the Western Province, had intended to come, but his brother died suddenly and he was unable to attend. Needless to say our prayers were with him.

Surprising Announcement

> *"And they were all amazed, so that they questioned among themselves, saying, 'What is this? '"* Mk. 1:27 (RSV)

What a surprise for us nuns when the invitation arrived at our monastery in West Springfield! Our prioress, Sr. Mary of the Immaculate Conception, O.P., announced that any sister who was interested in attending the retreat should submit her name. The community decided that we could allow three sisters to go and the names were put in a "hat." We had the drawing at recreation and one of our senior sisters did the drawing of the names. My name was the first one drawn and I was delighted! The two other sisters who went on the retreat were Sr. Mary of the Nativity and Sr. Mary Mannis.

Wonderful Welcome!

> *"Whoever welcomes one of these little children in my name welcomes me."* Mark 9:37 (NIV®)

The Dominican Sisters of Adrian Michigan opened their homes and hearts to receive us. In her opening welcome, Sr. Donna Markam, O.P., Prioress General, told of a trip she had made to Rome and how she and another sister had walked to a monastery of the friars. They were warmly welcomed and as the day drew on felt they had to get a cab to return to their abode, otherwise it would be too dark to return in safety. When they asked about calling a cab, the friar was taken aback. He exclaimed, "You are our sisters!" He had no intention of calling a cab; the friars themselves would drive their sisters back. Sr. Donna and her companion were deeply touched by this experience.

Sr. Donna and all the Adrian Dominican Sisters welcomed us in like manner. We were family and every one of the nuns felt welcomed into the Adrian Dominican family for this very special time. Words simply cannot be found to express this whole-hearted welcome and opportunity for such a unique retreat. It will live on in our hearts and in our lives.

Sr. Mary Pia, O.P. – Los Angeles, CA

The weeks following our return home from the Master General's retreat in Adrian were filled with wonderful memories, as we tried to convey to our sisters who had remained home, details of this magnificent spiritual experience.[1]

Sr. Mary Rose, O.P. – Lufkin

The enthusiasm with which the sisters welcomed us made me feel quite abashed. It was like meeting long lost relatives. May God reward them for all their goodness to us![2]

Corpus Christi Monastery - Menlo Park, CA

I think everyone agrees that our days together will remain as a number ten in our log of spiritual peaks. The tremendous generosity of everyone was exceptional in every aspect.[3]

Sr. Mary Assumpta, O.P. - Linden, VA

The hospitality of our Adrian Dominican Sisters could not be surpassed. As soon as I entered Weber Retreat Center, I knew that I was among family. They were joyful and gracious, catering to our every need. The beautiful grounds of over 100 acres were conducive to contemplative prayer and an ideal setting for a retreat.[4]

The Retreat Conferences

"I will run the way of your commandments,
when you shall enlarge my heart." Ps. 119.32 (AKJV)[1]

SR. MARY REGINA, O.P. – LANGLEY BC (CANADA)

Fr. Carlos offered us certain people in the Old and New Testament and built his talks around them, placing them in the context of their own contribution to spirituality and to spirituality relevant to our life as Dominican nuns. His choices were great. The talk featured Abraham, Joseph (OT), Moses, David, Elijah, Jeremiah, Jonah, Ruth, John the Baptist, the woman at the well, Mary Magdalene, Thomas the Apostle, Peter the Apostle, Saul/Paul, John the Apostle and the last retreat talk featured Mary as Mother of God, as the person and model for spirituality and as one who plays a role in our lives as Dominican nuns.[5]

BLESSED SACRAMENT MONASTERY - FARMINGTON HILLS, MI

Sisters appreciated his balance of humor with profound insights and wisdom. (Just when you were laughing your head off, he followed quickly with something very deep to think about).[6]

SR. MARY ASSUMPTA, O.P. - LINDEN, VA

Drawn from the lives of men and women of the Old and New Testament, and, filled with humor, the Master General's conferences had a unifying theme of Gospel teaching on charity, unity, peace and joy which are so essential to community life and are at the very heart of our Dominican Order.[7]

SR. MARY MICHAEL, O.P. – BRONX, N.Y.

The conferences with Fr. Carlos were truly a blessing. I

---

1   American King James Version in public domain Nov. 8, 1999

saw in him the deep joy of our holy Fr. Dominic and his love and concern for the nuns and a deep love for the Word of God, as we walked with the holy men and women of Scripture, receiving inspiration from them and asking them to help us open our hearts to the Lord.[8]

Sr. Mary Regina, O.P. – Langley BC (Canada)

The major parts of each lecture were concentrated on the serious, but when you would least expect, he delightfully turned into an impersonator, splitting our sides from the laughter. He was so superb at this, that we all wondered how the Dominican Order was blessed to have this enormously happy man instead of the greater stage in the world.[9]

Fr. Master and our Brothers

"But I am among you as one who serves."
Luke 22:27 (NIV®)

Sr. Marie of the Precious Blood, O.P. – Bronx, NY

I found the Master very charming AND disarming – a true brother who really listened to each of us. It was wonderful to meet and re-meet so many of our sisters who became more than just names but real sisters, and to share the same feelings and concerns that seem common to us all.[10]

Sr. Mary Regina, O.P. – Langley

Fr. Carlos is wise and sound, experienced and generous. He is willing to go beyond the line of exhaustion for the sake of love and responsibility. We all noticed this, expressed it to each other and stood amazed.[11]

Sr. Mary of the Sacred Heart, O.P. – Marbury, AL

Fr. Carlos, Fr. Manuel (Merten) and Fr. Ed (Ruane) spared no effort to make themselves completely available to each and every one of us. There was an almost palpable living charity that permeated the atmosphere during the entire retreat.[12]

Sr. Mary Augustine, O.P. – North Guilford, CT

(I am grateful for) Fathers Ed Ruane and Manuel Merten, who displayed a genuine interest and care for the sisters, and our gracious Master Carlos Azpiroz Costa, who agreed to come and pour so much wisdom and spirituality upon us, along with being such a vibrant and prayerful example of what he taught and preached.[13]

Elmira, NY Nuns

(I appreciated) Fr. Carlos', Fr. Merten's and Fr. Ed's generosity in making themselves available daily to anyone wishing to speak privately with them.[14]

Sr. Mary of the Sacred Heart, O.P. – West Springfield, MA

Your author was part of a committee of nuns, who had been working on a jubilee calendar for the US nuns. It was in process and set aside during the time of this retreat. I had spoken to Fr. Manuel about it during my private interview and Father gave me extra interview time slots. He showed me photos he had on his laptop, which he had taken of nuns and their monasteries in various parts of the world. He copied any I wanted on a thumb drive I had with me. These pictures were wonderful in helping to complete the 800th Anniversary calendar.

Special Penitential Service

"He told them, 'This is what is written: The Christ will suffer and rise from the dead on the third day, and repentance and forgiveness of sins will be preached in his name to all nations, beginning at Jerusalem. You are witnesses of these things.'"
Lk. 24:46-48 (NIV®)

Sr. Mary of the Nativity, O.P. – West Springfield, MA

One night we also had veneration of the Cross, which was laid on the altar for us. Each sister went up and venerated it.[15]

Sr. Mary Veronica, O.P. – Lancaster, PA

We had our own penitential service directed by Fr. Carlos with seven petitions for forgiveness responded to by the "Parce Domine"[2] and venerations of the Cross.[16]

High Point: Communal Prayer Experience

Let the word of Christ dwell in you richly, teach and admonish one another in all wisdom, and sing psalms and hymns and spiritual songs with thankfulness in your hearts to God. (RSV)

Sr. Mary of the Nativity, O.P. – West Springfield, MA

On another night, Fr. Master gave each of us a holy picture, asking us to write our motto on the back. After this he invited us to go up to the altar, placing our picture there with the Monstrance, and making an act of adoration. The choir sang as the sisters went up singly for their acts.[17]

Corpus Christi Monastery - Menlo Park, CA

The one powerful moment most often reflected upon was

_____
2   Latin antiphon sung at Compline during Lent.

Adrian Retreat Participants

Fr. Carlos Azpiroz Costa, O.P.

Sr. Donna Markam, O.P.

Sr. Mary Rose, O.P.

Concelebrated Mass

Holy Communion

Tech Support

Blessing of the medals

Holy Hour and presenting mottos

Liturgy of the Hours

Cemetery visit

Frs. Ruane and Merten

Penitential Service

Looking at calendar pages

Homily

White Sox fan and Paul's Aunt

Closing Mass & upper deck

the evening we spent before the Blessed Sacrament listening to scripture readings, singing from the depths of our hearts and holding tightly to our little "motto" holy card. When each sister and brother reverently approached Jesus in the monstrance and placed their personal motto on the altar, we intensely prayed for one another, knowing we are one family in St. Dominic.[18]

SR. MARY REGINA, O.P. – LANGLEY (CANADA)

I think all would agree that the night of adoration of the Blessed Sacrament stood out as central and special for each of us. That service lasted from 8 p.m. to 10:30 p.m., but the time value did not disturb us in the least. Fr. Carlos had asked us to write on a card the motto each one of us individually chose for ourselves at the time of our profession of vows. He then asked us to file in a line (up to the altar) and each put our motto at the base of the monstrance to pray to Jesus.[19]

SR. MARY ROSE DOMINIC, O.P. - SUMMIT

The procession of sisters was accompanied by the singing of beautiful hymns and readings from St. John's Gospel, especially from chapter 6 and chapters 13 to 17. Besides kneeling silently in adoration, the sisters variously prostrated themselves with arms in the form of a cross...or stood with arms outstretched or elevated in silent prayer. It was so moving that many wept.[20]

SR. MARY OF THE NATIVITY, O.P. – WEST SPRINGFIELD, MA

Finally, when the sisters got slower and the time was passing quickly, Fr. Master whispered to the sisters to please move along. It was 11:00 p.m. before we got to bed that night! I was so touched when everyone finished. Fr. Master took the Monstrance over to the organist for her turn.[21]

Sr. Mary Aimee, O.P. – Marbury, AL

The supreme joy of the evening of Eucharistic Adoration exceeded all other blessings. At the invitation of Fr. Master, each sister came forth to speak face to face to Jesus in the Monstrance. What graces she received at that moment only she can tell. After each had her conversation with Jesus, Fr. Master, in a moment of exquisite thoughtfulness, took the Monstrance to Sr. Mary Dominic at the organ. Surely the swelling of pride in belonging to such a family was not out of place.[22]

Praying Together

They all joined together constantly in prayer, along with the women and Mary the mother of Jesus, and with his brothers.
Acts 1:14 (NIV®)

Sr. Maria Joseph, O.P. – Lancaster

The singing with the sisters in the Rosary Chapel with those gorgeous stained-glass windows… it seemed to me angels were above our heads carrying our voices up to heaven. It was amazing to me that I had no problem singing with the Nuns I had never sung with before. There were 80 of us and it sounded so heavenly![23]

Sr. Mary Rose Dominic, O.P. – Summit

The singing at the Mass and Liturgy of the Hours was beautiful and devotional, with lovely psalm tones, all sung with a rich volume and perfect tempo; the two chantresses[3] were heavenly and blended well together. We sang "O Bread of life." Composed of my own words and Sr. Maria's tune, and I was happy to see that the sisters liked it very much. We all shared the various duties for the Liturgy; it was impressive

---

3   Sisters who lead the choir

to see how united in spirit we all were. On July 4ᵗʰ there was a special Vespers for peace and forgiveness.[24]

SR. MARY VERONICA, O.P. – LANCASTER

The special 4ᵗʰ of July Prayer for Peace liturgy planned by our Adrian Sisters began with a bang.[25]

Miscellaneous Moments

The sisters also spoke of the daily personal holy hour of rosary and adoration after supper: receiving the special commemorative medals designed by the Summit monastery and blessed by Fr. Carlos; receiving the Directories of the monasteries compiled by Sr. Mary of the Sacred Heart Desmond, O.P. of Menlo Park; the lovely remembrance cards by her as well as those by Sr. Mary Grace of the Bronx monastery. The sisters were also pleased to get a sneak preview of the 800ᵗʰ Anniversary calendar, which was in the making. Sr. Mary Grace Decuir, O.P. provided the calligraphy and Sr. Mary of the Sacred Heart Decuir, O.P. served on the committee, while Sr. Mary of the Sacred Heart Sawicki, O.P. did the computer layout designs and negotiations.

Remembering the Message

I want to remind you of the gospel I preached to you, the gospel that you received and in which you are firmly established.
1 Cor. 15: 1 (JB)

CORPUS CHRISTI MONASTERY – MENLO PARK, CA

We looked back on the words of the Master when talking about vocations. He said we have a tendency to judge our monasteries by numbers. Instead we should ask ourselves why we want vocations. Is it just for security? Or have we promised God that if we get vocations we will contribute to new foundations or assist other monasteries? Then there was the call to action, to foster unity in our communities, monasteries, among all of the Dominican family and in the whole church.[26]

Those Who Went Before

I always thank my God as I remember you in my prayers, because I hear about your faith in the Lord Jesus and your love for all the saints. Philemon 1: 4-5 (NIV®)

SR. MARY ROSE, O.P. – LUFKIN, TX

It was a touching sight to witness the Adrian Sisters walking to the cemetery every day, rosaries in hand. The cemetery itself, with its 1200 graves, staggers the mind. How many lives it represented! The concentric circles of the graves reminded me of ripples in a pond. Surely the gift of each one of those lives produced a ripple effect felt throughout the world. The Adrian novice who first showed us the cemetery said that they have no idea why they started burying the sisters in circles, but they kept it up. I liked it. It seemed to speak of the equality the sisters share under their constitutions. It was neat, too, that we were present praying in their cemetery, Adrian having sprung from Regensburg[4], it seemed like history had come full circle.[27]

SR. MAUREEN OF THE EUCHARIST, O.P. – BUFFALO

I had the Adrian Dominican Sisters for five years in grade school in Detroit, Michigan, and it is to them that I attribute my lifelong love for all things Dominican. It gave me great joy to be able to visit the gravesite of my much-loved eighth grade teacher, Sr. Elise Marie, O.P. And thanks to the "Cutting Garden" provided by the sisters (Where else have you seen a

4   The Regensburg monastery in Germany was a community of nuns. The Sisters fled to America in a time of persecution and engaged in an active ministry.

cutting garden, flowers free for the cutting?!) I was able to lay a bouquet of flowers at the grave, a thank you of sorts for someone who instilled in me a great love for the Order as well as for the English language and all its many facets – poetry, literature, and vocabulary.[28]

SR. MARY AGNES BAUDO, O.P. – BUFFALO

The beautifully formed cemetery has approximately eight huge sets of circles where the deceased Adrian Dominicans are buried. Our Master General arranged a time for the retreatants to meet on that sacred ground to pray for all deceased Dominicans, especially those of our communities.[29]

The Closing Mass and Social

We ought always to thank God for you, brothers, and rightly so, because your faith is growing more and more, and the love every one of you has for each other is increasing. 2 Thess. 1: 3 (NIV®)

SR. MARY VERONICA, O.P. – LANCASTER, PA

The Thanksgiving Mass at the Regina chapel with all the Adrian Sisters presided by the Master and concelebrated by the Provincials of St. Joseph, St. Albert and St. Martin's provinces and also by Fr. Michael Monshau was special. We sang the beautiful *Seignadou Mass*[5] composed for the 8th Centenary by Sr. Maria of the Cross of Summit.[30]

SR. MARY REGINA, O.P. – LANGLEY

On the last evening of the retreat, Fr. Carlos and the other friars (three provincials of the four Dominican provinces joined us for this) offered the Eucharistic Celebration for both the nuns finishing the retreat and all the Dominican Sisters at the Adrian Motherhouse at the time. The infirm sisters,

---

5   Latin texts with the music based on 13th Century French *chansons.*

too, attended and that made our celebration complete and so tripled our joy.[31]

Sr. Mary of the Sacred Heart, O.P. – West Springfield, MA

The infirm Adrian Sisters were in the "upper deck" of the large Chapel. At the close of the Mass, some of us went up there to greet those sisters. I met one wearing a Chicago White Sox hat. I told her that I was a Red Sox fan, but asked her if she knew Paul Konerko. Well, two other sisters standing at her side got quite excited. I told them that Paul's aunt (a nun) was here and went to get her. Sr. Mary Assumpta met them and promised to write to Paul and ask him to send them his baseball card.

We also prayed with the sister in the wheelchair, forming a chain of prayer with an Adrian Sister holding sister's right hand and myself her left hand with others in between. It was a very special time praying with this sister, who in a way represented all the sick and infirm sisters. Oh, and "Paul-ey," as the sisters called him, did send his Adrian Sister fans his autographed card!

Grateful Hearts

Let the word of Christ dwell in you richly…
with gratitude in your hearts to God. Col. 3: 16 (NIV®)

Sr. Mary Veronica, O.P. – Lancaster

All the above add up to ten special days of grace, peace and holy renewal for which I thank our dear Master Carlos Azpiroz Costa, O.P., as the worthy successor of St. Dominic, in continuing his love and care for all the monasteries.[32]

SR. MARY AGNES BAUDO, O.P. – BUFFALO, NY

Heartfelt gratitude to Sr. Donna, O.P., and our other Adrian Dominican Sisters and their employees for the welcoming hospitality, wherein nothing was wanting to us during our memorable stay at the Weber Center.[33]

SR. MARY VERONICA, O.P. – LANCASTER

Many thanks also to Sr. Mary Rose and Sr. Marie Dominic as coordinators of the retreat and to Sr. Mary John and the community of Lufkin for the arrangement of liturgical booklets.[34]

SR. MARY OF THE SACRED HEART, O.P. – WEST SPRINGFIELD, MA

One of the ways of expressing our ongoing gratitude to our Adrian Sisters was through a gift of our 800th Anniversary calendar. We designed a special custom cover just for them and filled it with love and prayers!

The Return Home

Walk as children of light: For the fruit of the Spirit is in all goodness and righteousness and truth. Eph. 5: 8-9 (KJV)

SR. MARY PIA, O.P. – LOS ANGELES, CA

The weeks following our return home from the Master General's retreat in Adrian were filled with wonderful memories, as we tried to convey to our sisters who had remained home, details of this magnificent, spiritual experience.

The spiritual treasure I carried home from the talks of our Master Carlos was a very deep conviction of HOPE, that God was indeed using our cloistered, contemplative life for the holy preaching and the salvation of souls, as our Holy Fr. Dominic had intended us. It is very necessary to keep this hope vibrant and alive, especially in places like Hollywood where the stellar attractions of power, pleasure and worldly success all tend to blur people's concept of a life of prayer and the eternal destiny for which God has created us. Though these haunts of sinful pleasure are but a walking distance from our cloister walls, still there are people hungering for God who come to our chapel in search of peace, and ask our prayers for their many needs.[35]

(Endnotes)

1   Sr. Mary Pia, O.P., "Master's Retreat, Adrian Michigan – 2006," Los Angeles, *Association Sharings*. 26.2 Fall 2006: 31. Used with permission.

2   Sr. Mary Rose, O.P., "Master's Retreat, Adrian Michigan – 2006," Lufkin, *Association Sharings*. 26.2 Fall 2006: 32. Used with permission.

3   Corpus Christi Monastery, "Master's Retreat, Adrian Michigan – 2006," Menlo Park: Retreat Reflections, *Association Sharings*. 26.2 Fall 2006: 38. Used with permission.

4   Sr. Mary Assumpta, O.P., "Master's Retreat, Adrian Michigan – 2006," Linden, *Association Sharings*. 26.2 Fall 2006: 31. Used with permission.

5   Sr. Mary Regina, O.P., "Master's Retreat, Adrian Michigan – 2006," Langley, *Association Sharings*. 26.2 Fall 2006: 29. Used with permission.

6   Blessed Sacrament Monastery, "Master's Retreat, Adrian Michigan – 2006," Farmington Hills: Community Sharings, *Association Sharings*. 26.2 Fall 2006: 26. Used with permission.

7   Sr. Mary Assumpta, O.P. 31. Used with permission.

8   Sr. Mary Michael, O.P., "Master's Retreat, Adrian Michigan – 2006," Bronx, *Association Sharings*. 26.2 Fall 2006: 21. Used with permission.

9   Sr. Mary Regina, O.P. 29. Used with permission.

10   Sr. Marie of the Precious Blood, O.P., "Master's Retreat, Adrian Michigan – 2006," Bronx, *Association Sharings*. 26.2 Fall 2006: 20. Used with permission.

11   Sr. Mary Regina, O.P. 29. Used with permission.

12   Sr. Mary of the Sacred Heart, O.P., "Master's Retreat, Adrian Michigan – 2006," Marbury: My Impressions of the Master's Retreat, *Association Sharings*. 26.2 Fall 2006: 36. Used with permission.

13   Sr. Mary Augustine, O.P., "Master's Retreat, Adrian Michigan – 2006," North Guilford, *Association Sharings*. 26.2 Fall 2006: 39. Used with permission.

14   Elmira, NY Nuns, "Master's Retreat, Adrian Michigan – 2006," Elmira: Snapshot Memories of the Master's Retreat, *Association Sharings*. 26.2 Fall 2006: 25. Used with permission.

15   Sr. Mary of the Nativity, O.P., "Master's Retreat, Adrian Michigan – 2006," West Springfield: Through Many Tribulations, *Association Sharings*. 26.2 Fall 2006: 43. Used with permission.

16   Sr. Mary Veronica, O.P., "Master's Retreat, Adrian Michigan – 2006," Lancaster: Impressions and memories of the Master's Retreat in Adrian Michigan, *Association Sharings*. 26.2 Fall 2006: 28. Used with permission.

17   Sr. Mary of the Nativity, O.P. 43. Used with permission.

18   Corpus Christi Monastery 38. Used with permission.

19   Sr. Mary Regina, O.P. 29. Used with permission.

20   Sr. Mary Rose Dominic, O.P., "Master's Retreat, Adrian Michigan – 2006," Summit: My Reflections on the Jubilee Retreat, *Association Sharings*. 26.2 Fall 2006: 41. Used with permission.

21   Sr. Mary of the Nativity, O.P. 43. Used with permission.

22   Sr. Mary Aimee, O.P., "Master's Retreat, Adrian Michigan – 2006," Marbury: Retreat with the Master of the Order June, 2006, *Association Sharings*. 26.2 Fall 2006: 37. Used with permission.

23   Sr. Maria Joseph, O.P., "Master's Retreat, Adrian Michigan – 2006," Lancaster: Remembering, *Association Sharings*. 26.2 Fall 2006: 27. Used with permission.

24   Sr. Mary Rose Dominic, O.P. 41. Used with permission.

25   Sr. Mary Veronica, O.P. 28. Used with permission.

26   Corpus Christi Monastery 38. Used with permission.

27   Sr. Mary Rose, O.P. 34. Used with permission.

28   Sr. Maureen of the Eucharist, O.P., "Master's Retreat, Adrian Michigan – 2006," Buffalo: Beautiful, *Association Sharings*. 26.2 Fall 2006: 23. Used with permission.

29   Sr. Mary Agnes Baudo, O.P., "Master's Retreat, Adrian Michigan – 2006," Buffalo: In Gratitude for the Retreat with our Master General, *Association Sharings*. 26.2 Fall 2006: 24. Used with permission.

30   Sr. Mary Veronica, O.P. 28. Used with permission.

31   Sr. Mary Regina, O.P. 30. Used with permission.

32   Sr. Mary Veronica, O.P. 28. Used with permission.

33   Sr. Mary Agnes Baudo, O.P. 24. Used with permission.

34   Sr. Mary Veronica, O.P. 28. Used with permission.

35   Sr. Mary Pia, O.P. 31. Used with permission.

CHAPTER 19

A Climatic Celebration with our Bishop

*They will celebrate your abundant goodness
and joyfully sing of your righteousness. Ps. 145:7 (NIV®)*

September 8, 2007, was the climax of our 800th Anniversary celebrations and marked our monastery's 85th Anniversary of being founded in the diocese of Springfield. The occasion was celebrated with a Solemn Mass of Thanksgiving with Bishop Timothy A. McDonnell, D.D. as the principal celebrant.

Bishop McDonnell has a deep appreciation for the life of a Dominican nun. Before he came to the diocese of Springfield he was an auxiliary bishop in the Archdiocese of New York and was familiar with the Dominican Nuns in the Bronx. Many bishops recognize the value of the contemplative life and the value of the nuns' life of prayer, and are eager to have a monastery in their diocese, knowing that it will bring great blessings to the diocese.

Flashbacks

Most Reverend Timothy A. McDonnell
Bishop of Springfield
Excerpt from the 800th Anniversary Mass homily

Consecrated Life makes one --- in the best sense of the

word — a professional, one giving herself entirely to the cause of Christ in a particular community, with a particular rule of life. The charism of the Dominican Nuns has been handed down and lived for 800 years since the days of St. Dominic. Here in West Springfield, you are the present day heirs of the traditions of the Holy Preaching of Prouilhe, you are the elder sisters of the Dominican friars, you are those who have given yourselves entirely in commitment to Christ. And as you renew your history, you enhance that tradition and make the world a more prayerful place.

SEPTEMBER 8, 1922: BISHOP O'LEARY WELCOMES THE NUNS TO SPRINGFIELD

Bishop Thomas Mary O'Leary received Mother Mary of the Crown, O.P. and her companion, Mother Mary Hyacinth, O.P. from Catonsville, Maryland and they discussed the possibility of a foundation of nuns in the diocese of Springfield. Bishop asked how much money the sisters had to begin the foundation. Mother Mary Hyacinth replied, "Five dollars." A bit shocked he responded, "Do you think you can start a foundation with just five dollars?" Mother Mary Hyacinth answered, "I can't, but our Blessed Mother can." After a few moments the bishop continued, "Come, come to Springfield in the name of God and of Mary. Today is Mary's birthday; this will be our gift to her."[1]

FEBRUARY 1, 1950: BISHOP CHRISTOPHER J. WELDON FROM NEW YORK

On February 1, 1950 we learned that Monsignor Christopher J. Weldon of New York was to be our new bishop. Like his predecessor, Bishop Weldon had a great appreciation of his nuns. On May 1, 1955, he officiated at the ceremony for the laying of the cornerstone of the new monastery. During construction he personally came to the site to keep an eye on the work being done and did not hesitate to make observations to those doing the construction.[2]

Ingersoll Grove
Springfield, MA

Mother Mary
Hyacinth Fitzgerald

W Springfield Monastery
(Nye Estate)

Laying of the
cornerstone

Blessing of the bell
September 8, 1926

Perpetual Adoration
Old Monastery

25th Anniversary Holy Hour
Rosary Sunday

Family members
at the 800th celebration

Sr. Mary Grace Power
and a family member
800th Anniversary Celebration
in the cloister courtyard

At our 800th Anniversary our Dominican brother James M. Sullivan, O.P. was the homilist and Msgr. Christopher Connelly served as Master of Ceremonies. There were a total of sixteen priests at the concelebrated Mass. Among these were the Vicar General, Msgr. Richard S. Sniezyk, as well as Msgr. Leo A. Leclerc. Sr. Mary of the Immaculate Conception's nephew, Fr. Joseph Dolan, also concelebrated. He is a priest in the diocese of Worcester. Fr. Marek Stybor, O.F.M.Conv. represented our Franciscan brothers and Fr. Francis X. Sullivan has been a long time friend of the community. Fr. Gerard A. Lefleur was a good friend of Sr. Maureen Magdalen. They were neighbors and in their early childhood days, and Sr. Maureen's brothers were playmates with the boy who was to become Fr. Lafleur. Fr. Richard A. Riendeau taught at Cathedral High School when the author was a student there. Fr. William Hamilton has had many a prayer offered for him at the monastery and has stated that his name has been placed under the monstrance so many times that he does not want to imagine what life would be like if it was not there. Fr. Gary Dailey has been instrumental in the sisters adopting particular seminarians to be remembered in their prayers. Completing our list of celebrants were Frs. William Lunney, Steven McGuigan and Philippe D. Roux.

Flashbacks

September 8, 1926: Blessing of the Bell — over 50 priests participate

On September 30, 1925, our community moved from 80 Ingersoll Grove in Springfield to a large residence in West Springfield. It took nearly a year for the dwelling house to be gradually transformed into a functional monastery. On September 8, 1926, there was a double ceremony. A large bell was to be blessed and perpetual exposition of the Blessed Sacrament in our small chapel was to be inaugurated.

The blessing of the bell, took place on the lawn outside

the chapel. Bishop O'Leary officiated and more than 50 priests participated. On one side of the bell the words "Venite, Adoremus" (O Come let us adore) had been engraved, and on the other side "Ave Maria." These names were symbolic of our double commitment of Eucharistic adoration and the praise of Mary through the rosary.[3]

SILVER JUBILEE MASS

With Bishop O'Leary's permission, Fr. John C. McMahon, a devoted priest-friend, took upon himself the full burden of preparing for a magnificent pontifical field Mass on Labor Day, September 1st. He had a beautiful altar erected on the monastery grounds. According to news reports, approximately 500 priests and 20,000 lay people participated. Bishop O'Leary was the celebrant, and the noted Dominican Fr. Ignatius Smith was the guest preacher.

On Rosary Sunday, October 5th, a Silver Jubilee Marian Holy Hour took place at the outdoor altar. Bishop O'Leary presided and the Very Reverend Robert J. Slavin, O.P., president of Providence College, Providence R.I., gave the meditations. The attendance was much larger than at the Jubilee Mass and there were an estimated 25,000 persons.[4]

Returning to our 800th Anniversary celebration was Deacon James W. Longe who proclaimed the Gospel. He was the seminarian whom Sr. Maria had adopted to pray for and she was delighted for "her seminarian" to have that honor. The Knights of Columbus again honored us with their presence in providing an Honor Guard. The Knights always add to the solemnity of the occasion and people are inspired by their presence.

Sr. Mary of the Immaculate Conception, O.P. was our prioress at the time and was the great organizer for this climatic celebration. Sr. Mary of the Pure Heart, O.P. worked with her in preparing the liturgical musical selections, which included Gregorian chant commons from the *Missa de Angelis* (Mass of the Angels) and *Cum Jubilo* (With Joy).

The Latin Motet "Ave Verum" was also sung. The responsorial psalm and communion hymn were in English. Sr. Mary Regina, O.P. was organist for this celebration. She has such a gift for playing the organ and the music reverberates in such ways that words cannot adequately express it.

Guests were invited by the prioress and community. Each sister was allowed a limited number of invitations. For a sister's jubilee celebration it has become a custom to have a tent on the monastery grounds for the reception with the jubilee sister and the prioress in attendance at the reception. Due to the nature of this particular celebration, an exception was made, whereby the tents were set up in our monastery cloister courtyard. This allowed sisters to be with their family and other guests at the reception and luncheon. The guests were not told of this beforehand and so it was quite a delightful surprise for them.

There were three tents with large white round tables and chairs underneath, all of which were rented. Tablecloths and linens were in two shades of blue: a royal blue and pastel blue. The courtyard also had an array of colorful potted mums provided by Dr. and Mrs. Stanley Swierzewski. Together with the gardens around the edge of the courtyard, it made for a delightful setting.

One of our sisters was at the Mt. St. Vincent Healthcare Center, which provided her with the care she needed. However, arrangements were made for a wheelchair van to bring her home to the monastery for the day. Dominican fraternity members Mary Beth Dillon and Linda Burr assisted in sister's transit. Sr. Mary Grace thoroughly enjoyed herself. It was quite a nice experience for her family members too, who had come from a distance.

Sr. Mary of the Assumption's family came from upstate New York and Sr. Mary of the Immaculate Heart's family from New Hampshire. Sr. Maureen Magdalen, who had been a Sister of St. Joseph for a number of years, enjoyed seeing many Sisters of St. Joseph who had come for the occasion.

(Endnotes)

1   "Golden Jubilee Remembrance" compiled by the nuns, (1972). 3.
2   "Golden Jubilee Remembrance" 13,16.
3   "Golden Jubilee Remembrance" 6-7.
4   "Golden Jubilee Remembrance" 11-12.

CHAPTER 20

Surprises of Prayer

The Impact of Prayer

If you believe, you will receive whatever you ask for in prayer.
Mt. 21:22 (NIV®)

When some of the sisters first entered the monastery, their families
did not all approve or understand. Some had questions or reservations.
Such was the case for Sr. Mary of the Sorrowful Heart. She prepared
to make a trip from Worcester to the monastery, bringing her mother
to meet the prioress. Mary's friend, Theresa, was to drive and Mary
was in the front seat to assist. As they drove down the street, which
was situated on a hill, Theresa said "Shift." Mary's job was to change
gears with the shift stick, but she was having a bit of trouble getting
it in place. They rounded the corner just in time for Theresa to crash
(gently) into another car! The crash was enough to fling Mary's mother
into the seat in front of her. Her face swelled up, quickly becoming
all black and blue. As they were not far from home, Mary's father
came running up with the family dog tagging along. Upon seeing the
situation, Mary's father said, "Don't you see that God doesn't want
you to enter!"

At the ceremony for her reception to the habit, Mary was given the
name Sr. Mary of the Sorrowful Heart, O.P. When Mary's matriarch

Aunt Nellie met her in the monastery visiting room after the ceremony, she looked sister in the eye and said of the new name, "Good enough for you!" I'm told that Nellie had a hard time keeping a straight face while making that remark. You would have to know sister to understand why Aunt Nellie would say this. Sister is known for her good natured personality and a most obvious "happy heart" filled with compassion and love. But sister's name is appropriate; she carries the sorrows of many who ask for her prayers (as do all the nuns) and brings them before the Lord in prayer.

Over the years numerous friends and relatives and even strangers, ask prayers from sister and the community. One such intention came for sister's niece and family. Their baby, Tommy, was seriously ill in the hospital with a variety of tubes connected to him. He was not expected to live. Tommy's mother prayed the rosary with the family, and from afar sister joined her prayers to theirs. At one point, when the nurse came into Tommy's room to check on him, a look of panic in her eyes and demeanor signaled to Tommy's mother just how desperate the situation was. But God heard the prayers of all concerned. Today Tommy is a healthy boy who just made his First Holy Communion. This youngster has a great devotion to Our Lady and her rosary. He often speaks of God as being his real Daddy. Tommy loves his earthly Father and says he is his second Daddy. In such a case as this, it seems that God not only granted healing to the baby, but something more than meets the eye.

Intercessory Prayer of the Nuns

I urge, then, first of all, that requests, prayers, intercession and thanksgiving be made for everyone. 1 Tim. 2:1 (NIV®)

The nuns in all our monasteries receive requests for prayer. Sometimes we actually hear about the fruits of our prayer, such as times when the doctors are surprised that the surgery went so well, or that the sick person made such remarkable progress, or even that a tumor once showing on an x-ray has somehow disappeared.

We get other requests and sometimes we receive joyful responses for favors received. These might be for the blessing of having met someone as a marriage partner, for the blessing of a baby, for the gift of faith. Sometimes an individual visits a monastery only to find blessings waiting there for them from the Lord. Such was the case for a friend of Sr. Mary of the Nativity's brother. Victor Julian and sister's brother had come to the monastery to perform with their traveling dog show. Victor was a very dignified gentleman and thoroughly enjoyed doing the show for the nuns. Upon departing from the monastery, Victor had a new desire within his heart and asked sister's brother Buddy, "What do I have to do to become a Catholic?" It was not easy to receive instruction while transversing the country with his traveling show, but Victor did, and was very happy to be received into the Church at the Easter Vigil about a year later.

For the most part, prayer requests are for trying or troublesome situations. These might include loss of a job or employment needs, need for reconciliation, a troubled child, substance abuse, addictions, etc. The list is long and the suffering great. In the many and varied crosses they carry, people find solace and strength knowing that the sisters are praying for them.

Sometimes the tragedies of our world are not that far from us. Such was the case on September 11th for a nun in the **Bronx, NY**, Monastery. She was in the garden and saw the second plane hit the Twin Towers. When the sisters turned on the TV, one sister in the Bronx Monastery felt overcome by what she saw, so she went to pray the rosary in the garden. While standing there, she saw the Towers crumble before her eyes. The sisters also pray for St. Catherine's Dominican Priory, where the ministry of the friars is connected with a cancer hospital. Healthcare issues touch on ethical issues regarding the value of life and stem cells. The friars counsel doctors, nurses and patients. The sisters are well aware of and pray for those in difficult situations arising from drugs and prostitution, which destroy so many lives. The sisters support the St. Ignatius Middle School, which reaches out to the people of the area by offering its classes free of charge for children who are part of the neighborhood. The children often come from a single parent home. The sisters are connected with the Hispanic community too, which joins them for Mass on the feasts of Our Lady of Guadalupe. The whole school attends on the feast of St. Francis. The sisters pray for the ministry of Fr. Benedict Groschel, C.F.R. and his friars. They also pray for the inmates at the correctional institution, which is visible in the distance from their back yard.

In 2003, while we were all moved by the tragedy of the Space Shuttle blowing up on its reentry, the nuns in **Lufkin, Texas**, heard the explosion, many of them seeing the smoke trail as the shuttle fell. Their two sisters from Tanzania are very much aware of the needs of the African community, keeping them in prayer. The nuns in **Lancaster, PA**, had their phone ringing non-stop for prayer intentions as soon as they arrived in Pennsylvania many years ago. The hearts of all the nuns went out to the Amish community of Lancaster County in their 2006 schoolroom tragedy. Prayers were offered for those grieving the loss of their children. In the sixties, priests and sisters asked the monastery in **Marbury, Alabama**, to pray before the famous Civil Rights March from Selma to the capital in Montgomery, AL, that such a march would be peaceful. As it turned out, the march became quite bloody (police with clubs and dogs), but not as violent as it could have been. The march diverted to the City of St. Jude which offered the marchers a safe haven. In and around **Elmira, NY**, there are a number of correctional facilities and prisons. The sisters there cannot help but pray for those serving time as well as for the correctional officers. Some of the guards come to Mass in the nuns' chapel and make intercessions for the prisoners. The nuns in **Farmington Hills, Michigan**, were originally founded in Detroit, the heart of the automotive industry. Many workers, who have lost their jobs or whose jobs are in jeopardy, are constantly asking the nuns to pray for them and their families. These are the people of faith who have supported our way of life through thick and thin.

All the nuns join together as one voice in offering prayers for every intention imaginable, from A to Z, for young and the not so young, for students and professionals, for moms and dads. The hearts of the nuns embrace them all and lift them up to God in prayer.

CHAPTER 21

Perpetual Rosary Monasteries

Tracing our Roots

> *"Nevertheless, God's solid foundation stands firm,*
> *sealed with this inscription: 'The Lord knows those who are his,'"*
> *2 Tim. 2:19 (NIV®)*

On October 3, 1857, Mother Mary Agnes of Jesus (Lasalle) and her twin sister, Mother Mary of the Angels, left the monastery in Nay, France, with ten sisters, seven of whom were novices, as well as five postulants, to found the Monastery of the Most Holy Rosary at Mauleon. This was to be the first Dominican cloister of strict observance after the (French) Revolution. The following year, on May 31ˢᵗ, the Perpetual Rosary devotion was established in the monastery by Fr. Marie-Augustin Chardon, O.P. From then on, the new foundation was to become known as the monastery of the Dominicans of the Perpetual Adoring Rosary. Years later, Mauleon would have to give up the devotion due to a severe epidemic that undermined the health and vitality of the community. The idea of founding a Third Order Cloister dedicated to the Perpetual Rosary was first conceived by Fr. Ambroise-Marie Potton, O.P. The dream and the reality would be fulfilled by Fr. Damien Saintourens, O.P., Director of the Perpetual Rosary Association in Lille, France. [1]

Fr. Saintourens, aware of the toll taken on the health of the Second Order Nuns of Mauleon by adding the perpetual rosary to their already full monastic life of strict observance, conceived the idea of a community of sisters whose life would be based on that of the Second Order Nuns, but with modifications that allowed for the added sacrifice of the perpetual rosary. In 1876 while preaching in Southern France, he visited the monastery in Mauleon and told Mother Agnes, the prioress, of his desired project. She suggested Sr. Rose of St. Mary as an associate in this work.[2]

Sr. Rose of St. Mary

Marie Wehrle was born of a good Catholic family on July 10, 1846, in Belfort, France. Her father was a university professor and her mother a woman of deep faith. At age 15, Marie was already thinking of a religious vocation in 1861 when Fr. Potton, O.P. preached at the Lenten services in the parish church at Belfort. On May 20, 1865, Marie entered the monastery in Mauleon. After a three month postulancy, she received the Dominican habit and the religious name, Sr. Rose of St. Mary. At the end of one year's novitiate, Sr. Rose professed perpetual vows on August 30th. Fr. Potton presided at both these ceremonies. As a young religious, Sr. Rose assisted in the revitalization of the Dominican Monastery in Cracow, Poland.[3]

The Beginnings of the Perpetual Rosary Sisters

It was after Easter in 1876 that Sr. Rose was told to prepare herself and place herself without reserve in the hands of her prioress because Jesus was asking her to make great sacrifices and would entrust her with a special mission. This she did without knowing what God desired of her. Later she was introduced to Fr. Saintourens and his plans. It entailed a big sacrifice for Sr. Rose, for it changed her status from a Second Order Nun to a Third Order Sister. The conditions for Fr. Saintourens project seemed advantageous; several wealthy women had promised all kinds of material resources, the permission of the diocesan superiors was granted and the date was set to leave in June, but insurmountable difficulties caused the foundation to fall through. In November of 1878, Sr. Rose was sent with nine other sisters to make a new foundation of nuns at Arles, in Provence. At the same time, Fr. Saintourens was making arrangements for a few of the candidates for his new order to receive training in religious life with Mother Mary of the Angels, Prioress General of the Third Order Teaching Dominican Sisters at Calais. His candidates would receive initial formation in Dominican religious life in the novitiate of the teaching sisters.

On September 11, 1880, while preaching the community retreat at Calais, Fr. Saintourens gave the habit to his first candidates after their three months postulancy. In October, Mother Mary Agnes, the prioress at Arles, told Sr. Rose of St. Mary that the new community was going to separate from the teaching sisters at Calais and that Fr. Saintourens insisted that she assume leadership. Her superior also insisted and begged her to accept. Sr. Rose of St. Mary was unable to make a decision. She was frightened at the responsibility, and her health was weakened from having typhoid fever. However, she abandoned herself to her superiors, acquiesced to their wishes and accepted the task.

To Bonsecours

At a time when the Dominican Fathers and all other orders of men were being expelled from France, it was expected that the same would happen to convents of women. So Fr. Saintourens chose the small village of Bonsecours in Belgium on the borderline of France for the new foundation. It was a very popular place of pilgrimage in honor of Our Lady.

In November of 1880, Sr. Rose of St. Mary left the monastery at Arles for Bonsecours. However, in her weakened condition she had to make the trip across France in stages, traveling only a few hours each day. At the same, time the Prioress of Calais was accompanying the group of novices on their journey from Calais.

On November 9, a cold and rainy night, their train arrived at the Bonsecours' station at nine o'clock in the evening with no one there to meet them. The Prioress of Calais made her way with the three young sisters to the house of Madame de Saint Ouen. She was a woman devoted to Fr. Saintourens and still residing temporarily at Bonsecours. At Madame de Saint Ouen's house, the sisters learned that no house had been rented for them. This lady had contacted different landlords at the request of Fr. Saintourens but had not yet met with any success. The Saint Ouen family provided something for the travelers to eat and then tried to procure a shelter for them. Among the prospective houses there was only one, which was furnished. The sisters had nothing with them except for the clothing they needed, so finally came to an agreement with the proprietors. The house in view had not been inhabited for a long time and needed to be aired for awhile. It was close to eleven o'clock before the sisters were able to finally get some rest.

After Mass the following day, they went again to Madame Saint Ouen's home. She provided for their meals for these first days, until the sisters were able to procure some provisions of their own. The day before Mother Rose of St. Mary arrived, the Prioress of Calais received a telegram recalling her immediately back to her community for grave matters. Therefore she had to leave the young sisters before Mother Rose of St. Mary arrived. Of the three young sisters, two were novices only two months and the third was a seventeen year old postulant. They were in a state of sadness and depression in their abandonment; at ten o'clock in the evening all three could be seen still sitting at the table where they had eaten their frugal meal, gloomy, silent and without energy to move or put the house in order.

Mother Rose of St. Mary Arrives

By the next day, November 17, two of their number met Mother Rose of St. Mary at the train station in Peruwelz. On the last leg of her journey Mother Rose had been accompanied by her own dear mother, who brought all kinds of kitchen utensils, cloth and other useful articles. A great sense of joy replaced the gloom with the arrival of Mother Rose of St. Mary and the group took the trolley to Bonsecours, walking to the house which served as their monastery.

Funds which Father Saintourens had counted on were withdrawn at the move to Bonsecours. Mother Rose of St. Mary had only 400 francs to buy food, pay the monthly rent of 125 francs, and buy furniture. Mother Rose was unable to keep back tears of gratitude as money arrived in the mail from friends. The sisters had none of the objects necessary for divine worship and had to attend Mass at the village church for many weeks. In the fairly large drawing room on the first floor, the sisters arranged a kind of little altar on which they placed a small statue of Our Lady with a small lamp in front. They assembled here for the Divine Office[1], rosary and meditation.

Two Dominican tertiaries sent donations to the sisters and became a great consolation to them. These women wanted to be the first to furnish the little chapel, so the sisters would be able to have the Blessed Sacrament[2] with them. Countess du Pare gave a beautiful chalice and Miss de Clock the sanctuary lamp. Madame Pombla, another friend of Fr. Saintourens, little by little donated a beautiful monstrance, a magnificent cope made of golden cloth, a censer and boat[3] as well as other items. However, the sisters' poverty was such that they never bought more than three or four eggs at a time, and then only rarely. On abstinence days they ate potatoes, boiled or otherwise, and butter was regarded as a luxury.

Mother Rose of St. Mary immediately tried to establish monastic regularity. The four sisters formed into two choirs and recited the Divine Office. Mother Rose instructed the novices in all the various elements

1   Liturgical prayer of the Church
2   Jesus present in the Eucharist under the species of bread
3   Items used in liturgical worship for offering incense.

of monastic liturgical prayer, gave them religious instruction, and also provided spiritual direction. They went to the village church twice a day, in the morning for Mass and in the evening for Benediction of the Most Blessed Sacrament.

In August of 1881, Mary Collin joined the community. She eventually received the habit and was given the name of Sr. Mary of Jesus. She would eventually be chosen as one of the Foundresses for the Perpetual Rosary Sisters in America.

January 1, 1882, was another new beginning for the sisters. For the first time the Blessed Sacrament was exposed all day in their small chapel. Later that month, on the 28th, a new postulant joined them. She left her family in Arles without telling anyone, for her parents were opposed to her vocation and would never have given their consent had she asked them.

Officially Established

In March of 1882, the new foundation was officially affiliated with the Dominican Order, and received certificates stating such from Fr. Joseph Marie Larroca, O.P., who was the Master General of the Dominicans. In March two postulants received the habit and two sisters professed vows for one year rather than perpetually. This had been advised due to the uncertainties and difficulties in which they lived as well as the hesitation of one of the novices. Fr. Bianchi also told Mother Rose of St. Mary that if the sisters wished to have their Rules approved by Rome one day, they would be required to take temporary vows before making them perpetual. Fr. Iweins, Prior of the Dominicans of Louvain and Director of the Rosary in Belgium preached at the profession ceremony of the first two novices. The reception of the habit by Sr. Mary of Jesus had immediately preceded it and proved to be a day of great joy.

On April 4th, Tuesday of Holy Week, Mother Rose went to Paris to see Fr. Chocarne, O.P., the Provincial of the French Province. She did so by the request of her superior, Monsieur Canon Guillaume,

Fr. Damien Marie Co-founders Mother Rose of
Saintourens, O.P. St. Mary Wehrle, O.P.

Bonsecours
de Peruwelz
Belgium - 1882

Mother Mary
of the Rosary

Sister Mary
Joseph

Louvain c. 1890

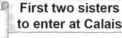

First two sisters
to enter at Calais

Union
City
Monastery

Milwaukee Community - 1903
Mother Mary of the Rosary - center

Hales Corners - 1903
Fr. Trimmberger

Hales Corners 1910

First Monastery
in Camden

Camden
Monastery

Baltimore Community
1913

Buffalo

Mother Mary
of Jesus Collin

Mother Mary
Louis Bertrand

Mother Rose of St. Mary
Mannion - First Prioress

who had discussed with her the necessity of receiving support and counsel before making the foundation. Fr. Chocarne advised that the foundation be placed under the protection of the Dominican Fathers in Belgium. Mother Rose of St. Mary wrote to Fr. Iweins, Prior of Louvain, concerning the matter. With the permission of his superiors he accepted the task. It was at this time that Madame Plomba and other benefactors withdrew their support, and the foundation was left utterly without resources. Should they continue? Fr. Iweins would not hear of dissolution and began collecting a small sum every week from his Rosary Associates in Belgium. This allowed enough to supply their needs, but towards the close of the month they often did not have a penny on hand.

Developments

The sisters considered establishing themselves at Louvain in order to be better known and aided by benefactors of the Order. The Provincial placed one condition on the move: Mother Rose of St. Mary had to be allowed by her superior, the Bishop of Bayonne, to continue the work for at least ten years. Keep in mind that Mother Rose was still a Second Order nun on loan for the new foundation. In May of 1881, Mother Emmanuel had been loaned by Mauleon to aid in the direction of the house and to take charge in the absence of Mother Rose of St. Mary. She was anxious to return to Mauleon and was given an obedience to do so by the Bishop of Tournai. She left on September 1, 1882. But the sisters at Bonsecours continued to receive vocations and were able to observe day and night Hours of Guard, during which they relieved one another in praying the rosary. Their numbers were such that in 1891, plans were underway for two foundations: one in Normandy at Bonsecours Rouen and the second in America.

Fr. Saintourens was the Director of the Perpetual Rosary at Saint Hyacinth in America. He obtained ecclesiastical approbation for a foundation and asked Mother Rose for sisters. He even threatened to establish a new branch of the Dominicans of the Perpetual Rosary if she did not agree. His pressing appeal was followed by a second one from the Bishop of his diocese, and Mother Rose could no longer resist.

A Foundation for America

Mother Rose presented the request to the monastery council and chapter. It was received with joy, and preparations began. Earlier, Mother Rose had established a new foundation in Normandy, and Mother Mary of the Rosary and Mother Mary Dominic had been part of the founding community. Mother Rose chose Mother Mary of the Rosary as prioress for the American foundation. Mother Mary Dominic, because of her experience as an active Dominican Sister and her background in mathematics, was chosen as Procuratix and bookkeeper for the new foundation. Mother Mary of Jesus was summoned from Louvain and made Sub-Prioress of the group. Mother Mary Gabriel, born in England, was an accomplished organist and would prove an asset because of her native language. After four days together, Mother Rose of St. Mary accompanied them to the harbor, where they boarded the steamship "Gascogne." The ten-day voyage proved to be a stormy one and not without seasickness. Near the end of the trip, the weather became favorable and on December 21st at 6 a.m., land was sighted.

Fr. Saintourens was waiting for them at the pier along with Sr. Juliana, an extern sister from Hunt's Point (Bronx), who did not understand their language. Nellie Tully, a promoter of the Perpetual Rosary, was also there. When the sisters took the ferry toward land, they thought they were in a waiting room until it started to move! They next took the subway to Hoboken, (now called Union City) and stumbled through a rubbish laden waste lot before arriving at the two small houses. Sr. Catherine, an extern sister, had prepared everything and was waiting for them at the door of their new home. Being a few days before Christmas, Fr. Saintourens surprised them with a simple wooden box at the feet of Our Lady's statue, in which laid a beautiful statue of the Infant Jesus, on straw. Mother Mary Emmanuel, prioress of the cloistered nuns in Newark, NJ, had sent things necessary for religious life. Both the Newark and Hunt's Point nuns sent their first provisions so that they might celebrate Christmas day joyfully.

The sisters in West Hoboken attended Mass every day in their small chapel, had the Blessed Sacrament reserved, and resumed reciting the Office in common. As far as it was possible, the sisters shared the Hours of Guard, day and night. Their resources grew daily. They requested the provincial that Fr. Saintourens be allowed to continue to assist them because of the strange language and customs of their new surroundings and permission was granted.

First American Vocations and Growth

On February 2nd, Catherine Fitch and Elizabeth Mannion entered as postulants. On February 11th, they received the rosary in a ceremony in their simple chapel because the sisters did not have a choir. [4] Other postulants entered soon after and more room was needed. The Bishop gave permission to buy property and authorized a loan. Mrs. Antoine sold her property to the sisters on trust, giving them fifteen years to pay off the debt, even lowering the price considerably. On March 17th, St. Patrick's feast, the contract was signed. On April 14th, the sisters moved into the new house, even before construction was finished. Mr. Rossi, a French architect, directed the work of construction. Despite all efforts to economize, the sisters needed more funds and the bishop gave his approval for them to borrow all that was necessary. The blessing of the chapel and convent was set for May 16th. The contractor had promised to have all ready by that day, but there was still much that needed to be done. The Sisters of Charity, seeing their plight, sent their school children to help them clean up and put the place in order. The children were eager to help, and despite the language barrier, set themselves to work. The convent seemed invaded by these little people, passing in and out, going about with much activity, cleaning, carrying rubbish, etc. Thanks to all the help, everything was in good order in

4   The cloistered nuns' section for worship.

time for the ceremony of blessing. Only the cells were unfinished. After the ceremony, the sisters hosted an open house for the constant flow of people. The busiest day of all was May 24th, when enclosure was established and even at that, the house was still filled with visitors at nine o'clock that night!

Mother Rose of St. Mary Visits from France

In early July, Mother Rose of St. Mary arrived from France to visit the nuns. It was only seven months since the founding sisters had left for America. Sr. Gabriel acted as translator, but Mother Rose surprised them all when she prayed a "Hail Mary" in English. Later that month, on July 20th, a double ceremony took place. The first three American sisters who had completed six months postulancy, received the habit. The bishop delegated Fr. Saintourens to replace him. Fr. Aloysius, C.P., superior of the Passionists sang the Solemn Mass and Fr. Harpes, S.J. preached the sermon, while Mother Rose of St. Mary played the organ. Catherine Fitch was given the name Sr. Mary of the Blessed Sacrament; Elizabeth Mannion became Sr. Rose of St. Mary; and Elizabeth Schendorf was named Sr. Mary Alain. Immediately afterwards, Sr. Mary Gabriel professed her perpetual vows.

Later that day the sisters sang the Divine Office for the first time, being aided by Mother Rose. They also prayed the rosary in English with a sister announcing the mystery, the community leading the first half of the prayers and the congregation responding with the second half. Statues representing the fifteen mysteries of the rosary were blessed and the "Te Deum" [5] sung. The ceremony was concluded with Benediction of the Blessed Sacrament. It was a full day, filled with joy and many blessings!

Before Mother Rose of St. Mary departed for France, she visited Mother Mary of Jesus at Hunt's Point and Mother Mary Emmanuel in Newark to thank them for all they had done for the new foundation. Three months later, three more postulants received the habit and at Christmas there was a double surprise in store. The sisters surprised

5   Hymn of praise to God

the prioress by secretly preparing a Christmas tree, which they led her to after Mass. The prioress had also prepared a surprise for the sisters, which she led them to at the end of the day. In her office, they beheld a Christmas tree all shining with lights. It was a joyful ending to the day and to the first year in America.

Eventually it became clear that it was not practical for the Perpetual Rosary Monasteries to be united under a Mother General. Fr. Saintourens decided that the Perpetual Rosary convents should be independent of one another, and made each house subject to the Bishop of the Diocese.

Something Brewing in Milwaukee

August 31, 1897 began as a joyful day for the community in Union City; it celebrated Sr. Mary of the Blessed Sacrament's reception to the habit. But the following day after Mass, the bell summoned the sisters to the chapter room. After the customary prayers, the Sub-Prioress announced that their Prioress, Mother Mary of the Rosary, and five other sisters would be leaving for a new foundation. The three professed sisters included Sr. Mary Imelda (Sub-Prioress), Sr. Mary Joseph, and Sr. Mary Alain. The two novices going were the newly clothed Sr. Mary of the Blessed Sacrament and Sr. Mary Aloysius, who would make her profession in Milwaukee in 1898. The sisters went to the parlor where they said their good-byes to the travelers. After their departure, the sisters learned they were headed to Milwaukee, Wisconsin, and that Fr. Saintourens was waiting for them. He would return after they were settled. Going to the community room, the sisters learned that their former Sub-Prioress, Mother Mary of Jesus, was now their Prioress by appointment of the Bishop.

The sisters arrived in Racine, Wisconsin, on September 1st, and stayed overnight with the Racine Dominican Sisters. They took the train to Milwaukee the next day, September 2nd, which day is considered the foundation day. Prior to their arrival, Fr. Saintourens had met with the Archbishop and obtained permission to rent a house for them. He searched for one that was near a church so that the sisters could attend Mass each day. After a week he rejoiced at finding the house, really a cottage, of former General Hobert, but failed to notice its condition. It had been vacant for a year and was in disrepair. The nearby Jesuits promised to help the sisters temporally as well as spiritually. The sisters were extremely poor and lived in this small house for nearly two years. It was not at all suited to their needs. During a novena the sisters were making for guidance and help, Fr. Trimmberger, pastor at St. Martin's, offered the sisters fifteen acres of land at Hales Corners, Wisconsin, provided that they would build a convent on the property. They accepted, and construction soon began for the first cloistered contemplative convent in the Archdiocese of Milwaukee. The sisters moved into the new convent in September of 1899. They did not have electricity or running water because they were too far from the city, so they used kerosene lamps and well water. Severe winters made the roads impassable for long periods of time and they were without access to supplies of food and fuel. In 1905, to keep from freezing, they chopped down trees in weather far below zero, and used the green wood to warm the monastery. They had installed a heating plant the summer before, but that fall and winter there was a coal strike, so they had a furnace but no fuel. Coal deliveries were sometimes late or missed, so the sisters kept a supply of seasoned wood for emergencies. During the winter of 1916-1917, while the sisters were clearing the roads of snow (The nearby farmers seemed to wait for the sisters to do this.), one member died of a heart attack. The undertaker could hardly get to the convent, so he directed the sisters to place the casket out on the grounds if he were not able to return on time for the burial!

With communication infrequent and unpredictable, the isolation proved a hindrance for the sisters' livelihood, as well as for vocations. These sisters had been faithful to their way of life for twenty-seven years. They had also tilled the land, raised their own vegetables, and sold some. Their hard labor had transformed the grounds into a place of beauty. But in 1924, the ecclesiastical authorities, aware of the hardships connected with the location, decided it was in the community's best interests to relocate nearer to the city of Milwaukee.

The new site was less than one half acre, the sisters buying fifteen city lots.[6] Due to unfortunate circumstances regarding the disposing of the Hales Corners convent promptly, the sisters had to resort to two mortgages on the new property. They moved into their new home on May 31, 1926, and began anew with the task of dealing with unkempt fields, while maintaining sewing and altar bread work for sustenance. Milwaukee Archbishop Sebastian Messmer, a friend of Fr. Saintourens and the former pastor of Sr. Mary Imelda, suggested collecting funds. Just two sisters went out to collect money---Sr. Mary Dominic (who could drive a horse and buggy and later a Model T Ford) and Sr. Mary Dolores. They made numerous friends for the community during those years. They began in 1921 and continued their collecting trips until 1944, when Archbishop Meyer, later Cardinal, had them return to the cloister. The Milwaukee Monastery is the only Perpetual Rosary Monastery that kept its original status. It has its own constitutions and the sisters profess perpetual vows.

Baltimore, Maryland

Fr. Saintourens had been trying to establish a convent of the Perpetual Rosary in the Archdiocese of Baltimore for a long time. He personally knew Cardinal Gibbons for about twelve years. When he finally succeeded in completing arrangements, he informed the Prioress of West Hoboken (Union City) and requested sisters. Thus on February 20, 1899, seven sisters left Union City under the leadership of Mother Rose of St. Mary Mannion, O.P., who had been Sub-Prioress there. Fr. Saintourens went with the sisters to their new home, which he had rented for one year. Despite their small numbers, the sisters recited the entire Divine Office and kept the hours of guard day and night. The Blessed Sacrament was always reserved in the sisters' chapel, but they were not able to have Mass every day. The Vincentian Fathers provided for the sisters to attend Mass in a side sacristy, where a large folding door looked out upon the sanctuary when opened. They also received Holy Communion from that location.

6   In Hales Corners they had 15 acres.

French Developments

Because of religious persecution in France, the sisters living there requested to go to Belgium. Unfortunately, the two convents there did not have enough room for them. Mother Rose of St. Mary Wehrle wrote to the Cardinal of Baltimore, asking for residence in his diocese, which was granted. The twenty one French sisters arrived in Hoboken on May 5, 1903. It was a Tuesday evening, and two extern sisters met them at seven o'clock. They arrived at the West Hoboken (Union City) convent at eleven o'clock, where the community was waiting for them. It was an exciting and joyful occasion, even though the French sisters could not speak English, and the American sisters had difficulty being understood. They were up until midnight.

Before the sisters arrived, cells had been prepared for them. Some of the generous lay sisters[7] slept in the barn. Others slept two in one cell and one on the floor, and still others on a board placed upon two boxes. Every board was taken to sleep on, even the door of the chicken house. (However, when the Procuratrix missed the door, she feared the chickens might catch cold and consequently searched the house until she found it. It was taken back and nailed to the chicken house so that no one could take it again!) In the novitiate, one of the postulants slept on two trunks, and a professed novice on a board placed upon two boxes. During the night, sisters were awakened by a terrible noise, which turned out to be the novice falling off her board! The next day revealed fifty-six sisters in the house! Sisters sat on both sides of the tables in the refectory. In the choir, benches were placed outside the stalls for the sisters to sit on. These arrangements lasted about a week.

The following Monday, the French sisters left for Baltimore. Mother Rose of St. Mary Wehrle was very touched by the sisters' charity on their behalf. She said that if the sisters of Hoboken should ever be obliged to return to France, the doors of their convent would be thrown open to them with as much charity as they had been shown.

---

7   Lay sisters did manual work and were not obliged to the recitation of the Divine Office. They had their own set of prayers. After Vatican II the lay sister distinction was discontinued.

The French sisters arrived in Baltimore sooner than were expected, with no one to meet them at the station. They found their way to the convent as best as they could. Since the French sisters had not obtained a dwelling place, Mother Rose of St. Mary Mannion, the American prioress of the Baltimore convent, invited them to stay with her until they could. Delays and language difficulties brought things to a head. Because the French sisters far outnumbered the American sisters, it was decided that the Union City sisters should return to their monastery and leave the Baltimore house for the French sisters. Mother Rose of St. Mary Mannion stayed on for a few months in Baltimore to help with the language and other matters, returning to Union City in October of 1903.

A few months afterward, the French sisters bought a larger house. It was at this period that Mother Rose of St. Mary Wehrle became prioress of the community and remained so until her death on April 21, 1909. She had previously requested that her body be sent back to France. Instead it was temporarily interred in Bonny Bray Cemetery in Irvington, Maryland. On August 2, fourteen of the French sisters accompanied her body back to France, where it was interred in the family plot. A volcanic eruption thwarted the sisters' plans to live in Nola, Italy, so they returned to Belgium and settled in Ghent. Meanwhile the remaining six French sisters in Maryland requested assistance from Union City. Mother Rose of St. Mary Mannion, who had been the first Prioress and Foundress of the Baltimore community, and three other sisters were sent from Union City. The sisters lived in a little cottage in Catonsville, Maryland, that was rented for one year.

Camden, New Jersey

On Tuesday, December 4, 1900, six sisters from West Hoboken/ Union City went to make a new foundation in Camden, New Jersey. Fr. Saintourens had requested specific sisters for this foundation with Sr. Mary Catherine of Sienna as Prioress. Among the six were two postulants, who were sad to leave Union City. They asked if they might be given the habit before starting for the new foundation. Fr. Saintourens left it to the community to decide. The request of the postulants was granted and on December 2nd they were clothed in the habit and given new names. Sr. Loretta became Sr. Mary Dominic of the Rosary and Sr. Marie received the name Sr. Agnes of Jesus.

Fr. Saintourens consecrated this foundation to St. Dominic and all the Saints of the Order. It rained heavily on the day the sisters left Union City. They arrived in Camden to be received by the Sisters of Mercy, where they received hospitality. The house which Fr. Saintourens had rented was not yet available. The lady who owned it, died a few days before their arrival, so the arrangements had not been finalized. They were able to move in on the second day, but were required to spend the night sleeping in one room on straw, which they had strewn on the floor.[4] Fr. Saintourens quickly got a carpenter, who converted a room into a chapel. He also made an altar, a table, some beds, and a little grille for the cloister. On Dec. 8th, the first Mass was celebrated and the Blessed Sacrament reserved in the little chapel. The house was so small that there was hardly room to move about.

Fr. Saintourens began searching immediately for a permanent place for the sisters. He found a beautiful place outside the city on Haddon Avenue. It was sold to the sisters, and Fr. Saintourens had two little wooden houses built, one for the sisters and one for himself. The sisters moved there on May 20, 1901. On Oct. 4, 1902, ground was broken for a permanent monastery and the cornerstone laid on the 26th of that month. Exactly one year later, the new chapel was opened and on February 2, 1904, the sisters moved into their permanent stone monastery. Fr. Saintourens continued as their chaplain and Camden became the center of the Perpetual Rosary in America. Fr. Saintourens died on September 26, 1920, and is buried at the foot of Our Lady's statue in the Rosary Shrine on the front lawn.

In 1927, Archbishop Walsh blessed and laid the cornerstone of the Perpetual Rosary Shrine Chapel. On that occasion he told the faithful, "Come often to pray here. One might say you can pray the Rosary anywhere – that is true, but when you pray here you pray in an atmosphere permeated with the Rosary because it is recited perpetually by the consecrated spouses of Christ. This is truly a university of prayer." [5]

A Unique Individual

Before proceeding with the next foundation made by Union City, it seems fitting to give some attention to one of the first three American women who entered the Perpetual Rosary Sisters in America. Her name was Elizabeth Mannion, and when she received the habit, she was given the name Sr. Rose of St. Mary (Mannion). The two women who entered with her were sent on the Milwaukee foundation. At that time Sr. Rose of St. Mary was named Sub-Prioress of West Hoboken (Union City). She was only five years in the convent. Less than two years later, in 1899 when the Baltimore foundation was made, Mother Rose of St. Mary was chosen as the first prioress. She proved admirable during the visit of the twenty-one French sisters, who were invited to stay temporarily in Baltimore. She even stayed on to help with language and other matters after the other sisters returned to Union City.

In May of 1905, Mother Rose of St. Mary was chosen as prioress of the new foundation to be made in Buffalo, New York. She did all she could to establish the community on a firm foundation. After three years in Buffalo, she was recalled to Union City.

In August of 1909, after the majority of French sisters left Baltimore for Europe, the few French sisters remaining in Baltimore again requested assistance from Union City, and Mother Rose of St. Mary, together with two other sisters, were loaned to the community, Mother Rose appointed the Sub-Prioress. She continued in this office until November 20, 1915, when she returned to Union City. She was then named Vicaress by Mother Mary of Jesus, who was Prioress.

When Mother Mary of Jesus died in October of 1917, Mother Mary Imelda succeeded her as Prioress and appointed Mother Rose as Sub-Prioress. She was either Sub-Prioress or Vicaress for the next thirty-six years. We are told that she was prayerful, fervent, and exact in the observances, that she possessed a real community spirit and always enjoyed the recreation periods. She had a gentle nature and was ever humble. She liked to sew and did her work well. She kept always occupied until cataracts in both eyes left her almost completely blind. She never complained, died a holy death on February 22, 1953 of a heart attack at the age of eighty-six.[6]

Buffalo New York

With the return of the American sisters to Union City from Baltimore in 1903, Mother Mary of Jesus felt it was time to begin a new foundation. In early 1904, she made her request to newly appointed Bishop Colton of Buffalo. As pastor of St. Stephen's Church in New York City, he was well known to the sisters and had established the Perpetual Rosary in his parish. In response to Mother's request, the new Bishop replied that it did not seem opportune at the moment, but to have hope for the future. After a few months, Mother Mary of Jesus engaged a Dominican Father in New York to approach the bishop on the subject. With that came a promise from the bishop that he would talk the matter over with her on a trip he would make to West Hoboken (Union City) in a few weeks. On his visit, he met with the sisters in the parlor, some of whom had been his parishioners at St. Stephen's. In July of that year he invited Mother to come to Buffalo and examine some property he had in mind. Accordingly, on July 5th, Mother Mary of Jesus obtained permission to make the journey together with Mother Rose of St. Mary, who had recently returned from Baltimore. The Buffalo foundation was entrusted to her. The property appeared very desirable. However, Bishop Colton went to Rome, and on his return informed Mother Mary of Jesus that he had changed his mind. He thought that another site should be chosen. At that, Mother again contacted the Dominican Father in New York and asked him to work with the bishop in selecting something. Together with the Vicar of the Diocese, this Dominican Father chose a most beautiful place, eight acres in size with hundreds of fruit trees. There was a spacious dwelling which could be very well adapted for the use of convent life.

On May 22, 1904, Mother Mary of Jesus, Prioress of Union City, left with the new foundation group for Buffalo. They received hospitality with the Franciscan Sisters at Sacred Heart Academy and received the bishop's blessing on the following day. The sisters found the grounds of their new foundation to be truly beautiful, but the house was devoid of everything. In a few days, Mother succeeded in procuring all that was necessary for the immediate needs of the community, and even went out collecting from charitable people in the city to obtain useful and necessary things for the house, the chapel and the altar. When the house was in order, Mother Mary of Jesus returned to West Hoboken (Union City). The Buffalo sisters consider her their foundress and Mother Rose of St. Mary the first Prioress. The week following her return to Union City, Mother Mary of Jesus sent four more sisters to Buffalo. In due time the first wing of their permanent monastery was finished in time for Easter Sunday 1922, and the rest of the monastery was completed by Rosary Sunday 1929.[7]

A New Foundation in 1907

This foundation originally began on April 9, 1907, when Mother Mary of the Angels and Sr. Mary of the Blessed Sacrament left Union City to negotiate for a place in Oregon. On June 7th, two novices were sent to join them. In September, Sr. Mary Agnes and a postulant were also sent. Other sisters were sent later, but it was obvious that the foundation could not continue in Oregon as the sisters were without support in Baker City. After two years, the bishop wanted the nuns to take on an active apostolate of teaching. They began to look elsewhere to continue their contemplative life and responded to the invitation of the bishop of La Crosse, Wisconsin. The foundation suffered many trials, and Mother Mary of the Angels died on May 18, 1943. Ten days later, Mother Mary Alphonsus was chosen to succeed her. In 1950 the sisters felt they needed more help.[8] A mandate came from the Master

General of the Order, Fr. Emmanuel Suarez, O.P., to the Monastery in West Springfield, MA to send six sisters.[9] Mother Mary of the Immaculate Conception[8] was sent as Prioress and the six arrived on June 22nd. Bishop Tracy of La Crosse gave the community an outright gift of seventeen acres of land near the new seminary in La Crosse. St. Dominic's monastery was completed in early 1954, and the sisters moved there in April. It was dedicated on May 30, 1954.[10]

In 1984 the nuns again relocated, but this time it was due to lack of vocations and the loss of priestly ministry. They were encouraged to settle in Washington, DC, and for nearly twenty years lived there in a transitional monastery. In 2001, the community was able to purchase a large tract of land in Linden, Virginia, within the Diocese of Arlington. But they needed funds to build a monastery. The solution lay in selling their property in order to have money to begin the new building in VA. The sisters would be literally homeless, but the community in West Springfield, MA, worked out a plan with them whereby both communities lived their monastic life in the West Springfield Monastery until the Linden Monastery was habitable. The one year projection timetable became two and one half years. The Linden sisters actually lived in West Springfield during the jubilee year celebrations. In June of 2008, the sisters left West Springfield for their new home in Linden, Virginia.[11] Hopefully their itinerant days are over and their new roots permanently established.

Summit, New Jersey

In 1919, Mother Mary Imelda of Jesus, prioress of Union City[9], had been looking forward to making a new foundation. At that time a beautiful house with spacious grounds in Summit, New Jersey, was offered to them at a very reasonable price. Bishop O'Connor granted permission for Mother to visit the place. She liked everything about it; the house and grounds seemed ideal for a new foundation. Negotiations

---

8   Sister later changed her name to Sr. Rita Mary
9   On Oct. 11, 1917 elected prioress, Mother Mary Imelda was the first American to succeed the French foundresses.

Oregon
- LaCrosse -
- Washington, DC -
Linden, VA

Foundresses
Mother Mary of the Angels
Sr. Mary of the Blessed Sacrament

Mother Mary of the Crown
and Mother Mary Hyacinth

Nuns to
LaCrosse

Old yields

Sr. Mary of the Immaculate Conception
(3rd from left)

to the new

Mother Mary Imelda
& her sister,
Sr. Mary Emilienne

Summit Foundresses
Mother Mary Imelda
(Front-center)

Old Monastery
Summit

Mother Mary of the Child Jesus
& Mother Mary Dominic
with postulants

Lancaster

Mother Mary of the
Immaculate Heart

Marbury
First
Monastery

Mother Mary
of the Crown

N. Guilford

Mother Mary
of
Jesus Crucified

Sisters work hard

were carried out and the property purchased,[12] with Mother Mary Imelda the chosen instrument for the new foundation. On October 2, 1919, in pouring rain, she and thirteen companions set out in three cars for the two hour journey. On Rosary Sunday, October 7th, the first Mass was celebrated and the Blessed Sacrament was placed in the tabernacle. The Divine Office was recited by the sisters and the Hours of Guard kept all night. Beginning on New Year's Day, the sisters were able to pray the rosary day and night.[13]

Soon after their arrival in Summit, Mother Mary Imelda, wishing to share her devotion of the rosary with the lay people, established a branch of the Perpetual Rosary for the laity. Many thousands of members keep an Hour of Guard each month in honor of Our Lady of the Rosary in union with the sisters at Rosary Shrine.[14]

In 1924, the community was growing and quarters were cramped. In December, the Manley estate was purchased through a loan. In 1925 on March 25th, the breaking and blessing of the ground took place. The cornerstone was laid eight months later, and the following year, the crypt chapel was blessed. The architect had drawn up a plan for a four-winged structure in the European monastic tradition. However, it became apparent that construction would have to be postponed until a two-year building debt was liquidated.

On December 23, 1928, Mother Mary Imelda's third term as prioress expired. In her place Mother Mary of Jesus Crucified was elected prioress, and held office for eighteen uninterrupted years. She was able to liquidate the debts of the monastery and then set to work revising the original architectural plan. The radical alterations both facilitated and complicated the construction of the chapel and monastery into what it is today. Permission to resume construction was granted on July 26, 1937, and Mother Prioress personally oversaw the work. On June 4, 1939, the new building was blessed and after a few days the monastery was ready for occupancy. On September 15th Archbishop Thomas J. Walsh solemnly dedicated the chapel. His closing address can be applied to many monasteries and is worth quoting:

I, personally, publicly, and officially invite all the clergy, the friends and benefactors, and all the people to attend all the public services held here at all times, and even to come here to make private visits to Our Lord. Come here often, come every day to visit Jesus in the Blessed Sacrament.

This magnificent chapel is not exclusively for the use of the nuns; it is for you to participate in the services. You may ask why they are here. The nuns are praying for themselves and for us and we have benefitted by their prayers. These nuns are behind the grille and do not see nor enjoy this magnificent chapel. This chapel of Our Lady of the Rosary is for you and for all who seek help. Come … for consolation, to ask advice and light in your difficulties.

I bless all the pilgrims who will come here in the future and all those who have come here in the past, and who have already been blessed by Almighty God. You have helped the nuns to raise this beautiful edifice.[15]

Union City's Granddaughter Houses

'Master,' he said, 'You entrusted me with five talents.
See, I have gained five more.' Mt. 25:19 (NIV®)

The Union City Monastery, the first Perpetual Rosary foundation in the United States, made six daughter foundations. In 2008, there was a Mass offered to mark the monastery's closing, but the life of the nuns lives on in its daughter houses. Those daughter houses have also made foundations, totaling another six monasteries. Though the Catonsville foundation closed on November 20, 1980, it founded three additional monasteries which are still active in prayer and religious life.

West Springfield (see Chapter 19)

In 1917, two years before the Summit Foundation was made, Sr. Mary Hyacinth (Fitzgerald) was sent from Union City to the monastery in Catonsville to serve as Novice Mistress. The exercises and prayers there were in French and Sr. Mary Hyacinth was needed for the English speaking girls who were pursuing their vocation. Eventually it became obvious that an English speaking foundation was needed, and Catonsville would be Union City's first daughter house to establish a foundation itself. There was a sister in the Catonsville community, who was considered to be very holy. While the prioress discerned which diocese would be best to make a new foundation, a meeting of the bishops took place. The local newspaper published the event full page, with very small pictures of all the bishops in attendance. This newspaper with the photos was shown to the "holy sister," and she was asked in which diocese the new foundation should be made. Without hesitation she placed her finger on the photo of Bishop Thomas Mary O'Leary of the Springfield, Massachusetts, diocese and said, "This is the diocese where the foundation will be made." On September 8, 1922, Mother Mary of the Crown came to Springfield, Massachusetts, accompanied by Sr. Mary Hyacinth. Bishop O'Leary appointed Sr. Mary Hyacinth as the prioress of the new community. She was then twenty-nine years old. Mother Mary of the Crown soon returned to Catonsville.

While the two sisters were meeting with the bishop, a young girl, named Rita Fitzgerald, waited for them in St. Michael's Cathedral. She was asked to pray that the bishop would say "yes" to their request. She was the younger sister of Sr. Mary Hyacinth, and would later enter the monastery in West Springfield and receive the name Sr. Mary of the Immaculate Conception (she was among those sent to LaCrosse in 1950, and was appointed prioress at that time, and was responsible for the building of the permanent monastery as seen above in the 1907 foundation).

On October 22nd in a downpour of rain, Mother Mary Magdalen, Sr. Mary Lucie, Sr. Mary Hyacinth of the Blessed Sacrament (a volunteer from the Camden, NJ, monastery), Sr. Mary of the Assumption, Sr. Mary of the Sacred Heart, and a postulant named Sr. Hazel Shaw, who would later become Sr. Mary of the Rosary, arrived from Catonsville. They joined Mother Mary Hyacinth (Fitzgerald) at the convent of the Sisters of the Good Shepherd, where they received hospitality until the vacant house found for their use was ready for occupancy. On November 9th, then the feast of All the Dominican Saints, the sisters moved into the house adapted into a monastery. With a minimum of furniture and utensils donated by the Sisters of the Good Shepherd, the Sisters of Notre Dame and other friends, they began community life with the singing of Vespers. Within three months, the first postulant entered, and in the next two years many more vocations followed, making the need for more room. This blessing was especially due to the fact that Fr. Walsh (a priest in the Boston area) had a sister who was an active teaching Dominican. He was familiar with the new community founded in Springfield and directed vocations both to the teaching Dominicans as well as to the nuns in Springfield.

With more room needed due to the influx of new vocations, Mother Mary Hyacinth, looking for possibilities, approached the Nyes and asked them if they would be interested in selling their property which was situated on a lovely hill in West Springfield. They replied they had no intention of selling. Within a very short time, Mr. Nye died suddenly, and Mrs. Nye feeling she could not remain alone on the large estate, changed her mind. The Springfield Country Club also showed interest in the property and offered to pay cash, while the Dominican Nuns had only promises. Bishop O'Leary was initially hesitant to give his approval, since the nuns were so poor, but the nuns, for their part, continued to pray and to hope. While aboard a ship in the Atlantic Ocean on a voyage to Rome, the bishop had a change of mind and authorized the sisters to proceed with the purchase. Late in October of 1925 the community, which by then had doubled, moved into their new home. Many renovations took place, with a high solid fence added or the enclosure[10]. Vocations abounded and by the end of 1927 the community numbered nearly thirty. Vocations continued to come, and

10   Monastery space reserved exclusively for the Sisters into which the public is not allowed.

eventually the monastery proved too small and overcrowded. In 1954 on the feast of the Rosary, ground was broken for a new monastery. Friends of the community sent donations to buy a brick, helping the monastery become a reality. There was one big surprise that came the sisters way though. A priest by the name of Msgr. Bell had visited the monastery and had seen a model of the planned building. He spoke with Mother Mary of the Immaculate Heart, who was prioress, about the expense of such an undertaking. Monsignor loved the Blessed Mother very much. He wanted to make a substantial donation to build her a monastery that would be a lasting monument. When the prioress asked how much he wanted to give, she was overwhelmed by his reply. Monsignor was not in good health and told her that he was going to fix it with the bank.

It was a matter of a day or two when the prioress noticed Monsignor's name in the obituary notices. She called the bank and was told, "It's all right, Mother, he was in here at ten minutes of three and signed all of the papers." Mother nearly collapsed with relief and summoned the community to tell them of Monsignor and to have the sisters offer the Office for him. Monsignor's name has always been spoken of with deep gratitude and reverence by the community. His actions made a big difference in the building of the present monastery. In 1956, the sisters moved into the new building, which was located on the same property and which could be observed during its construction.

Lancaster, PA

In June of 1925, the Baltimore community made a second foundation. Mother Mary of the Crown was chosen as the Prioress and left Baltimore on June 10 with seven other sisters for South Enola, Pennsylvania. Bishop McDevitt of the Harrisburg diocese had granted permission for the new foundation. It was situated in the country, making life hard because of its isolation. In need financially, the sisters worked very hard and steadily to earn enough to support themselves. Vocations were slow in coming and the generosity of the early sisters was taxed almost to the breaking point. However, Mother Mary of the Crown was able to add an extension to the house, including a large community room with several cells above it.

In 1946, the Union City community was called upon for some nuns to help out. Accordingly, Mother Mary Raymund, Mother Mary of the Immaculate Heart, Sr. Mary Theresa and Sr. Mary Bernadette left for South Enola on July 25th of that year. With this added help things began to change for the little community. Mother Mary Raymund became ill toward the close of 1947 and had to return to Union City. Two more sisters were sent from Union City in 1949. Mother Mary of the Immaculate Heart, who succeeded Mother Mary Raymund as prioress, spared no efforts until she succeeded in securing a new location nearer the city and in suitable surroundings, where the sisters could live their cloistered life as needed. Through the solicitude of Bishop Leech, the Eschelman property in Lancaster was bought, and the community moved there on January 22, 1952. The house had been remodeled to accommodate the sisters for their monastic life. They lived there for over two years when, in January of 1954, ground was broken for their new monastery. On May 9, 1955, the community was able to move into their new home. The dedication and blessing of the chapel and monastery took place on May 22nd, with the Apostolic Delegate, the Most Reverend Amleto Giovanni Cicognani, presiding. Assisted by several monsignori and accompanied by Bishop Leech, he dedicated the new monastery in honor of the Immaculate Heart of Mary. The main altar was consecrated on June 21, 1955.

Marbury, Alabama

The Dominican Monastery of Saint Jude was founded on August 17, 1944, by Mother Mary Dominic, O.P., and Mother Mary of the Child Jesus, O.P. from Catonsville, Maryland, who had a bold vision in mind: having a community where those who aspired to the contemplative life could enter regardless of race. Many bishops were contacted and asked if such a community would be welcomed, however the replies were not too encouraging. Many thought it a noble idea, but unsuitable to their area or the time or to the people of their diocese. In 1944, the foundresses were finally welcomed by Archbishop Thomas Toolen of Mobile, Alabama. With the cooperation of Fr. Harold Purcell, founder of the City of Saint Jude, a place was found in the (then) Diocese of Mobile.

Fr. Purcell intended to establish the cloistered sisters in a building adjoining the Church of Saint Jude in Montgomery. He could not build, however, because of the shortage of materials in wartime. There was a house available in Marbury, 30 miles north of Montgomery. All he needed to do was to make suitable adaptations in order to turn a frame farm house into a temporary monastery.

The two foundresses left the monastery at Catonsville, Maryland, on August 17, arriving in Marbury the next day. The small frame house was ideally situated in a quiet, country spot. On August 28, 1944, the feast of St. Augustine, the small monastery was dedicated under the patronage of St. Jude, patron of Impossible Cases. The monastery remains proof of his powerful intercession. The sisters were enclosed the same day and began anew their cloistered contemplative life in Alabama. The privilege of Perpetual Exposition and Adoration of the Most Blessed Sacrament was given especially for the conversion of the South. With the bishop's approval the community decided to remain in Marbury.

In time, the sisters asked permission to build a permanent monastery. When he gave permission, Archbishop Toolen said to Mother Mary Dominic, "Mother you have my wholehearted permission to go ahead, and my blessing. Now your headaches, heartaches and worries begin. But don't give up. When your friends hear that you have actually begun to build, they will help you." In the early 1950s, the nuns began to solicit funds for the permanent monastery on the adjoining hilltop. There were countless responses to the request, "Just throw a brick at us! Each one is 14 cents." Bishop Toolen turned the first spadeful of earth on November 13, 1952.

When Monsignor Rogers visited the nuns they shared the good news with him. No time was lost in helping the sisters get started. In fact, it happened so fast that they could not believe their eyes or ears when the bulldozer began work on January 1, 1953. The sisters well remember the building days. One of the early lessons they learned was that the first thing to do when building anything is to dig a hole. "If it's a foundation to be poured, dig a hole; if it's a pipe to be laid, dig a hole; if it's a line to be laid out, dig a hole." This sounds funny until one learns that their ground is so hard and gravelly that they wore out several new pickaxes and shovels in the first months – just digging holes. The sisters actually helped in the building. They laid cement blocks and laid them right! They made bucks for windows, filled floors, shellacked and varnished cupboards, painted woodwork, ran the tractor with a scraper, put in electric wires, fixed an organ, put up and took down doors, planted one thousand pine trees, and designed the entire kitchen layout. Today the unions would probably object and other complications would most likely arise. But on October 28, 1953, the Feast of Saint Jude, the community moved into this new monastery. The Most Reverend Thomas J. Toolen, Archbishop of Mobile, officiated at the dedication, which took place in March, 1954. The sermon was preached by the Right Reverend James B. Rogers, P.A., who was the pastor of Saint Peter's Church, Montgomery, and Dean of central Alabama.

Fr. Rogers said, "Everywhere around us in the great thoroughfare of life is chaos, confusing and arresting evidence of cold, cruel materialism. Truly you are laying up treasures here. It is refreshing indeed, in the calculating strife, to find a peaceful asylum and a sanctuary of love where the parched spirit may find solace, rest, and peace."

Bishop Toolen told the nuns, "This monastery was built through your sacrifice and hard labor. Your prayers and devotion will bring unknown and untold blessings to the Diocese of Mobile in a spiritual way. God has especially blessed you, you who are continuously praying the rosary for an end to the evils in the world. As Christ worked the miracle His Mother asked at the marriage feast of Cana, so will He work miracles for you." [16]

Syracuse

On September 24, 1924, Mother Mary Louis Bertrand, O.P., prioress of the Camden, N.J. Monastery requested permission of the bishop of Syracuse, N.Y., Most Rev. Bishop Daniel Curley, D.D., to make a foundation of nuns in his diocese. On Thanksgiving Day, November 27th, Bishop Curley sent a telegram to Mother that his Consulters had approved the request for the nuns to make the foundation. Shortly afterward on December 4th, Mother Mary Louis Bertrand examined the property, which was destined for the foundation, and decided that it was an ideal place for Our Blessed Mother's Sanctuary.

On December 4, 1925, eleven sisters from the Dominican Monastery in Camden, N.J. received a mandate in virtue of holy obedience, and under formal precept[11] to proceed to establish a monastery in Syracuse, N.Y. Fr. J. S. Moran, O.P., National Director of the Perpetual Rosary, delivered an encouraging sermon, which was followed by Benediction of the Most Blessed Sacrament. He accompanied the sisters to the Reading Terminal in Philadelphia, PA, and they left for Syracuse, N.Y.

Upon entering their new home, the sisters chanted a "Te Deum" in thanksgiving for the privilege of starting a new foundation to the honor and glory of God and Our Lady, Queen of the Most Holy Rosary. However, there was much work to be done in constructing and preparing a suitable building. The Sisters of St. Francis provided hospitality for the sisters at their Franciscan convent during the period of construction. The Sisters of St. Mary's Hospital on Court Street also offered their services and hospitality.

On February 1st, Bishop Curley surprised Mother Mary Louis Bertrand when he presented her with a check for $5,000.00 as a gift from the Diocese of Syracuse for the construction of the Monastery. He made a most welcome visit and was pleased to see carpenters rapidly at work. On March 18th, two statues arrived, one of St. Joseph and the other of St. Theresa of Avila. These were donated by Mr. and Mrs. Kleinhans of Rochester, N.Y, parents of one of the sisters.

---

11 A binding formal command.

Mother Mary Louis Bertrand blessed the whole house with holy water. It was bare with only one chair and a small table…no dishes or food. With happy hearts the sisters went back to St. Anthony's Convent to borrow a few dishes and on their way back they stopped at a grocery store on Court St. for some food and supplies. They then partook of their first meal in the new foundation. Afterwards they recited the rosary and spent a half hour in meditation. Every evening they said prayers in honor of St. Joseph, asking him to bless the new foundation.

After many weeks of trial, suffering and hardship caused by a severe wintry cold and sickness, the formal opening of the new monastery took place on March 25, 1925. Rt. Rev. Bishop Curley celebrated Holy Mass, assisted by his Secretary, Rev. H. McDowell. The first Hour of Guard of the Rosary was recited by Sr. Mary Augustine, O.P. After Mass, Bishop Curley blessed every room in the monastery and the community accompanied him to the enclosure door. The door was opened to the public for an "open house" and a large crowd visited the monastery.

On Saturday, March 28th, Chapter was held for the first time in the new monastery and Mother Mary Louis Bertrand exhorted the sisters to great fervor and zeal. After the formal opening, people had taken interest in the work of the community and the Perpetual Rosary, and hundreds entered their names in the register to be part of Mary's Guard of Honor of the Rosary.

On March 25, 1954, a new wing was finally constructed and the first postulant was admitted to the Syracuse Monastery. Prior to this, all candidates were sent to the Camden Monastery in New Jersey for their formation. Pearl Worhach entered on March 25th and became Sr. Mary Augustine of the Passion, O.P. More young women followed and the Novitiate grew under the watchful care of Sr. Mary Theresa Ferguson, O.P. Mother Mary Paul was appointed prioress and was a person of foresight, common sense and genuine holiness. She held the position of prioress many times during her life and started a building fund, used to construct the present Monastery, which was completed in 1986. The special Mystery of the Rosary given to this monastery is reflected in its full title: Dominican Monastery of the Perpetual Rosary of the Holy Spirit.[17]

North Guilford

In January of 1947 vocations were so numerous in Summit, N.J., that a new foundation was made in North Guilford, Connecticut. Fr. Charles Gabriel Moore, O.P., the former chaplain at Summit, had urged Bridget Rice to offer her 197 acres of farm and woodland to Mother Mary of Jesus Crucified for a monastery. After a year of negotiations, Mother and the Council accepted Bridget's "deed of gift" on July 16, 1946. In exchange, the sisters agreed to provide the donor with living quarters at the monastery guest house in Summit. The deal was closed. As plans for the new foundation began to expand in speculation, the number of vocations more than doubled between 1945 and 1946. It became clear that God wanted a new foundation.

Mother Mary of Jesus Crucified was prioress and on January 21, 1947 she and fourteen companions left for North Guilford. The number of fifteen was significant for the fifteen mysteries of the rosary[12]. The weather was sleety and raw when they boarded a large bus early that morning. They were fasting[13] so as to be able to receive Holy Communion at the end of their journey.[18] The rosary was said on the way. They had Mass and Communion when they arrived. Then at two o'clock in the afternoon, they had breakfast and dinner combined.[19]

In North Guilford, they found a seventeenth century farmhouse that could be converted into a monastery at the corner of Hoop Pole and Race Hill Roads, names that had come down from the pre-Revolutionary days when the Native Americans inhabited the Connecticut Valley. In addition, there was a smaller house that could serve as temporary quarters for their chaplain, Fr. Moore, O.P. Two empty barns, one for horses, and the other for cows, completed the new monastery complex. These were transformed and served as the

---

12 The five luminous mysteries had not yet been promoted.
13 Pre Vatican II regulations stipulated that fasting was observed from midnight before receiving Holy Communion.

inside choir and outside chapel. Thus, the first Dominican monastery in the Diocese of Hartford came into being. The welcoming bishop was the Most Reverend Henry O'Brien.[20]

Preparations were well under way for a new monastery when, on the evening of December 23, 1955, the original monastery was totally destroyed by fire (see Chapter 4). From Rome, the Most Reverend Michael Browne, O.P., Master General of the Dominican Order expressed his sympathy and offered assistance. On December 24th, the Very Reverend W.D. Marrin, O.P., Provincial of Saint Joseph's Province wired the Dominican Fathers to extend all possible assistance. He later visited the community personally. Saint Vincent Ferrer's Priory promptly provided breviaries for everyone, vestments and altar equipment, etc.

Before the stranded nuns returned from the funeral on the morning of December 24th, Dominican nuns of Union City and Summit, New Jersey, had both sent truck loads of essential clothing and other necessities, together with substantial financial aid. Practically every Dominican cloister in the United States contributed necessities and money. Even the nuns in Portugal and Scotland responded. Active Dominican Sisters sent clothing, blankets and money, some of them so poor themselves that their gifts required real deprivation.

Catholics and non-Catholics alike in the Archdiocese of Hartford were most generous in responding to Archbishop O'Brien's moving appeal. Organizations of every sort contributed to the building fund and with the continued generosity of friends a new monastery was eventually built on the original site. The nuns were able to take possession of their new monastery in the summer of 1958.

It is of special interest that after the devastating fire in 1955, a burnt page from a Missal used at Mass was found among the debris of the destroyed farmhouse. The only remaining legible words were *Sanctus, Sanctus, Sanctus*. When the time came to carve words over the entrance of the new monastery chapel, the sisters recalling the scrap of burnt paper, and believing that such special words were the most appropriate choice for the inscription, chose: *Sanctus, Sanctus, Sanctus*.[21]

(Endnotes)

1   Sr. Maria Agnes, O.P., "The Story of Rosary Shrine 1919-1994," (Summit, N.J., MPD Printing: 1994) 7-8. Used with permission.

2   Mother Mary Aloysius of Jesus, O.P. 43.

3   Sr. Maria Agnes, O.P. 8. Used with permission.

4   Mother Mary Aloysius of Jesus, O.P. 46-162.

5   "100th Anniversary Monastery of the Perpetual Rosary 1900 – 2000" 9-11. Used with permission.

6   Mother Mary Aloysius of Jesus, O.P. 245-249.

7   Mother Mary Aloysius of Jesus, O.P. 178-185.

8   Mother Mary Aloysius of Jesus, O.P. 186.

9   Information provided by a Sister from the West Springfield, MA Monastery.

10   Mother Mary Aloysius of Jesus, O.P. 186.

11   Information provided by sisters from the Linden and West Springfield Communities.

12   Mother Mary Aloysius of Jesus, O.P. 188.

13   Sr. Maria Agnes, O.P. 12, 14. Used with permission.

14   Mother Mary Aloysius of Jesus, O.P. 188, 190.

15   Sr. Maria Agnes, O.P. 17-20. Used with permission.

16   Mother Mary Aloysius of Jesus, O.P. 156-159.

17   Information provided by Sr. Mary Augustine Worhach, O.P. of the Syracuse Monastery. May 2009.

18   Sr. Maria Agnes, O.P. 23-24. Used with permission.

19   Mother Mary Aloysius of Jesus, O.P. 192.

20   Sr. Maria Agnes, O.P. 24. Used with permission.

21   Mother Mary Aloysius of Jesus, O.P. 192, 196, 198-199.

CHAPTER 22

The Rosary: A Surprising and Powerful Prayer

...and he answered our prayer. Ezra 8:23 2 (NIV®)

The rosary is special to the heart of every Dominican. We trace that devotion back to our Holy Father St. Dominic. Tradition tells us that as he preached against the overwhelming odds and entrenched errors of his day, he had little success. One day in prayer, Dominic complained about this to Our Lady. She replied, "Wonder not that you have obtained so little fruit by your labors, you have spent them on barren soil, not yet watered with the dew of Divine grace. When God willed to renew the face of the earth, He began by sending down on it the fertilizing rain of the Angelic Salutation. Therefore preach my Psalter composed of 150 Angelic Salutations[1] and 15 Our Fathers, and you will obtain an abundant harvest."[1] This revelation took place at the shrine of Our Lady at Prouilhe in 1208. As a result, St. Dominic and his followers have preached the rosary and its mysteries through the centuries.

---

1   Hail Marys

Prayers composing the Rosary

"When you pray, say..." Lk. 11:2 (NIV®)

The rosary is a scriptural prayer: the first half of the Hail Mary is from the Angel Gabriel's greeting to Mary as recorded in the Gospel according to St. Luke, and the Our Father was taught to us by the Lord Jesus. The second half of the Hail Mary, "Holy Mary, Mother of God, Pray for us sinners now and at the hour of our death" had been included by the ordinary person as "Holy Mary, Mother of God pray for us sinners", and forms similar to this long before it was made official by the Church. The prayer book for the dying, by St. Anselm of Canterbury, a native Italian (1109), contains a Latin prayer in verse in which the last line is a petition to Mary for assistance at the hour of death. Very much like the "Holy Mary," it runs as follows, "Mary, Mother of Grace, Mother of Mercy, protect us against the Evil Spirit and take us to heaven at the hour of our death." The "Glory-Be to the Father, to the Son, and to the Holy Spirit..." was added and approved by the Church through the years.[2]

At Fatima on July 13, 1917, the children were given a vision of hell. Our Lady instructed them, "When you pray the rosary, say after each mystery: 'O my Jesus, forgive us, save us from the fire of hell. Lead all souls to heaven, especially those who are most in need.'[3]

The Rosary Confraternity

Devote yourselves to prayer,... Col. 4:2 (NIV®)

The Confraternity of the Most Holy Rosary is a world-wide movement of prayer, which was entrusted to the Dominican Order by the Holy See more than 500 years ago. It is a spiritual association in which its members strive to pray the entire rosary during the course of each week.[2] In addition to their own intentions, faithful

---

2   Members are not obliged to the luminous mysteries but are encouraged to pray them.

members throughout the world include the intentions and needs of all the members, and are in turn prayed for by them. Each member also includes deceased fellow members, and knows in turn that he/she will be remembered by countless others. People can now enroll in the Confraternity on the internet. (http://www.rosary-center.org/index.htm)

Fr. Saintourens, the Confraternity and the Nuns

...pray for us that the message of the Lord may spread rapidly and be honored, just as it was with you. 2 Thess. 3:1 (NIV®) .

Fr. Damien Marie Saintourens, O.P. was a great apostle of the rosary. His real life work began in his native France in 1875, when he was appointed Director of the Perpetual Rosary by Fr. Boulanger, the Provincial at Lille. In 1886, he was requested to preach Lenten conferences in the cathedral of New Orleans. At the same time he was commissioned to propagate the rosary devotion in the Western Hemisphere. For four years he preached in Canada, going from diocese to diocese and enrolling millions as associate members of the Confraternity. After giving the Lenten conferences at Guadalupe, he established Rosary Confraternities throughout Jamaica, San Domingo, Santa Lucia, and Cuba. He finally returned to the United States to carry out his apostolate.

When Fr. Saintourens realized that the members of the associate could give only a limited time to praying the rosary, he envisioned a congregation of Dominican Sisters who would devote themselves to the rosary day and night, every day of the year. Thus did the Dominican Sisters of the Perpetual Rosary come into existence as described in the previous chapter. Part of Father's dream included the sisters helping in the administration of the Rosary Association by supplying clerical aid in copying lists, preparing data for the press, answering correspondence, and the like. [4]

A Gift Given and Gifts Received

Follow the way of love and eagerly desire spiritual gifts, ...
1 Cor. 14:1 (NIV®)

Our Lady gave us the gift of the rosary because she knew it would bring us innumerable benefits. In an encyclical Pope Leo XIII dedicated the month of October to the Queen of the Holy Rosary. He ordained that every year during the entire month of October, including the first and second of November, in every cathedral and parochial church, and in all other churches and chapels which are dedicated to the Blessed Virgin Mary, five decades of the rosary and the Litany of Loreto are to be recited in the morning during Mass or in the afternoon while the Blessed Sacrament is exposed. A plenary indulgence can be obtained on the Feast of the Holy Rosary or during the octave for those who, during the entire octave, recite five decades daily and fulfill the other usual conditions.[3] A plenary indulgence can also be gained on any other day of the month for those who, after the octave of the feast, recite five decades of the rosary for at least ten days.[5]

Through these means, anyone can receive the gift of a new start in one's spiritual life through Our Lady's prayer. A plenary indulgence remits all punishment due to sin. A true sacramental confession frees the soul from sin and guilt, and the reception of Holy Communion unites a person sacramentally to Jesus present in the Blessed Sacrament, strengthening him/her in living his/her Christian life. Our Lady's promises are listed at the end of this chapter.

---

3   Confession and Holy Communion within 8 days

Rosary Sunday

The only thing that counts is faith expressing itself through love.
Gal. 5:6 (NIV®)

Many Dominican parishes and monasteries still observe the first Sunday of October as "Rosary Sunday." By maintaining this feast, the sons and daughters of St. Dominic continue their centuries-long tradition of promoting devotion to Christ through the daily recitation of the Rosary.[6]

"Rosary Sunday" was the day of our celebration for the month of October. We were pleased to have Bishop Bertrand Boland, O.P., as our guest preacher and officiant for the service. Bishop Boland had been a dedicated missionary for many years in Pakistan. We supported him with our prayers and on various occasions, when he visited the States, he shared his stories of the vibrancy of the Pakistani people's faith with us.

For many years our "Rosary Sunday" service has been preceded by an organ prelude played by Sr. Mary Regina Thomas, O.P., our gifted organist. In the Jubilee year, she played the Praeludium und Fuge in G-Moll by J. S. Bach. The Holy Hour itself began with the familiar Lourdes Hymn, "Immaculate Mary." A Scripture reading was made and then Bishop Boland preached on the rosary. The traditional blessing of roses followed.

Each year the community orders a large quantity of red roses for the occasion. Early that morning a group of sisters arranged the flowers, making two large floral displays. The roses, placed in the chapel near the altar rail, are distributed after the blessing by members of the Dominican Fraternity. Each person was also given a leaflet with a prayer and an explanation of the blessed rose as a sacramental, and its efficacy especially for the sick and the troubled.

During this distribution, the sisters sang a number of Marian hymns. The rosary was then recited by all, and benediction of the Blessed Sacrament followed. The recessional hymn was the traditional "Holy God, We Praise Thy Name." There was an atmosphere of peace

Rosary Sunday Devotions at Ingersoll Grove - 1922

**Roary Sunday
1952**

**Rosary Sunday
Ingersoll Grove**

**First Known Rosary Pilgrimage
Summit , NJ - May 22, 1921**

**Fr. Saintourens is buried
at the rosary shrine in
Camden, NJ**

and joy as Sr. Mary Regina played the organ recessional, "Te Deum Laudamus" by Dietrich Buxtehude. Years ago, the Rosary Sunday devotions took place outdoors at the Rosary Shrine on the monastery grounds. Mr. John Sullivan and Mr. Robert McBride, outstanding among our devoted friends, helped set up wooden folding chairs and benches. The uncertainty of the weather was always a concern. A young girl was privileged to crown the statue of Our Lady at the service. Attendance at such devotions proved a powerful manifestation of the people's love and devotion to Our Lady and her ability to bring down many blessings on them.

Rosary Shrine - Summit, N. J. Monastery

In 1920, a group of visitors from Paterson, New Jersey, asked to make a procession on the exterior grounds. They recited the rosary and sang Marian hymns during the procession. Before leaving, their spokeswoman, Mrs. Grape, announced that this was to be the prelude for future pilgrimages. Since Prouilhe, the cradle of the Dominican Order, had been a pilgrimage site for the faithful, Mother Mary Imelda and the sisters were delighted to foster this devotion to Mary with the assistance of the Dominican Fathers. On January 31, 1921, Bishop John O'Connor gave permission for the erection of a chapel-like grotto on the grounds. It was blessed and dedicated by Fr. Thomas a Kempis Reilly, O.P. on May 22nd of that year with about 2,000 people present. This was the earliest authenticated record of an outdoor pilgrimage in honor of Mary, Queen of the Holy Rosary, held in the United States. Pope Benedict XV, a Dominican tertiary, sent his Apostolic Blessing granting a plenary indulgence "to all the faithful who participate in the pilgrimage to the shrine of Our Lady of the Rosary in Summit, New Jersey." Special medals had been struck to commemorate this event. That same year, on October 2nd, Fr. Reilly addressed the pilgrims and publicly gave the monastery its identifying title, *Rosary Shrine*. He also erected the Rosary Confraternity and established the Rosary Shrine Pilgrimage League. On this occasion, copies of the *Rosary Pilgrim*, an eight-page bi-monthly magazine, were distributed for the first time. Since then, Rosary Shrine has become widely known, drawing as many as 50,000 pilgrims during the May and October devotions from 1923-1934. [7]

One Successful Stop, One Giant Journey

And God is able to make all grace abound to you,
so that in all things at all times, having all that you need,
you will abound in every good work. 2 Cor. 9:8 (NIV®)

It seems fitting to relate a simple but profound and true story of a struggling addict, whom I will call Gloria[4]. During her time in rehab, someone introduced her to the rosary and offered her a selection. She selected a purple one, and some time down the road she wrapped the rosary around her wrist. One day after that she met the person who had given it to her. When asked how she was doing, she told a story of a recent struggle.

A few days earlier Gloria was being badly tormented by a drug addiction. She found herself stopped at a red light, where she saw a man she didn't know crossing the street. She knew she could get what she wanted from him. Addicts know what to look for: the walk, etc. She checked him out again and noticed he had a set of rosary beads wrapped around his wrist, just like she did. Gloria started to cry. She knew he was struggling too. Then she stuck her arm out the window for him to see and yelled, "Hey," and waved her rosary beaded wrist to him. He picked up his arm and with a big smile waved his rosary laden wrist at her and said, "God bless." The desire was gone.

Gloria knows she will deal with this battle every minute for the rest of her life. She got through that moment with Mary's help and gives God credit. A simple act can give another human being the strength to continue on a healthy path, a path of freedom and love. And that is Mary's wish for all her children. For those who reach out to take a rosary, it is like reaching out to take Mary's hand. She is just an "Ave"

4   Not her real name.

within earshot and will never abandon those who call on her.

Impossible?

Jesus replied, "What is impossible with men is possible with God."
Lk. 18:27 (NIV®)

Another true story involves a man whom we will call Zeek[5]. He was in rehab through the instrumentality of a psychiatrist and his family, and was in total denial. His attitude was, "I'll show them. I'll go away and complete this program to keep the family and people off my back." But he had no intention of quitting his addiction; it was "Just for now!"

During that first night in rehab, Zeek decided to stand up at group so he could check out and go home. He stood up and announced, "Hi, I'm Zeek, an alcoholic. That is step one. I admit it. Now I want to complete all 12 steps and get out of here. You guys can stay." Another hulk of a man towered over Zeek and said, "Sit down, stupid, and shut up. You don't know what you're talking about. Get down on your knees and pray!"

Zeek said that on that August night "it was as hot as hell." There was no air conditioning, no fans – just a bed with plastic sheets and plastic pillows. After group therapy, Zeek went to his room. As he reached into his pocket, he felt a rosary and remembered that his friend Jose had given it to him. Jose, who was Portuguese, had gone to Fatima, Portugal to visit his family earlier that year. He had offered Zeek a pair of rosary beads he'd brought back before Zeek left for rehab.

As Zeek touched the beads in his pocket, he had a flashback of the speech given him by the big guy at group. "Get on your knees and pray!" Yes, he heard that message again. Zeek considered himself a macho man and he didn't want his roommate to know that he might try this "prayer stuff." So he made sure that he was **ALONE**. He didn't want *anybody* to know he was going to pray.

Zeek said the rosary as best he could and NOTHING HAPPENED!

5   Not his real name.

BIG DEAL! With no place to go and nothing to do, he decided to just lie down and go to sleep. Now, alcoholics and druggies DON'T SLEEP! They need drugs or alcohol to kill the pain so they can pass out. At least that's what Zeek did. As he lay in bed, he started to pray the rosary again, laying there in bed on those plastic sheets and the plastic pillow. The next day he awoke and found to his amazement that he had slept eight hours straight; and now found himself in a pool of sweat. That's impossible! "What is impossible for man is possible for God." Zeek decided not to tell anyone, but he decided that since it worked one night, it might be worth it to try again. That was twelve years ago. Zeek has been sober ever since, praying one day at a time.

Making it Happen

For we are God's workmanship, created in Christ Jesus to do good works, which God prepared in advance for us to do.
Eph. 2:10 (NIV®)

It would be negligent on my part if I did not express a word of thanks to Henry and Linda Sansouci, members of our Dominican Fraternity, for their dedicated service in making rosaries. They have been instrumental in providing rosaries for distribution to many people whom they have never met or known. One of their latest projects was to make camouflage rosaries for members of the military. Each decade was made of different colored beads to blend in with the troops' uniforms. A dark brown cord strung the beads together and a dark colored plastic crucifix was attached.

FIFTEEN PROMISES OF THE BLESSED VIRGIN TO CHRISTIANS WHO FAITHFULLY PRAY THE ROSARY

1. To all those who shall pray my Rosary devoutly, I promise my special protection and great graces.
2. Those who shall persevere in the recitation of my Rosary will

receive some special grace.

3. The Rosary will be a very powerful armor against hell; it will destroy vice, deliver from sin and dispel heresy.

4. The rosary will make virtue and good works flourish, and will obtain for souls the most abundant divine mercies. It will draw the hearts of men from the love of the world and its vanities, and will lift them to the desire of eternal things. Oh, that souls would sanctify themselves by this means.

5. Those who trust themselves to me through the Rosary will not perish.

6. Whoever recites my Rosary devoutly reflecting on the mysteries, shall never be overwhelmed by misfortune. He will not experience the anger of God nor will he perish by an unprovided death. The sinner will be converted; the just will persevere in grace and merit eternal life.

7. Those truly devoted to my Rosary shall not die without the sacraments of the Church.

8. Those who are faithful to recite my Rosary shall have during their life and at their death the light of God and the plenitude of His graces and will share in the merits of the blessed.

9. I will deliver promptly from purgatory souls devoted to my Rosary.

10. True children of my Rosary will enjoy great glory in heaven.

11. What you shall ask through my Rosary you shall obtain.

12. To those who propagate my Rosary I promise aid in all their necessities.

13. I have obtained from my Son that **all the members of the Rosary Confraternity** shall have as their intercessors, in life and in death, the entire celestial court.

14. Those who recite my Rosary faithfully are my beloved children, the brothers and sisters of Jesus Christ.

15. Devotion to my Rosary is a special sign of predestination. [8]

(Endnotes)

1   Catholic-pages.com, "St. Dominic and the Rosary," <http://www.catholic-pages.com/prayers/rosary_dominic.asp> (accessed May 13, 2009).

2   "The History of the Rosary." Christians Pray the Rosary. http://www.prayrosary.com/rosaryscapular/history.php3. (accessed May 13, 2009).
    http://www.catholicfamilygifts.com/therosary-1.aspx

3   Kondor, Louis (editor). <u>Fatima in Lucia's Own Words: Sister Lucia's Memoirs.</u> Postulation Centre (1995).

4   Mother Mary Aloysius of Jesus, O.P. 14-15, 18, 7.

5   "Special Devotions for Months: October." Catholic Encyclopedia. http://www.newadvent.org/cathen/10542a.htm. (accessed May 18, 2009) Used with permission.
    Holweck, Frederick. "Special Devotions for Months." The Catholic Encyclopedia. Vol. 10. New York: Robert Appleton Company, 1911. 30 Sept. 2009 <http://www.newadvent.org/cathen/10542a.htm>. Used with permission.

6   "Rosary Sunday." CSVF blog – Church of St. Vincent Ferrer. http://www.csvfblog.org/2008/10/05/rosary-sunday/ (accessed May 18, 2009). Used with permission.

7   Sister Maria Agnes, O.P. 14-15. Used with permission.

8   "Fifteen Promises of the Blessed Virgin to Christians who faithfully pray the Rosary." Rosary Center. <http://www.rosary-center.org/nconobl.htm#prom>. (accessed May 13, 2009).

CHAPTER 23

Our International Family: United in Diversity

"The Dominican Family then, consists of friars, nuns, sisters of apostolic life, members of secular institutes, priestly fraternities and laity who belong to fraternities or new groups accepted by the Order. [...] Thus, as if arising from a tree planted beside living fountains, the branches of the Dominican Family are numerous. Each one has its own character, its special status, its autonomy. However, since all participate in the charism of St. Dominic, they share the very same vocation to be preachers in the Church."

~ Acts of the General Chapter of Friars (Mexico, 1992)

Attracted to Dominic

Philip found Nathan'ael, and said to him,... "Come and see."
Jn. 1: 45,46 (RSV)

When someone finds a bargain or has some really good news, they want to share it with others and spread the word. Today a lot of this happens via email. But there is something special and contagious about the message when one sees the expression, hears the excitement, and witnesses the enthusiasm of the speaker. It communicates a desire in the heart of the listener, who wants to hear more. They, in turn, want to share the news with others. Such was the case with those who encountered Dominic de Guzman. His face was radiant; his personality attractive and impressed others, and his words convincing. So when a Polish Bishop met St. Dominic in Rome, he was inspired to ask Dominic if he could send some of his friars to Poland. But Dominic's brethren had already been dispersed to various countries, and he had none to send. Seeing the two priest brothers who accompanied the bishop, Dominic made a proposal. Give me these two priests and I will send them back to your country. As a result, the two brothers became Friar Preachers, and Poland became the richer for it. Today these two friars are known as St. Hyacinth and Blessed Ceslaus.

Many and varied are the vocation stories of the early friars, but a common element may be found in their stories: they were touched by the holiness of life of St. Dominic. When an overloaded ferry boat sank, someone ran to St. Dominic, who was praying in a nearby Church. He ran to the river, and at his prayer, the victims rose to the surface of the water. One of those was Lawrence the Englishman, who then joined Dominic. Gomes of Portugal was a soldier on the riverbank and helped to pull victims in with his lance; others used boathooks. When Gomes finished his time of service, he too joined the band of friars and brought the Order to his home country. Matthew was prior of the monastery at Castres, where Dominic used to go and pray. On one occasion, Matthew saw Dominic raised above the ground and wrapped in prayer. Shortly afterwards, Matthew resigned his office as prior, and joined Dominic. Others were taken by Dominic's preaching. But whatever the reason, they came because of the holiness of the man whose life spoke volumes and whose way of life they desired to follow. They knew his way would lead them closer to God and so they desired to develop a Dominic-like zeal for souls. They sought to learn more in order to give that knowledge and love of God to others.

The Lord spoke to St. Catherine of Siena about Dominic and those on his "ship"[1]. "In this way of life one is more perfect than another, and both the perfect and the not-so-perfect fare well on this ship.... He (Dominic) made his ship very spacious, gladsome, and fragrant, a most delightful garden."[1]

---

1   Image used to represent the Order.

Diversity in the Call

*And you also are among those who are called to belong to Jesus
Christ. Romans 1:6 (NIV®)*

Through 800 years, women from all walks of life and countries
have followed in the footsteps of Dominic, with the nuns who have
preceded them. They have sought holiness of life for themselves as
well as blessings for the world. They have prayed for the conversion
of sinners so that they might know true joy of heart, soul and mind.

One has only to read stories of those early women to catch their
burning love for God. Blessed Diana D'Andalo wanted to enter religious
life but could not get parental consent. So she set out secretly to enter a
Benedictine monastery. Her Italian brothers pursued her and used such
force to retrieve her that some of her ribs were broken. Eventually she
recovered and later, when she asked to become a Dominican nun, her
family consented.

Other vocation stories of contemporary nuns can be read in a book
published at the close of our jubilee year. The book is entitled <u>Vocation
in Black and White</u> and can be obtained from various Dominican
monasteries or from amazon.com

Women and men are still following Dominic 800 years later. We
asked some of the nuns, who are in formation, to share why they
entered the monastery.

Sr. Joseph Marie Nguyen, O.P.
Menlo Park, CA

*The words of St. Paul and St. Augustine summarize my vocation
journey to live for God alone, "The love of God impels us" (St. Paul)
and "Our heart is restless until it rests in God" (St. Augustine). Truly
my heart was restless, empty and longing for the only one, true love,
even while I was surrounded with earthly success and love. Looking at
Jesus in the Blessed Sacrament, waiting day and night to embrace His
own creatures, I was impelled to return that awesome love for me, and
for the whole human race.*

Sr. Joseph Marie is one of the boat people who escaped with just her life from Vietnam, when the Communists took over. She finished school, and became a US citizen when she was in college. She obtained her degree in science and worked for a while in a lab. When she moved to California, she got a better paying job as an accountant in the water department of the State of California.

Sr. Karyn Yager, O.P., Postulant
Farmington Hills, MI

The first time I met the sisters, I felt the fruits of the Spirit were present in this group of women---especially great joy, kindness and love for each other. These are the fruits of their contemplation, and it is what I want to develop in myself.

Sr. Karyn hails from Iowa and was a school teacher before she entered the monastery in February, 2009.

Sr. Carri, postulant
Summit, New Jersey

There are three elements, aside from Divine Intervention, that pulled me towards the Dominican Order. The first is the emphasis St. Dominic placed on study. The importance of always keeping the mind sharp, and using the knowledge acquired for meditations, are gateways for contemplation. Second, I've always had a deep devotion to the rosary, finding it a brilliant form of prayer. What better Order than one founded by the man with whom this devotion is associated? Third, though the character is hard to capture, I've heard the Dominican Order described as "balanced." The blessed Father held a beautiful balance between profound contemplation and zeal for the conversion of sinners. It's this same balance that represents my personality, making it ideal for righteousness.

Sr. Diana Marie of the Most Blessed Sacrament, O.P.
Summit, New Jersey

When I first began discerning a vocation to religious life, I had no real knowledge of any particular Order, save Mother Angelica's Poor Clares of Perpetual Adoration, since I was a regular viewer of EWTN. As I began to conduct some research on the Internet, the first thing I had to come to grips with was that it seemed as though I was being drawn to cloistered contemplative orders—and a mighty struggle it was! I wrote to a total of six monasteries/convents in five different orders: PCPA, Passionists, Visitation, the "Pink Sisters," and Dominican (two different monasteries). One by one each of the monasteries fell off my list, and I was down to the two Dominican monasteries (Summit, New Jersey, and Lufkin, Texas), so I decided to make a "Come and See" weekend to the Dominican monastery in Summit, a stone's throw away from my former childhood home on Staten Island (New York). It was then that I began to learn about the Dominican Order and its charism, but it wasn't until I made my aspirancy that I knew for certain that I was drawn to Dominican spirituality: chanting the Divine Office, the importance of study, and the fact that we are encouraged to be ourselves—and not forced to conform to some type of cookie-cutter austerity—as we journey together in seeking a life of perfection. After that, the Order and monastery our Lord was calling me to was no longer in doubt, and all that was left was the struggle of giving Him my "fiat."[2] Through the gift of His grace, I said "yes" to His call, and was blessed to be allowed to make my First Profession in early 2009. May He continue to give me the grace to give myself to Him each and every day for the rest of my life.

Sr. Diana Marie, O.P. went to college for several BA and AA degrees and worked in several different fields. She is from Florida and worked as an editor for a library research company prior to entering in 2006.

Sr. Mary Austin, O.P.
Los Angeles, California

My family and I came to Southern California from the Philippines when I was 13 years old. In my mid-twenties I started to go to daily Mass because I was intrigued by the priests' homilies. I also wanted

---

2   *Latin, Let it be done*

to dress up in cute outfits since I had to wear scrubs when I went to work as a registered nurse. My life was busy then, and I had to work and go to school at the same time. I was not rich, but I was able to buy whatever I wanted. So I did. I tried to fill the void within me with material things. I would feel happy, but after two seconds of happiness I felt empty again. On the other hand, whenever I went to the three-day religious convention, I would feel happy and filled. At the convention, which I attended yearly, I would see a lot of religious[3], but I never talked to any of them. I can't really tell when the vocation to the religious life was planted in me, but I remembered seeing religious men and women at the convention. There was a glow in their faces that exuded peace, happiness and love. It was only later that it clicked---the things of God made me happy and the things of the world left me feeling empty. Then one day my mom, sister and I went on a bus that toured Los Angeles. We went to the cathedral, etc. and to the Monastery of the Angels because of the pumpkin bread and chocolates which the nuns made. While my mom and sister were busy looking at the things in the gift shop, I had this idea to ask the sister at the counter about their life. From that time on, I would go to the monastery on Sundays to talk with the sister. She told me about their life, and I felt that this is where God wanted me. I have been with the sisters now for five years and I am very happy with my vocation.

Sr. Joseph Maria, O.P.
Summit, New Jersey

I started looking at Dominican cloistered life because of a suggestion from a friend who is now a Dominican brother. I didn't even know cloistered Dominicans existed but had always thought that there were only active Dominican Sisters. Having found this out, I was elated. After contacting a Dominican monastery and learning more about cloistered life, I was hooked! Our Lord truly caught me with the joy that radiated from each Dominican nun that I met. I wanted to have that same joy so I had to enter and learn their secret of being so joyful!

---

3   A member of a religious order or congregation.

Sr. Joseph Maria is Vietnamese by way of Texas and was attending college majoring in biology before entering in 2007.

Sr. Maria Teresa, O.P.
Summit, New Jersey

It was one word, "Veritas", the battle-cry of our Order that held attraction for me. In this post-modern world where each person feels a right to their 'own personal truth,' my spirit was crying out for absolute truth—for Truth Himself.

The saying, "the truth will set you free," says it all. The Order of Preachers has, for 800 years, been the lighthouse of the Church, shining the splendor of truth into the darkness of the world. By severing the chains of ignorance and heresy with the sword of truth, the Order set men free to truly know and love God. I wanted to be a part of this great work.

Sr. Maria Teresa is a native of New Jersey and attended college majoring in religious studies and biology before entering in 2008.

Sr. Mary Gabriel, O.P., Temporary Professed
Lufkin, Texas

Jesus calls us and loves us just as we are. He does not call us because we are great or smart. He simply loves us into life. St. Dominic was truly a man fully alive. God was able to do marvels through him because he allowed the Lord to enliven his spirit and empower him with His love, thus giving light and life to the whole Church. My joy, my challenge, my call is to allow God to do the same in me.

A Syracuse Sister describes Dominican life

"Monastic life is a journey into the heart in order to be transformed by the mystery of Christ."

Sr. Ann of the Cross, O.P.
North Guilford, CT

My interest in religious life began when I was an adolescent, but I did not encounter Dominicans until my junior year of college. Eucharistic adoration, *lectio divina*, and community living attracted me to the Dominican cloistered nuns in general. .

Sr. Sarah David of Truth Eddy, O.P.
North Guilford, CT

What drew me to the Dominican monastic life and to Our Lady of Grace Monastery was the *desire to love God*. Certain that God was calling me to the religious life but unsure as to *where*, it seemed that, so far as an apostolate was concerned, for me the doing was secondary to the being. In calling me to the Dominican monastic life, God also called me particularly to this monastery - something that became clear to me only as I learned to live this contemplative life.

Diverse Circumstances

> *I press on toward the goal to win the prize for which God*
> *has called me heavenward in Christ Jesus. Phil. 3:14 (NIV®)*

At different times some monasteries (Prouilhe among them) have numbered over one hundred nuns at a given time. On the other hand the monastery in Lagundo, Italy in the sixteenth century was decimated by the plague so that **all but one** of the nuns died. Fortunately, many vocations soon came and the community began to flourish once again.

Yes, the life of a Dominican Nun is still valid today. Even though monasteries had experienced a decline in vocations, the Lord continues to call women to follow Him through living the charism of St. Dominic. God's grace is still present drawing women to seek his face, to ponder his Word, to grow in holiness of life and to pray for the salvation and needs of all God's children.

Unity in Diversity

All these are the work of one and the same Spirit, and he gives them to each one, just as he determines. 1 Cor. 12:11 (NIV®)

Each monastery is autonomous, yet all are united in living the spirit of St. Dominic, and following the Rule of St. Augustine and the Constitutions of the Nuns of the Order of Preachers. Nevertheless there is diversity among sisters and among monasteries as has been reflected in their stories. In addition, some monasteries have a unique element or two.

BUFFALO, NEW YORK

The Buffalo Monastery *Madonna Hall* houses a collection of Marian statues from all over the world, showing how Mary is always a Mother.

Within the enclosure there is a Nativity statuary scene in an oratory off the cloister. Mother Mary Agnes, one of the founding sisters, had a great devotion to the Infant and the mystery of the Incarnation. She highly influenced the community as prioress, and the oratory became a permanent part of devotion to the Word Incarnate. The Nativity group has been the center of Christmas recreations and celebrations. It is a special nook where the sisters can pray and meditate as they gaze upon the representation of the mystery of our God Incarnate.

CAMDEN, NEW JERSEY

The Chapel of the Monastery is a true work of art. The all-stone structure is one of the most beautiful church buildings in the Camden area. Even though the current chapel was built in 1927, it has a centuries-old feel. The sanctuary is flanked by curved stairs that lead to the Rosary Shrine above the main altar. Here the carved marble statute of Our Lady, crowned as Queen of Heaven, holds the child Jesus as she gives the rosary to Saint Dominic and Saint Catherine of Siena.

The chapel is also home to an encased statute of Our Lady of Fatima. This statute is one of only five in the world like it. It was a gift of the Dominican Nuns of Fatima, Portugal.

CAMDEN'S SPECIAL STORY

When Fr. Damien Marie Saintourens, O.P. was dying, Mother Catherine, the prioress, and her sisters were praying and crying at Father's bedside. He said to them, "Don't cry; Our Blessed Mother told me that another priest just as devoted to the rosary would be sent here to carry on the work of the rosary." When Mother Catherine asked what his name was, Father said, "Fr. John Stephan Moran."

Mother told the sisters after they went outside the door, that Fr. Moran was very sick with tuberculosis, and wasn't expected to live. God chose otherwise; Fr. Moran, O.P. was their chaplain for 25 years. He carried on the rosary work just like Fr. Saintourens, O.P. had done. Fr. Moran, O.P. died on January 5, 1953.

The Monastery in Camden is the Shrine of the Perpetual Rosary and is the burial place of Fr. Damien Marie Saintourens, O.P., founder of the Dominican Nuns of the Perpetual Rosary.

ELMIRA AND DELAWARE

The nuns in Elmira and Delaware are making history, in the founding of the new Caterina Benincasa[4] Monastery. Although US nuns have made foundations abroad, it has been over sixty years since a new foundation has been made in the States. It is significant that the new monastery is in Delaware. Americans think of George Washington and his crossing of the Delaware River. It was at that time that Thomas Paine wrote, "These are times that try men's souls; the summer soldier and the sunshine patriot will, in this crisis, shrink from the service of his country;…yet we have this consolation with us, that the harder the conflict, the more glorious the triumph." In many ways, these are hard times in our country and in the Church, yet, by the grace of God, the nuns faithfully stand firm in responding to their calling.

In December of 2007, three nuns were welcomed by his Excellency,

---

4   Better known as St. Catherine of Siena

Michael Al Saltarelli Bishop of Delaware, and Fr. Timothy Nolan, pastor of Holy Spirit Church. The nuns had the blessing of the prior provincial, and the assistance of Fr. Manuel Merten, O.P. in founding the Monastery of Caterina Benincasa in New Castle. Like the nuns of Prouilhe, they are at the center of the holy preaching, situated near the Dominican Friars at the University of Delaware.

In April of 2009, Fr. Carlos Azpiroz Costa, O.P., the Master of the Dominican Order, visited the nuns along with his assistant Fr. Edward Ruane, O.P., and Sr. Miriam Scheel, O.P., the prioress of Elmira. Fr. Carlos encouraged the sisters in their mission, promising support and guidance.

Elmira, NY

Sr. Miriam, O.P. designed the stained glass windows for their chapel, as well as the monstrance that is used for adoration in their chapel.

Lufkin, TX

The Monastery in Lufkin, Texas has the honor of providing the Conference of Nuns with its first president, Sr. Mary Catherine, O.P. When the Conference of Nuns developed into an Association, the membership elected Sr. Mary John, O.P. another Lufkin sister, as president.

Marbury, AL

The Canonization of Saint Katharine Drexel has special significance for the nuns in Marbury. Many of them attended schools operated by her Sisters of the Blessed Sacrament. Some even met Mother Katharine when she made her annual visitations to the classes. The Josephite Fathers also had a notable part of the early history of Saint Jude's monastery. One member remembers reading about the new monastery in their magazine *Colored Harvest*, as it was known then. The article inspired her to write to the monastery and seek admission.

MENLO PARK, CA

Menlo was the first granddaughter house of Newark. The Archbishop of San Francisco had the expressed intention of fostering devotion to the Blessed Sacrament in accord with the desire and practice of the nuns living in the Bronx, since their monastery had the privilege of Perpetual Adoration. These two monasteries on the coasts of the US both bear the name of "Corpus Christi Monastery." Menlo Park's twenty-four hour adoration did indeed foster devotion to the Blessed Sacrament as is evident from the fact that two other local churches, one just across the street, have also begun twenty-four hour adoration.

This monastery also enjoys a unique Dominican Family link. A community of Dominican Friars lives in a house located on the front of the property. Two of the friars serve in full-time campus ministry at nearby Stanford University. Another friar is full-time Director of Vallombrosa Retreat and Conference Center just across the street. A third friar is semi-retired, serving in part-time ministry at Stanford, and serves as chaplain to the monastery. The Chapter of Dominican Laity meets monthly at the monastery and joins the nuns for mid-day prayer and the rosary. Public ceremonies or celebrations are well represented by the Dominican Family.

SUMMIT, NJ

Sr. Maria of the Cross, O.P., of the Summit Monastery, compiled *The Summit Choirbook* in response to the need of the nuns for quality hymns to use with the vernacular Divine Office. It was published in 1983, the Extraordinary Jubilee Year of the Redemption, and contains 534 Latin and English hymns for the Church year, along with those for the feasts of the saints.

Sister composed a wide variety of liturgical pieces in 1970, when Dominicans commemorated the eighth centenary of the birth of St. Dominic. Commissioned by James A. Burns, Sister also composed the *Mass of the Holy Spirit* and *Missa Caritas* for Christmas of 1970. Mr. Burns gave copies to the monasteries he taught music lessons to, including Hunt's Point, Lancaster, Newark, Summit,

Union City, and West Springfield.

WEST SPRINGFIELD, MA

Sr. Mary of the Pure Heart, O.P., composed simplified chant adaptations for our singing of the Divine Office. The psalm tones, based on the Gregorian psalm tones, are very easy to sing, thus allowing for reflection on the words while we are chanting. She has shared her work with a couple of our other monasteries.

SYRACUSE, NY

The Feast of Our Lady of Lourdes, February 11th, is the anniversary of Fr. Damian Marie Saintourens' all night vigil at her grotto. Each year the Syracuse community makes a solemn procession through the monastery in honor of the eighteen Apparitions of Our Lady to St. Bernadette. They do so for the needs and intentions of the Dominican Order and of the Diocese, as well as for friends and benefactors of all faith communities in the Universal Church.

MILWAUKEE, WI

Because of the Milwaukee Monastery's close association with the nuns we make mention of a special shrine to Our Lady which is still very active. In 1947, the shrine was dedicated to Our Lady of Fatima and to peace, following the end of World War II. Originally the community owned the shrine, which served as the center for numerous activities there. In 1970, the La Salette Fathers began directing the shrine, and in 1979, the Archdiocese of Milwaukee purchased the land and assumed direction of it, making it an Archdiocesan Marian Shrine. An enthusiastic group of volunteers maintain the grounds, which are very beautifully landscaped.

A Common Purpose

Just as each of us has one body with many members, and these
members do not all have the same function, so in Christ we who are
many form one body... Romans 12: 4-5 (NIV®)

The Dominican Family's common purpose is to communicate the love of God to all people, as preachers of the Catholic Church. Each branch of preachers, whether nuns, sisters, laity, youth, or friars, determines how it shall preach the Good News of Christ in their time and place. So, all Dominican preachers are in mission together. Each of us joins the branch of the Dominican Family as one feels called.[2]

JUBILEE VISIT

On January 27, 2007, Sr. Corinne, Sr. Valerie and Sr. Joan, Dominican Sisters from the Congregation of St. Mary of the Springs in Columbus, Ohio, visited us in honor of our 800th Anniversary. They brought with them a special surprise, a gift of art, painted by Sr. Thoma Swanson, O.P. It depicts Dominicans enfolded in Our Lady's mantle. Their presence made it a doubly joyful day.

The Dominican Fraternity

They devoted themselves to the apostles' teaching and to the
fellowship, to the breaking of bread and to prayer. Acts 2:42 (NIV®)

Many monasteries have a Dominican Fraternity attached to them. (See Chapter 14) The monthly meeting of each chapter usually includes Mass, rosary, community formation, spiritual instruction, fellowship time and Benediction of the Blessed Sacrament.

(Endnotes)

1   Excerpts from *Catherine of Siena, The Dialogue*, translation and introduction by Suzanne Noffke, O.P. Copyright © 1980 by Paulist Press. Paulist Press, Inc., New York / Mahwah, NJ. Reprinted by permission of Paulist Press, Inc. www.paulistpress.com Used with permission.

2   "The Dominican Family." Crossroads. http://laici.op.org/eng/about-us/family.php (accessed May 22, 2009) Used with permission.

CHAPTER 24

A Surprisingly Large Family

We always thank God for all of you, mentioning you in our prayers.
1 Thess. 1:2 (NIV®)

In November, the month in which we celebrate Thanksgiving Day, we resumed our monthly celebrations. We have much to be thankful for and many blessings to be counted. During the various monthly preparations for the Holy Hour celebrations, I thought of other groups that could be invited.

Homeschoolers

We proclaim him, admonishing and teaching everyone with all wisdom, so that we may present everyone perfect in Christ.
Col. 1:28 (NIV®)

Since we had invited Catholic elementary schools, Catholic high schools and colleges as well as CCD representatives, it occurred to us that it would be good to include homeschoolers. We were able to have fifteen families come as our honored guests: the Brazeaus, Cottrills, Demers, Dowdys, Driscolls, Ezeugwus, Heaths, Jacques, Kozubs, Mazzers, Mongeaus, Pelcs, Perkins, Ransoms and the Rose-Fishes. That was quite a large contingent!

Seniors

Seniors

Seniors

Gentlemen of St. Joseph

Daughters of Mary

KNIGHTS OF COLUMBUS

Procession

Homeschoolers

International Group

Homeschoolers

Homeschoolers

The Gentlemen of St. Joseph

Joseph her husband was a righteous man… Mt. 1:19 (NIV®)

We were surprised to learn about the "Gentlemen of St. Joseph" group. Mr. Robert Pietraszek leads the group and became my contact person. Those who were able to join us as honored guests were Ed Cottrill, Rob Demers, Sean Driscoll, Robert Heath, Yves Jacques, Sean Mazzer and John Rose-Fish as well as Mr. Pietraszek.

The Gentlemen of St. Joseph are a fraternal group of men who enjoy meeting once a month for a Holy Hour, fellowship, supper and discussion. They usually schedule some kind of speaker, although someone from the group usually suggests a topic for discussion. The Gentlemen of St. Joseph are dedicated to praying the rosary, to seeking St Joseph's intercession and are zealous for the conversion of souls and for families.

The Daughters of Mary

You are her daughters if you do what is right
and do not give way to fear. 1 Peter. 3:6 (NIV®)

The family --- Because St. Joseph and Our Lady are the protectors and patrons of all families, we invited the Daughters of Mary as honored guests. These included Christina and Maddie Cottrill, Katie Dowdy, Emily Rose and Kayla Driscoll, Aimee and Emilie Jacques and Rachel Pelc.

The Seniors

Rise in the presence of the aged, show respect for the elderly and
revere your God. Lev. 19:32 (NIV®)

We wanted to be sure to include the group of "seniors." There were

37 of them. It was nice to begin our celebration in December of 2006 with Expectant Mothers and to draw it to a close with our seniors. There were guests of all ages in the months between.

The International Family

*Bring my sons from afar and my daughters from the
ends of the earth… Is. 43:6 (NIV®)*

This month we had a special surprise in the form of a multi-lingual decade of the rosary, which represented the International Family. We invited guests who represented ten different countries. For one decade of the rosary, each guest prayed the first half of the "Hail Mary" in a foreign language. All in the congregation responded in English. Mr. Manuel Mendes, a long time friend of the community, prayed in Portuguese. Sr. Mary of the Nativity's cousin George Bresnahan taught Gaelic, so he prayed in that language. Gladys Les from St. Stan's in Chicopee prayed in Polish. Through Carole Raffaele of Our Lady of Mount Carmel, we had Lia Addeo, who prayed in Italian. Mary Lou Bueno prayed in Filipino/Tagalog, and because our Spanish speaker was absent, Mary Lou also graciously prayed the Spanish "Hail Mary." Two of the Daughters of the Heart of Mary joined us in the multi-lingual rosary decade. Blandine Adjou prayed in French and Itsu Tada in Japanese. Miriam Mboya, who is Kenyan and a student in a local school, prayed in Swahili. The tenth bead was prayed by Poan Guyen in Vietnamese.

While we received favorable comments on the singing and other various aspects of our monthly celebrations, the multi-lingual rosary decade was a favorite mentioned by many.

Mr. Manuel Mendes, So. Hadley, MA
("Hail Mary" in Portuguese)

Looking back some sixty years or so, my first visit to the monastery was as an altar boy. We were from the former Our

Seniors

Pauline Bacon
Lauria Chapman
Maurice DeMontigny
Mary Beth Dillon
Ellen Doyle
Cecile Durocher
Laura Giuggio
Roberta Haywood
Shirley Hebert
Val Hebert
Jane Hendrick
Mary Hickson
Florence Kaplan
William Kelly
Barbara Kuras
Gloria Lafleur
Joseph Lake
Laura Landry

Barbara Lane
Theresa LaValley
Nelson Letendre
Eva Miner
Dorothy Mozden
Catherine Murphy
Rose Marie Nathan
Felipe Pantoja
Marguerite Rivest
Beatrice Rush
Rita Rose
Lucille Roy
Marguerite Surprenant
Yvonne Therrien
Anna Tierney
Stella Torres
Elaine Trottier
Gail Waterman

Mary-Rose Hurley-Landers

Lady of the Rosary Parish in Holyoke. Together with others in procession, we witnessed a ceremony by the late Bishop of the Springfield Diocese at that time.

Now as I put pen to paper, I find that words in any language do not suffice to describe the essence of the Dominican Sisters at the Monastery.

Their path and homage is to always serve the Lord and the secular community in which they reside. The sisters' mission from their origin and destiny, is their living example of unending faith, hope and love.

Upon entering their monastery, one immediately senses an aura which, again, cannot be expressed in words! While in the presence of only one of their nuns or collectively in the presence of the entire community while listening to their clear voices at Mass or other celebrations, one feels a direct contact with the Divine…

Upon reading this, I am sure you will agree to the emotion, feeling and experience I make reference to. It is captivating!

Finally –If you have not had the opportunity and honor in meeting with Sr. Mary of the Sacred Heart, you cannot but come away "inspired," with a special sense of spirit!

I thank the sisters for their indulgence and ongoing prayers over the years.

Lia Addeo
("Hail Mary" in Italian)

It was a most beautiful experience! After receiving our instructions, I went back into the church and I asked myself, "Where am I?" I thought I was in paradise because of the atmosphere.

Knowing Sr. Mary of the Sacred Heart was a big gift and I felt very connected to the other people. For me it was an act of fraternity. God is great!

Fr. Donald Lapointe, the Diocesan Director for the Society for the

Propagation of the Faith, was our guest officiant.

REV J. DONALD R. LAPOINTE
DIOCESAN DIRECTOR OF THE PONTIFICAL MISSION SOCIETY
FOR THE PROPAGATION OF THE FAITH

How do you celebrate eight hundred years? Consider that Columbus discovered America more than five hundred years ago and yet the Religious Dominican Order had already been in existence nearly three hundred years. When we also note the fact that both were from a land across the great Atlantic, we come to appreciate that the Church of God is not limited by the confines of time and place.

How do you celebrate eight hundred years? You celebrate it with the most precious gift you have. You celebrate it with the gift of the Mass. You celebrate the gift of God the Son to God the Father in God's Spirit of love Eternal. You celebrate it in the Liturgy of Benediction where God participates in the celebration. And you celebrate it with as many people as possible.

It is for this reason that the Dominican Sisters chose to welcome the entire surrounding community to an unprecedented celebration that would last the whole year through. They chose to celebrate this occasion with people from all walks of life and from various Apostolic Ministries in the Church.

It was my privilege to participate in the Apostolic Theme of Evangelization during the month of November. We celebrated by reciting the World Mission Rosary, a rosary of five different colors to represent the five Continents of the world. Each Hail Mary of one rosary decade was prayed in a different language, again symbolic that people of all nations, members of the family of God, came to celebrate these eight hundred years. God so loved the world that he sent His own begotten Son and Jesus so loved the world that He told us to go out and tell the good news to all people. And so, the family came to celebrate with our Dominican Sister who themselves are international.

Let us thank our God and let us be grateful for our Dominican Sisters.

Faithful Servers

...to love the LORD your God and to serve him with all your heart and with all your soul... Dt. 11:13 (NIV®)

Henry Sansouci once again served as our Emcee. Alexander Sawicki, Sr. served as incense bearer and Mike Vezzola as cross bearer. Sean Devine of Redding, CT, served as acolyte together with Michael Broer of Chicopee, MA.

The Knights of Columbus

A scroll of remembrance was written in his presence concerning those who feared the LORD and honored his name.
Mal. 3:16 (NIV®)

We were pleased once again to have the Knights of Columbus join us in the celebration. The Knights add so much to the solemnity of the service in which we honor Our Lord, present in the Blessed Sacrament. As we mentioned in our January service, the Infant King has said, "The more you honor me the more I will bless you." And many blessings did indeed go out to our guests!

Knights of Columbus

Sir Knight Donald Gladdu
Commander
Sir Knight Roger Fontaine
Faithful Navigator
Sir Knight Richard Beaudry
Sir Knight Matthew Blaney
Sir Knight Edward LaFromboise
Past Faithful Navigators
Sir Knight Richard Fulton
Sir Knight Ronald Grenier
Honor Guard

Foreign Foundations from the US Monasteries

He will love you and bless you and increase your numbers.
Dt. 7:13 (NIV®)

The Monastery of the Perpetual Rosary in Camden, New Jersey, was the first to make a foreign foundation. Mother M. Louis Bertrand was the foundress, and took six or seven sisters with her to Rome in 1930.

At one point the monastery in Rome had a number of Irish sisters. Some were sent to Camden, N.J., prior to the outbreak of W.W.II, for their safety. Those left behind had a very hard time, as did all the people. There was a tremendous shortage of food, heavy bombings, and great insecurity. All sisters had a small bag with lay-clothes, in case there was need to make a hasty retreat. The Blessed Sacrament was reserved in a special secret place in the basement, where the sisters kept up their Rosary Hours. The Irish sisters were very young at the time, and their health became very much affected by the shortage of basic food and the harsh environment in which they lived. All the events affected most of them for most of their lives. This, as well as a lack of Italian vocations, necessitated the closing of the monastery in Rome.

As Italian vocations were lacking, and by 1962 the sisters in Rome were struggling for survival, the community made a request for help. Two sisters from Glasgow and Sr. M. Rose O'Connor O.P. from the Monastery of St. Catherine of Siena in Drogheda, Ireland, went to their assistance. Within a short time, however, it became clear that the monastery in Rome would have to close. Sr. M. Rose returned to her monastery in Drogheda, and shortly thereafter was followed by Sr. M. Visitation, originally from the Glasgow Monastery. Sr. Mary Joseph, the other Glasgow sister, responded to an appeal by the Bishop of Karachi, Pakistan. He had visited the monastery in Rome and had requested help for a new foundation in his diocese. The monastery in Rome was officially closed by the Apostolic See in 1964. Several of the remaining elderly Irish sisters transfiliated to the monasteries in Glasgow and Fatima.

Glasgow and Beyond

The See of Glasgow, Scotland, was designated by Pope Alexander III in 1175/76 as the special daughter of the Roman See (Specialis filia Romanae Ecclesiae). Kindliness and hospitality are prime Glasgow traditions, along with dynamism. With a "Hullo there," Glaswegians freely greet strangers by extending both hand and heart. Servicemen in two world wars voted Glasgow the friendliest city, compassionate, cosmopolitan, welcoming and warm. Glaswegians show they believe that people count.

Among its famous men, St.Kentigern, its patron saint, must be mentioned---a Celtic Prince of royal blood (also known as Mungo) meaning "dear friend." Inscribed on St. Mungo's bell, which was

To Glasgow

Mother M. Louis Bertrand (center), one sister (Camden) & three Irish nuns from Rome

First Monastery in Glasgow

Pakistan
Mother Mary Gabriel,
Mother Mary Imelda
and
Sr. Mary Michael

Nuns travel from Los Angeles to Bocaue in the Philippines

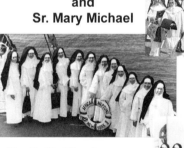

North Guilford nuns make new foundation in Nairobi, Kenya

Dominican Nuns and
the Monastery
in
India

Sr. Maria Rosaro
(left) in Cuba

Trinidad

Langley
Foundresses

received from an ancient Pope is the city's motto *Lord, let Glasgow flourish through the preaching of Thy Word and the Praising of Thy Name* (now, sadly abbreviated to, "Let Glasgow flourish.")

It was fitting, then, that this friendly city with a motto truly Dominican, Archbishop Donald Campbell D.D. extended an invitation in December 1947 (only two years after World War II ended). He asked for a Foundation of Dominican Nuns of the Perpetual Rosary to be made in his Archdiocese of Glasgow. His visit to the Dominican Monastery in Rome on the Gianicolo Hill provided the inspiration behind this invitation.

Mother M. Louis Bertrand O.P., the prioress of the monastery in Rome, had been searching for some time for a suitable property in England for a foundation but could not find any. She responded happily to the warm invitation of Archbishop Campbell. A suitable Victorian House in a residential area of the city was purchased and adapted to the needs of cloistered life.

The Monastery of St. Dominic was officially opened on December 14, 1948. At the opening ceremony, the Archbishop expressed his great joy to the assembled crowd, and explained how he had felt while in Rome, "that Our Lady had taken him by the hand and led him to carry out this work of the rosary for his beloved city of Glasgow."

On the same occasion, Fr. Tindal-Atkinson O.P., representing the Master General of the Dominican Order Fr. Emmanuel Suarez O.P., conveyed the Master's "sincere gratitude to the Archbishop and Chapter of the Archdiocese, the Clergy and Laity of Glasgow for the gracious welcome given to the Nuns." Fr. Tindal-Atkinson spoke also of his own immense joy "because the Catholic life of this great city is to be enriched by the coming from Rome itself of a tiny group of contemplative nuns, whose life is dedicated to unceasing prayer, especially the prayer of the most holy Rosary of the Blessed Virgin Mary." The small group was comprised of both American and Irish nuns led by Mother M. Louis Bertrand O.P.

A few months later on March 9, 1949, Mother M. Louis Bertrand received a letter from Fr. Emmanuel Suarez O.P. Master General, thanking her for her letter, which gave details of the new foundation "the first of the Second Order in Scotland since the Reformation." He went on to say, "I congratulate you and the nuns of the Federation anew, and with great pleasure send all of you the blessing of St. Dominic."

Great as the welcome was from the Catholic community, such was not the case from the local residents! A lengthy petition was signed against the sisters taking up residence in the neighborhood. However, when the local folk realized that the nuns did not go off the premises, their anxiety subsided!

The new foundation suffered utmost poverty, with the sisters working hard and often into the night doing various art and craft works to try and raise funds for daily expenses. It took long years of struggle to build up this Scottish foundation. Then came the shock of dry rot, discovered in the foundations of the house, and practically all the floors had to be pulled out. Christmas was celebrated in a house which had a tarpaulin in place of a roof and only a partial floor! Many good people, not only in Scotland but from Ireland and England as well, rallied to support the nuns, not only financially, but with donations of food and joining in prayer.

Throughout these early years of struggle, the sisters' trust in God's Providence never faltered. Their dedication to the life of prayer and community living was carried out in a spirit of joy and generosity so characteristic of our holy father, Dominic.

The first postulant from Glasgow entered in October, 1951, and the second, from England, entered Christmas Eve of the same year. This was indeed an encouraging time. There were several American sisters in the early years, and the community in Glasgow celebrated the 4th of July, and Thanksgiving Day in November, complete with pumpkin pie. One of the new postulants from Scotland had never heard of it!

In 1954, Mother M. Louis Bertrand founded the Fatima Monastery, which she always referred to as her "Benjamin."[1] Several sisters from Glasgow were sent on this new Foundation, including two sisters in the novitiate. The depletion of numbers after only six years in the new foundation was a heavy cross. From 1956 onwards, several postulants entered and a few sisters from Apostolic Congregations tried their

1   Benjamin was the name that Israel (Jacob) gave to his youngest son, and thus very dear to him.

vocation to the cloistered way of life, but most did not persevere.

In 1963, the Glasgow nuns were able to purchase the house adjoining their property with the hope of joining both houses by a link-block, giving much needed space. However, upon a thorough investigation, both properties were discovered to be riddled with dry-rot. Thus in 1967, work began on a completely new monastery on this site, and was designed to accommodate thirty sisters. Long years of fund-raising followed, amid increasing costs and ever higher interest rates. Many good people, not only in Scotland, but from Ireland, England and beyond, worked hard to help the sisters raise funds for this new house of prayer.

The second property was demolished and the first phase of the new monastery commenced. When sufficient living accommodation was completed, the sisters moved in. Then the second phase began, which included the chapel, choir, and extern quarters. Amid great rejoicing, the new monastery was finally completed in 1970, though the heavy debt continued for many more years.

A week of "Open House" allowed local clergy, religious, family, friends, benefactors and neighbors to view the new monastery. Neighbors especially appreciated this opportunity to meet the sisters and have the nuns' way of life explained to them. Feelings of hostility from the 1940's quickly evaporated! Many of these good people were happy to support the on-going fund-raising with their own craft work and baking, whenever such was organized in local parishes. It meant a lot to them to know they would be remembered in the sisters' prayers. After the Open House, the sisters resumed their normal monastic life and were relieved of the stress and pressure of living on site during the building.

Six annual novenas were continued, three of them preached by the Dominican friars. They were always well attended. On Sundays, there were often two to three hundred persons in attendance, with many traveling great distances to hear the Word of God. Tea and refreshments were served afterwards in the extern quarters by two dedicated Lay Dominicans, Kathleen and May. The sisters continued their vestment making, arts and crafts, and printing work.

Lack of vocations and an aging community began to take its toll. After much prayer and seeking advice, the decision was made in 1987 to close the monastery in what had always been "Glasgow's friendly City." Like Abraham of old, like Mary and Joseph, the nuns too placed their faith in God's indisputable ways.

Archbishop Thomas J. Winning (later Cardinal Winning), Fr. Damian Byrne, O.P. Master General of the Dominican Order and numerous clergy, religious, benefactors and friends expressed their sadness at the news of the closure, and at the same time, spoke of their deep gratitude for the powerful support of the sisters' lives of prayer for over forty years in Glasgow.

The sisters were deeply grateful to those monasteries who welcomed them. One sister transfiliated to the monastery in North Guilford, CT (USA.), one to the monastery in Fatima, Portugal, and four sisters to the Monastery of St. Catherine of Siena in Drogheda, Ireland. Two elderly sisters needed nursing home care and were given a warm welcome at our Dominican Sisters in Fatima Home, Co. Kerry; two others received an equally warm welcome with the Dominican Sisters of the Stone Congregation in England.

The Monastery of St. Dominic in Glasgow was sold to the Irish Carmelite Fathers for use as a retreat house. The sisters felt happy that a prayerful apostolate would continue in their monastery. On February 3, 1988, a special Mass of Thanksgiving was celebrated for all God's blessings through the years, after which, the remaining sisters welcomed the Carmelite Fathers. The friars were overwhelmed to have everything left in such readiness for their occupation, including food in the fridge!

At the present time, only two sisters from the Glasgow Monastery remain, the very first postulant of 1951 and the sister who entered in 1956. We are grateful to Sr. Kathleen, who is one of those two, for providing us with this history.

Karachi, Pakistan

In the early 1950's, Bishop Cialeo, O.P. from Pakistan made the acquaintance of the nuns in Los Angeles, California. He stopped to visit the community every time he came to Los Angeles and at each visit asked if the sisters would like to make a foundation in Pakistan. At that time, the community was large enough to consider the request. The prioress, Mother Mary Gabriel, had no particular interest in Pakistan, though. Her sights were on Australia.

When the late Joseph Cardinal Cordiero became Archbishop of Karachi, Pakistan, one of his first decisions was to invite a contemplative community to his diocese. Bishop Cialeo heard of his desire and immediately contacted him saying he thought he knew just the community.

Eventually, Archbishop Cordiero made the formal invitation to the nuns in Los Angeles. In order to better evaluate the possibility, Mother Mary Gabriel and Sr. Mary Imelda traveled to Pakistan in 1958. They both decided that, though it would be difficult, there was potential for a community of cloistered Dominican nuns to flourish in this predominantly Muslim country. In 1959, after much preparation, Mother Mary Gabriel and nine sisters left the monastery in Los Angeles for Pakistan.

Originally the community was situated in Karachi proper, on Ingle Road in a rather large house. The sisters learned to adapt to the many different ways of living they encountered. It proved both a challenging and difficult time. Gone were the many conveniences they had known, and yet, they found the strength of mind and soul to overcome the many obstacles. In time, it became imperative that the community move to a more permanent location. They did so in the 1960's, when they built a new monastery in an area outside the city.

The community has been through many hardships and dangerous situations, wars, floods, etc. But the sisters believe in their call to be witnesses of God's presence as most valued and needed. They are greatly supported by their many Muslim friends. The monastery in Karachi was well founded. At present, the prioress and all of the sisters are Pakistani.

Bocaue, Philippines

In the 1970's, a group of five Filipina sisters from the Dominican community of Saint Catherine of Siena, a Third Order community, asked their superior for permission to live according to the rule of the Second Order nuns, with the possibility of eventually founding a Dominican Monastery in the Philippines.

Initially, the sisters were encouraged by Fr. Cirilo Almario, (later bishop), and Fr. Harold, CP. In their quest to find a place where they could eventually live, Monsignor Honoring offered his home and property for their use. The property was situated in the town of Bocaue in Bulacan, in the diocese of Mololos where Fr. Almario had recently been made bishop.

The sisters moved into the two-story house in Bocaue and promptly began living the cloistered life according to the 1933 Constitutions, the only Constitutions they could find. After a period of time, they became convinced of their desire to become cloistered Dominican nuns. They then proceeded to look for a Dominican monastery which would officially give them formation in the Dominican monastic way of life.

Fr. Harold, CP, made many trips to the US. always stopping at any Dominican monastery he knew. One such monastery was the one in Los Angeles. Sr. Mary Thomas, prioress at the time, welcomed Father's proposal and arranged to go to Bocaue to evaluate the situation. She found the sisters in the Philippines willing and eager to become Cloistered Dominican nuns, so invited the sisters to come to Los Angeles for formation.

A few weeks after Sr. Mary Thomas returned to the States, the sisters from the Philippines arrived. Though the time seemed short (only a year) close ties were forged between the two communities. Their numbers increased to six with the acceptance of a sister from another congregation. At the end of the year of formation, the sisters returned to the Philippines, welcomed by Bishop Almario at the airport along with many other well-wishers.

The Filipina nuns bought the property from Monsignor Honoring. About a year later, three nuns from the Monastery of the Angels, Sr. Mary of the Cross, Sr. Mary Elizabeth and Sr. Mary Augustine, went to the Philippines to assist in establishing the new foundation. The first wing of the permanent monastery was built, but construction was delayed at times due to floods and typhoons. The finished monastery was blessed in 1982. The foundation was blessed with many vocations, and the prioress and all the nuns are natives of the Philippines.

Nairobi, Kenya, Africa

In 1962, the community in North Guilford, CT, blessed with an abundance of vocations, began to consider a foundation. In July of 1963, the Most Reverend Maurice Otunga, Bishop of Nairobi, happened to visit the community of fifty plus. He requested some volunteers, and in January of 1965, twelve sisters were selected as foundresses. On April 30th, 1965, the sisters boarded a bus that took them to New York, where they embarked on the S.S. African Neptune. "The Africans" arrived at their destination on May 28, but two years passed before they moved into their new building, named Corpus Christi Monastery. Now, more than forty years later, the foundation is fully African, the foundresses are back in North Guilford, and the Nairobi community continues to flourish.

Cainta, Philippines

The Cainta foundation came about by a simple congratulatory letter from Sr. Mary Lucina, which she sent to the newly installed Philippine provincial Fr. Rogelio B. Alarcon, O.P. in 1972. The province was newly erected as an offshoot of the Holy Rosary Province which was founded from Spain in the late sixteenth century. In her letter,

Sr. Mary Lucina expressed a desire to have a Dominican monastery in the Philippines. At the first Provincial Chapter held later that year, the prospect was mentioned. On December 8th, Mother Marie Rosaria presented the prospect of making the foundation. It would be the first perpetual rosary monastery in Southeast Asia. On January 10, 1973, the monastery chapter voted in favor of a new foundation with the stipulation that the Summit monastery would train Filipino women in the Dominican monastic contemplative life.

On October 20, 1975, Sr. Maria Aurea of the Nativity (Perez), O.P. was admitted by the community with the new foundation specifically in mind. Since there were not enough sisters to staff the proposed monastery, the solemnly professed Filipino nuns in Summit were chosen to form the core group under the leadership of Mother Marie Rosaria. On August 4, 1977, five nuns --- Mother Marie Rosaria, vicaress, Sr. Mary Lucina, Sr. Maria Agnes, Sr. Maria Guadalupe and Sr. Maria Aurea --- left Summit, and after an overnight stay in California, resumed their trip to the Orient. On hand to meet them were Fr. Rogelio Alarcon and Mother Stella Salao, O.P., Superior General of the Dominican Sister of St. Catherine of Siena, and the families and friends of the Filipino nuns. Garlands of *sampaguitas* (Philippine national flower) were hung around the necks of the foundresses.

They stayed at the motherhouse of the Siena Sisters in Quezon City for about three weeks until they found a rent-free house that belonged to the Zaide family of B.F. Homes, Quezon City. The four-bedroom house was converted into a convent which the nuns occupied for ten months. On June 29, 1978, they moved to Manaoag, Pangasinan. Upon the suggestion of Fr. Alarcon, Mother Marie Rosaria began the search for a suitable monastery site. The purchase of land and the construction of a monastery would be a considerable expense and the Philippine economy had slowed down under the martial law regime of President Marcos. At this point Fr. Jordan Aumann, O.P. and Bishop Leonardo Legaspi,O.P. came to the nuns' rescue. They petitioned Cardina Jaime Sin to receive the founding group into the Manila archdiocese. The Cardinal gave the nuns a piece of land for perpetual use in Cainta, Rizal, a suburb of Manila. The construction of the monastery began in 1980. Meanwhile, the nuns stayed in a little convent attached to the village church in Laoac, Pangasinan.[1]

Langley, Canada

Master General Timothy Radcliffe, O.P. requested volunteers for an English speaking foundation of nuns in Western Canada. On November 27, 1999, nuns came from different monasteries in the United States, and the new foundation was begun. The Monastery of the Blessed Sacrament in Farmington Hills, MI, accepted the responsibility as "Sponsoring Monastery." It gave this new foundation generous financial support. Other monasteries in the States did likewise.

The foundation began in Rosemary Heights in Surrey, BC, where the nuns lived in a very small house. Two years later they acquired a home on Agricultural Land Reserve in the Fort Langley area. The nuns chose to raise sheep in order to maintain their farm status and tried to support themselves through the sale of monastic arts: prayerfully created sculpture, liturgical linens, cards, and icons.

The community has outgrown the house in which they are presently living, and are facing various problems which make expansion unfeasible. Building restrictions in the Langley area exclude a multiple member dwelling. Families only are permitted and a growing monastic family does not qualify. They are searching for land on which to build a permanent monastery in the hope that the new monastery will also provide a monastic welcome to those who are seeking a place of silence and prayer, coupled with the natural beauty of God's creation, which speaks so eloquently to the heart.

Vietnam

Fr. Manuel Merten came to Farmington Hills, MI to officiate at Sr. Maria Rose's Solemn Profession. She was the first Vietnamese to make solemn profession as a nun. It was due to her initiative that the monastic foundation began. In 1999, Sr. Maria Rose approached

Fr. Timothy Radcliffe, Master at that time, for permission in investigate possibilities. She had the blessing of the Provincial Chapter in Vietnam for the project. It was she who asked Sr. Mary Thomas, who was prioress at that time for permission to begin her novitiate as a cloistered nun at the Farmington Hills Monastery. The monastery Chapter approved, and not long after that Sr. Theresa Tam joined her in Michigan in May of 2000.

Sr. Maria Rose was a former Superior General of her Congregation in Vietnam. Sr. Theresa Tam was an Assistant Mother General and former novice mistress in her congregation. These were experienced sisters, capable of bringing their dream to fruition, and the dream became a reality in 2002.

Assistance to Trinidad

The monastery in Lufkin, Texas has been blessed with vocations from a variety of countries including Mexico, Cuba, Tanzania and Vietnam. The presence of these sisters has been both enriching and challenging, and has given the community the opportunity to see themselves from new and different perspectives.

One of the sisters from Tanzania responded to a call from the Dominican monastery in Trinidad, West Indies, to assist them for three months; their numbers were few and most of them were elderly, ill and/or incapacitated. At the end of the three months, she was asked to renew her assistance for another three years. This entails a double gift, the gift of the sister on the mission as well as the gift of the sending community, who allowed her to go.

Cuba

Sr. Maria Rosaria, O.P., who is a native of Cuba, went from the monastery in Lufkin, Texas, to assist the nuns in Cuba for a period of time. The political situation in Cuba has not been conducive for religious life, and has necessitated the assistance of other monasteries.

Nuns who have assisted the Cuba monastery, include Sr. Carmen Yoland Sandoval of Columbia and Sr. Ofelia Perez of Mexico.

The Monasterio de Santa Catalina de Siena in Havana, Cuba was founded in 1689. It has continued without interruption for the 320 years of its existence. It began when five Cuban women wanted to live the Dominican monastic life. They asked permission of the Holy See and permission was granted. Since the Poor Clare Monastery was the only contemplative one in Cuba at the time, it provided for their monastic formation. At present there are seven nuns; two are Cubans and five are Mexicans.

A Michigan Mission Mosaic

From June of 2006 to May of 2009, Sr. Mary of the Savior of the Farmington Hills Monastery in Michigan was in southern India at the request of Fr. Master Carlos Azpiroz Costa, O.P. Sister's mission actually began in 1993, when she went to the Maria de Guadalupe Monastery in Nicaragua and resided there until 1996. The monastery was founded from Mexico, and the sisters were young and the only Dominican nuns in Central America.

Fr. Manuel Merten, O.P., Promoter of the nuns, became acquainted with Sr. Mary of the Savior's missionary interests while visiting nuns in the United States. In the name of Fr. Master Carlos, and at the request of the founding Cangas Monastery in Spain, Fr. Merten invited the Farmington Hills community to consider sending Sr. Mary of the Savior to the new foundation in India for at least three years. It was the first Dominican Monastery of nuns in India. After prayerful consideration, with the blessing of the prioress and community and with a warm welcome from the community in Spain, Sister accepted the request.

It was necessary that Sr. Mary of the Savior go first to the founding Monastery of the Incarnation in northern Spain (Cangas del Narcea). She lived Dominican life there for a total of five months, which she needed to do in order to fulfill India visa requirements. Sr. Mary of the Savior also introduced the community in Spain to English hymns and to the sung Divine Office as already in use in Kerala, India. The Indian sisters would eventually go to Spain to complete their formation there.

From Spain, Sister went to the Convent of Santa Maria in the State of Kerala, India, which is a formation house for young women in their first four or five years in the Order. Sister's task was to facilitate the reception and formation of English-speaking candidates, and assist the foundresses with translation needs. Sister's Spanish and English skills provided the help needed for the task.

Having taken the reader on an international tour of some Dominican monasteries, it is time to return to our West Springfield monastery so as to conclude our November celebration story. As you may recall, the theme was centered on the international family.

Mini Concert

Joy and gladness will be found in her, thanksgiving and the sound of singing. Is. 51:3 (NIV®)

Our mini concert had an international flavor to it. Verse two of "I Am Filled With Joy" was sung in French. This symbolized the first Monastery of Nuns, which began in Prouilhe, France. The "Irish Alleluia" signified the Monastery in Drogheda, Ireland. In keeping with monthly feasts, "Sing to the Lord of Harvest" was an expression of thanking God for all of his blessings to us in honor of Thanksgiving, a secular feast dear to Americans. "Be Exalted," accompanied by organ and guitars, was sung in praise of Christ the King, the ecclesial feast which culminates our liturgical year.

During November, we pray especially for the Holy Souls in Purgatory. Nuns all over the world are regularly asked to pray for the deceased members of family, friends and benefactors. Sr. Theresa Marie Gaudet, O.P. was our soloist and sang "Pie Jesu" (Loving Jesus). He is the "Agnus Dei" (Lamb of God) who takes away the sins of the world. Sister has such a beautiful voice and sings in such a way that many are moved by her singing.

(Endnotes)
1   Sister Maria Agnes, O.P. 41-44. Used with permission.

CHAPTER 25

Surprising Transitions

In our profession we promise obedience to the Master of the Order according to our Constitutions, and thus preserve the unity of the Order and of our profession which are dependent on our common obligations of obedience to one head. LCM 17. II

Brother Dominic, the First Master

In his home country of Spain, St. Dominic was a canon of St. Augustine when he accompanied Bishop Diego of Osma on a journey. That journey changed his life, when in Southern France he encountered an innkeeper who had been misled by errors. Dominic spent the whole night disputing with him, and when morning dawned, the innkeeper saw the light of truth. Southern France was plagued by errors and by those spreading them. Bishop Diego and Dominic joined with a band of Cistercian monks, whom the Pope had sent there for the purpose of preaching against the erroneous and immoral teachings. Eventually discouraged, the Cistercians gave up and went back to their monasteries. Dominic, however, continued preaching, while Bishop Diego went back to his diocese to obtain help for the mission. Diego died before he could rejoin Dominic.

Though now alone, Dominic continued preaching because of his great love for the salvation of souls. The fruits of his preaching were small and slow in coming, but little by little people were drawn to him. When a few of them asked to join him, Dominic asked them to pledge fellowship and obedience to him. They did. From that small beginnings grew the international Order of Preachers.

In documents we read of our founder being referred to as *Master Dominic*, but he designated himself as *Brother Dominic*. So likewise have a number of Master Generals, greeting us saying, *I am your brother, Timothy or Carlos*. They have held the authority of St. Dominic, but have acted in the spirit of brotherly service and humility.

Fr. Anicetus Fernandez, O.P.

In 1970, the Master of the Order, Fr. Anicetus Fernandez, O.P., established a commission of friars and nuns from all over the world. Participants would meet in Rome and work on bringing the Constitutions of the Nuns into line with the new Code of Canon Law and the needs of the times. The constitutions had not been reviewed since 1930. The Master requested Mother Mary of the Trinity of Menlo Park, CA, to work on this Commission, as she was fluent in Latin, Spanish, French and Italian. The other American nun on the Commission was Sr. Mary of the Eucharist, aka Sr. Lee of North Guilford. The commission's work produced a large, yellow, paperback book. At the General Chapter of the Order of Preachers at Tallaght, July 22, 1971, Fr. Anicetus Fernandez, O.P. said, "With great joy we present to you dearest sisters the completed new Constitutions." This happened on the feast of St. Mary Magdalen, a saint dear to the heart of all Dominicans, but more especially the nuns who, like Mary, listen to the words of the Lord.

Fr. Vincent de Couesnongle, O.P. and Fr. Damian Byrne, O.P.

In 1982, after the nuns had lived with the new text for some time, requests were made for some adjustments, and the Commission met again under Fr. Vincent de Couesnongle, who was then Master. Mother Mary of the Trinity again served on the commission and additional revisions were made. It was the work of that commission. Additional revisions were made, resulting in the present Book of Constitutions. In 1987, the book was "published by direction of Brother Damian Byrne, Master of the Order."

Fr. Timothy Radcliffe, O.P.

In 1992, Fr. Timothy Radcliffe, O.P. was elected Master of the Order. He wanted to meet with as many of the nuns as possible. The monasteries in Bronx, New York and Summit, New Jersey, provided hospitality. Fr. Timothy wanted to speak to the nuns but he also wanted very much to hear from them. He asked them how the brothers could be of better service in helping them. Fr. Timothy was the driving force behind the Vietnam and Langley foundations. He was instrumental in getting the priests and Dominican Fraternity enthused about the Vietnam foundation and decided on Vancouver as the place for the Canadian foundation, which later moved to Langley.

Fr. Carlos Azpiroz Costa, O.P.

We have already mentioned Fr. Carlos' retreat to the nuns in Adrian, Michigan. Previous to that event, he met with the US prioresses at one of their meetings. Fr. Carlos has been very supportive of the nuns and has written an introduction to the vocation book produced by the nuns, as well as to this current publication, for which we are most grateful.

Profession and the Master

In the Dominican tradition, the formula for profession mentions only the vow of obedience; poverty and chastity are understood as included. We promise obedience to God, dedicating ourselves to him, to the Blessed Virgin Mary, the Mother of our Order, to St. Dominic in fidelity to his spirit and mission. We also promise obedience to the successor of St. Dominic, the Master of the Order, and to the prioress of our monastery.

Solemn Vows

No one claimed that any of his possessions was his own, but they shared everything they had. Acts 4:32 (NIV®)

At the end of the eighteenth century, solemn vows became illegal because of the turmoil and unrest caused by the French Revolution. When monasteries were restored in the 19th century, it was still illegal and therefore not possible for the nuns to make solemn vows. Such was the case for all religious orders, even those in countries outside of France. When the French "second order" nuns and Perpetual Rosary Sisters began foundations in America, they professed "perpetual vows." Eventually, individual monasteries in the United States sought to restore the profession of solemn vows. The principal distinction between the two types of vows concerns property--- it is not that solemn vows are in a sense "superior vows," but it means that the professed religious in question disposes of all his/her property and that after profession, any income or inheritance goes to the monastery.

First American Monastery to pronounce Solemn Vows

The nuns of Corpus Christi Monastery, Menlo Park, were the first community of nuns in America to profess solemn vows. This was in response to the Indult published by the Holy See on June 23, 1923, which allowed nuns of religious orders originally possessing the privilege of solemn vows to re-assume that sacred obligation. As soon as the Indult came to the notice of Mother Mary of the Rosary, she took prompt measures to reclaim this age-old inheritance.

All the necessary communications were made with Rome under the sanction of his Excellency, Archbishop Hanna, D.D. The decree arrived from the Sacred Congregation of Religious, and on April 30th, 1929, the Feast of St. Catherine of Siena, His Excellency came to the Monastery to read the official papers to the nuns assembled at the grille. They had just completed their preparatory Retreat, which the Very Reverend Fr. Henry Ayrinhac, S.S., President of St. Patrick's Diocesan Seminary at Menlo Park, had conducted. It was under the guidance of Fr. Ayrinhac, revered for his piety as a priest and celebrated for his learning as a canonist, that the Prioress took the successive steps which brought them to this moment.

The Archbishop made a beautiful address to the nuns, congratulating them who, already bound as loving spouses of Christ, were happy to bind themselves still more closely by solemn vows. Mother Mary of the Rosary, as Prioress, then made her profession of solemn vows in the presence of His Excellency as reigning prelate of the diocese, after which each of the ten professed nuns of the community made solemn profession to their Prioress in the presence of the archbishop. The eventful ceremony closed with a full-hearted Te Deum.[1]

First Perpetual Rosary Monastery to make the Transition to Second Order[1]

Our Monastery in West Springfield was the first Perpetual Rosary Monastery to make the transition from the status of Third Order Cloister to that of Second Order monastery. It began in mid-1923, when the community voted to begin, with Bishop O'Leary's approval and encouragement, and a three-year trial period of observing the Second Order Constitutions along with the perpetual rosary obligations. At its conclusion, definite negotiations were begun with the Master General of the Order in Rome who, in turn, presented our petition to the Holy See. Bishop O'Leary sent his full support and endorsement with our petition. The decree, issued on November 26, 1928, by the Sacred Congregation for Religious

---

1   Term formerly used to designate nuns of the Order who follow the primitive observance.

authorizing the transition, arrived shortly before Christmas. It was an occasion of great joy and thanksgiving for the community of thirty-four members.

At that time, Pope Pius XI had expressed his willingness to grant or restore solemn vows to any community which could qualify. He himself granted our monastery this privilege, in addition to the one we had requested.

A delay of several months was required to allow for the further enlargement of the original building and to provide for the requirements of papal enclosure. Finally, all was in readiness, and the feast of St. Dominic, August 4, 1930, was selected as the date for the first solemn profession. Bishop O'Leary offered Mass in our chapel and then presided at the simple ceremony which followed. Mother Mary Hyacinth and the nine perpetually professed members of the community pronounced their solemn vows. A young temporarily professed sister named Sr. Mary Reginald, was close to death and was also allowed to make solemn profession.

A Word about the Summit Monastery

The Summit community received permission for solemn vows in 1923. However, they were delayed due to building needs which necessitated their leaving the enclosure to inspect the building process. In the meantime, their Bishop died. When the sisters attempted to follow through with solemn vows, they were surprised to find that the new Bishop was violently opposed to such. They had to wait patiently for years. After he died, they approached his successor, who eventually granted permission. Thus it was not until November 21, 1955, that the sisters pronounced their solemn vows.

The French Nuns and Solemn Vows

The French nuns were not able to pronounce solemn vows until the middle of the 20th century. Communities progressively made the appropriate requests and were granted permission to make solemn vows again. They organized ceremonies at which the whole community - or those who wished - would make vows together.

(Endnotes)
1   <u>Dominican Nuns in their Cloister</u> 284.

CHAPTER 26

The Surprising Finale

Praise the LORD from the earth, ... lightning and hail, snow and clouds, stormy winds that do his bidding, ... Ps. 148:7-8 (NIV®)

The Lord threw in a rescheduling surprise due to the inclement weather. There was no doubt about it, the prediction was certain, and although I can't remember the actual details, it was something along the lines of a nor'easter! We were not going to miss this one! So I had to contact as many people as I could via phone and email. We couldn't reschedule the celebration before Christmas, and so the date was set for January 6th, the actual closing date of the Jubilee Year! It was the liturgical feast of the Epiphany of the Lord, the day on which we recall the visit of the Magi to the Infant King. So it fit in perfectly for retaining our Christmas Pageant Guests!

The Nativity cast included some who came from afar! Such was "Mary" played by Marie Domina, who came from New Hampshire with her mother. "Joseph" was played by Jacob Broer, who was a student at St. Stanislaus School in Chicopee, MA.

With all the details for coordinating this closing event, I evidently generated some confusion. Of course, I could not provide costumes for the Nativity guests and had asked if some could bring their own. Since Marie was a homeschooler, she and her mother provided for Mary's robes. I thought that Jacob would get Joseph's from St. Stan's. So when the children were getting dressed for the service, Jacob's parents approached me and asked where Jacob's robes were. Dumbfounded I said, "Didn't you bring them?"

With 86 guests swarming around during the preparation time, it was a relief to have the adults pitch together to solve the problem. I did manage to contact Sr. Mary of the Sorrowful Heart and ask if she could find some cloth to help out. Two Shepherdesses, Joanne Granato and Giulia Verde, were from Mount Carmel Academy. The school principal, Carole Raffaele, gave permission for us to borrow the three shepherds costumes. Our Angel was Kristine Swierzewski and her Dad, Paul, assured me that he would see that she had her costume. Homeschoolers Vincent Bussolari, John Henle and Timothy Dowd were to be the kings. Because of the time crunch, we asked Mount Carmel if we could also borrow the kings costumes and again they graciously provided. Matthew Ransom was the third shepherd. Scout Master James Perkins took care of getting the children together for their practice session.

James Perkins:

While setting up for the manger portion, little things happened. It was a good situation for Divine Providence and for trusting in the Lord. While gathering up the kids, we came short of accessories for the costumes. We had to swap some of the kings props, robes and head pieces. I forget which sister was running around looking for items to help us out, but every time she came up with something, I had already remedied the situation. Some of the moms helped to fix things up. Suddenly, we noticed we were missing a king. Tim Dowd hadn't arrived yet. One father said that if we needed another boy, his son could fill in. I told him not to worry, that he would be here soon. While waiting for Tim, I brought the rest of the cast to the sanctuary so they would learn their spots. I then sat the kids down and ran back for Tim. Tim was having a costume malfunction. Tim, being pleasantly plump, didn't quite fit into it. I told him not to worry and to suck in that gut. He did and, with a smile on his face, proceeded to join the others. They did a great job posing. While leaving the chapel, John Henle, one of our kings, lost his crown due to a gust of wind. He grabbed it, recrowned himself and kept on moving. Kids adjust to any situation and keep on ticking.

The Nativity cast was seated in the front pew just in front of the Knights of Columbus. I'm told that at one point our "Angel" pulled her wing forward so she could look backward to see her Dad. Not only did white robed Kristine have golden angel wings, she also had a glorious silver halo hovering above her head.

Prior to the third joyful mystery of the rosary, the Nativity cast took their places. The angel was on the top step leading to the altar. From our vantage point on the other side of the grille, all we could see was her sparkling halo gracefully moving around. The Nativity cast offered a visual meditation for our guests as they prayed the third Joyful Mystery of the rosary, which was led by religious women. (Sr. Madeleine Joy, S.P. announced the mystery with its reflection).

Giulia Verde- Shepherdess

I am so glad that I could be a shepherd in the play. I learned that God is important and [that] Jesus is with us all the time. I am so happy that I was a part of such a beautiful day. Thank you for letting me share it with you.

Newly ordained Fr. James Longe was our guest officiant for this closing jubilee celebration. Father had come in June as a deacon, and was ordained a priest on November 3, 2007. Henry Sansouci served as Emcee, Valmore Hebert as incense bearer, Mark Ecker (father of SGT Mark Ecker II) as cross bearer and Michael Broer and Scott Lozyniak as acolytes.

For this closing celebration, we tried to invite guests who had been represented throughout the year from all walks of life. Some had come for earlier celebrations while others came who could not come before.

We were delighted again to have a Knights of Columbus Honor

Guard! Knowing how full their schedule is, I hoped to have the two Knights who first came for the opening celebration. We did. Sir Knight Joseph Babineau was the Commander in purple and Sir Knight Eugene Murphy, who had celebrated 50 years as a Knight during the year, was a member of the Honor Guard. Past Faithful Navigators were Sir Knight Delfo Barabani and Sir Knight Robert Boulay. Sir Knights Emery Filarsky, Roger Korell, John Smus and Charles Walton completed the Honor Guard.

The Rosary Led by those Serving our Country

Above all else, guard your heart, for it is the wellspring of life.
Prov. 4:23 (NIV®)

Our first joyful mystery of the rosary was led by those serving our country. Sr. Judy Rosenthal, S.S.J. who had served with the 104th Fighter Wing at Barnes Air National Guard before retiring after 20 years of service, introduced the mystery. This decade was prayed for all those who answered the call to serve our country and for the repose of the souls of those who gave their lives in doing so.

We were honored to have Capt Matthew Mutti, Wing Executive Officer of Barnes Air National Guard, as one of our honored guests as well as MSG Michael Cutone, SOD-G of the US Army Rhode Island National Guard.

Representing the Disabled American Vets, Chapter 11 was Robert Durocher. James "B.J." Hoar represented Voiture 862 40/8. The American Legion was represented by Charles Kovitch of Post 337. Also on the program was John Sasso of the WMass Korean Veteran Association Chapter 2000 and Lee Vance of American Legion 275 / DAV Chapter 11. James G. Berrelli, Jr. of the US Army, a Vietnam Veteran was unable to be present due to illness. He is Director of Veteran Services.

SR. JUDY ROSENTHAL, S.S.J.

**Language Guests and
Sgt. Michael Cutone**

**Firefighters and Police
Serving the Local Commu-**

Servers

Officiant

**Women Religious
Serving God and his People**

**Knights lead
procession**

Knights of Columbus

**Our Lady's
Messengers**

**Serving our country and
the local community**

Veterans

MSgt., USAF, Ret.

My introduction to the Dominican Nuns began many years before I entered the Sisters of St. Joseph. I attended the October Rosary Sunday Services at the monastery. I remember this service being held outside at the statue of Mary and St. Dominic near the parking lot area. I recall how peaceful it became as you left the very busy Riverdale Road and drove up the hill. It seemed like you entered into a little bit of heaven. You could feel the peaceful, holy atmosphere.

A few years went by when I was able to join a military unit in the local area. I worked in the medical section and on one occasion was taking care of an officer from a unit in Worcester. During our conversation, after he found out I was a sister, he told me he had a sister who was a Dominican Nun in West Springfield, MA. I wrote a letter to Sr. Mary of the Sorrowful Heart and told her about my meeting her brother, hence a long lasting friendship was born.

I worked in a parish, where Fr. Brian Boland talked about a sister whom he directed and knew from her high school days. Sr. Mary of the Sacred Heart entered religious life the same year as I did. On one of my visits to the monastery, I met her and another lasting friendship was formed. I feel it is a blessing to know these two sisters and I try to visit when it is possible. This monastery is a very special place, and how can God not answer their prayers for all of us.

When Sr. Mary of the Sacred Heart called and explained what she had planned to celebrate the nuns' 800th Anniversary of their founding, I told her this was a wonderful idea. The sisters could reach many people who probably didn't know much about the Dominicans, but would come to know them by their attendance and participation. I'm sure many who drive by their sign on Riverdale Road, don't know much about this community of women on the hill. Sister asked if I would be willing to participate in the month they were going to recognize those who serve by being in the military, and would

I represent them. I was thrilled and honored to be asked and said certainly. But as it was early spring, there was an ice storm and I wasn't able to attend, for which I was disappointed. I thought my chance to be a part of this celebration was over, when I received a call asking if I would be able to represent the military for the close of that year in the grand finale, where a representative from all the groups would be in the service to close this year. Needless to say, I was thrilled to be asked. I feel it was an honor to assist in this undertaking in this special place.

Sister worked very hard in getting everything together and all I heard were positive reactions from those who attended. As I look back, I am grateful to God for reconnecting me to this community of prayerful women in this holy house on the hill. I am grateful for the friendships I have been able to form with these wonderful women of God.

For the rosary we included an international flavor by having the Our Father of each decade prayed in a foreign language. Blandine Adjou prayed in French again touching our French roots of Prouilhe. Lia Addeo prayed in Italian. Lia came to my rescue on more than one occasion. When I discovered that our Spanish voice was missing, Lia recruited her niece to cover for us. Itsu Tada nearly prayed in Japanese to replace our German speaking voice, but with things so intense at preparation time, it was too much to coordinate. However, Toan Guyen was once again our faithful Vietnamese voice for the prayer.

Lia Addeo:

My niece teaches Spanish and she was here with her daughter, who was one of the shepherdesses. I went to ask her if she would do the Spanish "Our Father" for Sr. Mary and she loved it!

Patrizia Verde

My name is Patrizia Verde and I am Lia's niece. My daughter

Giulia and I participated in a beautiful ceremony for the 800th anniversary of the foundation of the Dominican Nuns. It was such a beautiful experience and I wanted to take a moment to officially thank you for letting us be a part of such a wonderful memory. That beautiful day will always live in our hearts.

Led by those Serving the Community

Each one should use whatever gift he has received to serve others, ...
1 Peter 4:10 (NIV®)

The Second Joyful Mystery was led by those serving the community. Police Officers included Lt. Steven Parentela of the South Hadley Police Department and Ofc. Robert Vogel, Jr. of West Springfield. Firefighters included Retired Firefighter Donald Bourcier of Wilbraham and Firefighter Robert Germano wearing Badge No. 1 from the West Springfield Fire Department. Those in health care serve the community too and Dr. & Mrs. Robert Donohue in Ophthalmology, Dr. David C. Momnie in Optometry and Rebecca Sawicki, P.T. represented the medical staff. Anne Sweetman, principal of St. Patrick's in Chicopee represented educators serving the community.

Lt. Steven Parentela
South Hadley Police Dept.

When I received a telephone call to be part of the 800th Anniversary of the founding of the Dominican Nuns, it felt special to be part of such a great event. For me, it has always been my honor to help serve the Dominican Nuns. In the mid 1980's, I was blessed to have become part of the buildings and grounds maintenance team that worked for the nuns. Over time, I eventually became the Head Buildings and Grounds Keeper who worked very closely with Sr. Mary of the Sacred Heart and Sr. Mary of the Precious Blood. During those few years just prior to becoming a full-time police officer, I learned the special meaning the monastery and the sisters' prayers had for me.

While working for the sisters, I saw small miracles happen day in and day out that some would call coincidence. However, after seeing firsthand the frequency of "coincidence," I truly believe there is something magical and holy in the prayers the Dominican Nuns hold for us every day.

One such "coincidence" came to my knowledge very shortly after taking the maintenance job with the Dominican Nuns. When my parents heard I took a job working for the nuns, I learned that my father had proposed to my mother in the new Chapel just prior to their marriage in 1959. Coincidence? I think not. Something that started in the Chapel came full circle when I came to work for the Dominican Nuns. It is one of the many "coincidences" that help me believe in the holy work being done within the monastery.

When I was told that we would be leading parts of the rosary during the Holy Hour, I recall being nervous about keeping the count on the Hail Mary's. However, by sharing the event with fellow police officers from various Police Departments in the area, I am happy to say, we got the count right. I think Sr. Mary of the Sacred Heart got a kick out of hearing how nervous I was about something so out of the ordinary from the duties I face at work each day. When I participated in the second Holy Hour, the nerves were rock solid, the count was again right and to this day I remember the sense of peace and happiness I had during my drives home from each Holy Hour.

I am truly blessed to have been asked to serve the Dominican Nuns in many ways. The Dominican Nuns of the Monastery of the Mother of God have my undying love and thankfulness for the prayers they offer for each and every one of us. To share in the 800th Anniversary Celebration was a privilege and my honor. God bless the Dominican Nuns.

Led by Religious Women Serving God's People

Because of the service by which you have proved yourselves, men
will praise God for the obedience that accompanies your confession
of the gospel of Christ, and for your generosity in sharing with them
and with everyone else. 2 Cor. 9:13 (NIV®)

The Third Joyful Mystery was led by Religious Women Serving God's People. Sr. Madeleine Joy, S.P., who serves in Pastoral Care at Mercy Hospital, introduced the mystery. Sr. Eleanor Dooley, S.S.J., a long time friend of our community, is an international lecturer and Professor Emeritus of the Elms College. Sr. Edith McAlice, S.S.J. is dearly loved by many and was among the Sisters of St. Joseph contingent. Sr. Marie Martin, S.S.J. has been a friend of the community from her earliest days and Sr. Jane Thomas, S.S.J. has been a long time friend too. Sr. Mary Janice, D. M. is the principal at St. Mary School in Ware, MA. Other Daughters of Mary listed in our program were Sr. Mary Clare, D.M., Sr. Mary Gloriosa, D.M., Sr. Mary Joseph, D.M. and Sr. Mary Philomena, D.M. Itsu Tada represented the Daughters of the Heart of Mary.

Led by Lay Leaders

We have different gifts, according to the grace given us....if it is
leadership, let him govern diligently... Rom. 12:6,8 (NIV®)

The Fourth Joyful Mystery was led by lay leaders. Assistant Cub Master James Perkins introduced the mystery. Included in this group was Joseph Lake, President of the Dominican Fraternity and Scoutmaster Ron Boissonneault. Robert Bonfitto speaks to groups about Our Lady and George Morrow teams up with him as "Juan Diego" in their Marian ministry of promoting devotion to Our Lady. "Juan Diego" wore his tilma for the celebration. Peggy Weber is a leader with her journalism gifts as she inspires many with her articles in the *Catholic Observer*. Her daughter Elizabeth too has leadership qualities and was responsible for recruiting students from Providence College the previous January. Mary Hickson, a member of the Dominican Fraternity, certainly led the way for me in contacting so many guests through the year. It made my challenging job a lot easier. George Beauregard, a cousin of Sr. Mary of the Nativity, and his wife Doris were also pleased to join us. Roberta Page, a cousin, is very active in community service programs.

Led by Those Making a Difference

There are different kinds of working, but the same God works all of them in all men. 1 Cor. 12:6 (NIV®)

There were many people who could have been in our Fifth Joyful Mystery. We called this group "People Making a Difference." Yes, each one makes a difference in his or her own way, using the gifts God has bestowed on them. Joshua Perkins of Troop 32 does this as a Boy Scout and Zachary O'Connor of Pack 15 as a Cub Scout. MagicAl Sawicki touches hearts with fun and laughter and leads them to a deeper love for God and Our Blessed Mother. Richard Butler has repaired many statues for various churches as well as for our community. Those touching the lives of family, friends, neighbors, the Dominican Nuns and so many others included Dave and Andrea Broer, Bruce and Maureen Smith, Paul Swierzewski and his family, Judith Deshaies, Edward Napolski and the Seavers.

REGINA AND ARTHUR LOURENCO:
It started with a simple telephone call inviting us to the first monthly celebration or the 800th Anniversary of the Dominican Nuns and it ended with a year full of excitement.

At SonRises we tried to co-ordinate efforts for the sisters. These included soldiers – state troopers, homeschoolers, statue refinishers and general public relations plus our own

Lay Leaders

"Mary" & her Mother

Scott' Lozyniak

Sgt. Michael Cutone

The Webers

Joshua Perkins
Zachary O'Connor

The Sawickis

Scouts

The Smiths

The Broers

The Dowds

The Seavers

The Nativity Cast

Sisters of St. Joseph
and the Donohues

appearances as Catholic Retailers and CCD Teachers. It is just one more outreach by our Dominican Nuns to enter and remain in our lives.

I wanted to invite as honored guests the scouts who so graciously helped us out in April when we had the inclement weather, so I had Robert Embury listed as representing that group of scouts. Sometimes good plans do not always materialize and unexpected sickness prevented Robert's driver from bringing him. However, we want to take a few words here to express our gratitude to Robert and his fellow scouts for being such a special part of our celebration. Leader Ron Boissonneault and Alex Parker, as well as Matt and Jacques Lafleur of Troop 303 of South Hadley will not be forgotten.

Nor will Leader Michele Kapper and scouts Josh Carpenter and Tyler and Nick Kapper of Troop 424 of Chicopee. We thank you for "making a difference!"

Mini Concert

Sing to the LORD a new song, his praise in the assembly of the saints….For the LORD takes delight in his people…
Ps. 149:1,4 (NIV®)

Our mini concert centered on the Christmas Epiphany theme with a Dominican orientation. Everyone is familiar with the light of the star leading the Magi to the Infant King. However, people may not be familiar with St. Dominic being called "Light of the Church." He is called this not only because he preached the light of truth, but because a star was seen on his brow at his baptism. That is the reason you see statues and pictures of St. Dominic portrayed with a star on his forehead. And so our concert began with the Gregorian Chant antiphon "O Lumen" (O Light), a hymn we sing every night to end our liturgical night prayer.

"Cry Out With Joy and Gladness" was sung to demonstrate the ministry of the nuns in praying that the Gospel proclamation be fruitful.

That was our ministry from the beginning - giving prayerful support to our preaching brothers. Sr. Mary Hyacinth Denmark, O.P. played the chime tree, which added a little extra flourish, while Sr. Mary of the Immaculate Heart Boudreau, O.P. and I accompanied it with guitars The song was written by James V. Marchionda, O.P., one of our Dominican friars.

"Born is Jesus" is a French Christmas carol we sang because it touches home with our foundation roots of Prouilhe. We made this month's concert extra special by adding various musical instruments, and I played a soprano recorder during an interlude on this piece.

Devotion to Mary is a strong characteristic of Dominicans, so we showed our love and devotion to her by singing "Hail Holy Queen." She is addressed as the "Mother of Mercy," and "mercy" is a very strong theme dear to Dominicans. St. Dominic used to address God saying, "My Mercy, what will become of sinners?" It is a reminder of our early days in formation, when at the beginning of each stage of our spiritual journey, we prostrated before the community and were asked the question, "What do you ask?" Our everlasting response, "God's mercy and yours."

Each month our mini concert was designed to build to a climax with a solo by Sr. Theresa Marie Gaudet, O.P. For this grand finale Sister sang "O Holy Night." The star-filled night reminds us of the star on Dominic's brow at his baptism. It also reminds us of St. Paul's exhortation for us to shine in the world like bright stars because we are offering it the word of life (Phil. 2:15). Sr. Mary Regina Thomas, O.P. played the organ for this piece and throughout the service. Her talents on the keyboard bring us tremendous blessings!

Peggy Weber:

Our family attended several of the anniversary holy hours. Elizabeth, a junior at Providence College, represented her Dominican-run school in January of 2007. My husband, John and I were there as well. In March, my daughter, Kerry, 26, who was an associate editor at *Catholic Digest*, at the time, and myself came as communicators. I am a reporter and producer for the *Catholic Communications Corporation* for the Diocese of Springfield. In June, I, my daughters, and my son, Matthew, 25, watched John pray the rosary as part of a group of fathers. This was my favorite holy hour because our whole family was together in prayer and we got a chance to acknowledge John, who is such a good and faithful man – and an awesome Dad.

I attended the July holy hour that recognized patriots and was impressed with an injured Iraq War veteran who carried the cross in the procession. I was reporting on this event and got a chance to interview so many people who were touched by the holy hours. Many had never been to the monastery so I thought that this year-long celebration had touched the lives of so many people in such a positive way. I heard people comment on how "real" and how much "fun" these nuns were. I just smiled knowingly, because I have been around the good Dominican Nuns since I was an infant.

My mother was friends with many of them when they lived in Springfield and used to go door-to-door to people and collect egg and butter money for the nuns. We visited Sr. Mary John Dominic as a family and brought our small babies to see her, and later Sr. Mary of the Sacred Heart and Sr. Mary of the Sorrowful Heart. To this day, we enjoy going to the monastery to be connected to the powerhouse of prayer and these good and kind women.

I attended the closing holy hour in January of 2008, with my daughter Elizabeth. It was nice for her to be there because she is such a student of the rich Dominican tradition. And I was glad to see all of the hard work and 800 Year Anniversary celebrated in such a wonderful way. I appreciated the warmth I felt on each visit.

I loved the cookies that were served. But most importantly, I was glad that so many people got a chance to encounter the good women up on the hill. I hope they keep their hearts and doors open to the people who admire them and need them.

CHAPTER 27

Surprising Rebirth

For the LORD will rebuild Zion and appear in his glory.
Ps. 102:16 (NIV®)

During the French Revolution, the nuns of Prouilhe were dispersed and their monastery was totally destroyed with not one stone left upon another. There is only one fragment of stone that remains from the original monastery (it bears the image of the risen Lamb on it). The large stones from the monastery had been taken away, some used for local farmhouses, others for streets. The rioters went so far as to tear down the line of trees leading to the monastery, so that there would be nothing to mark even the place where the monastery once had been. But in time, God miraculously designed that the monastery's original location be made known.

From Destruction to Construction

In Chapter 11, we mentioned Pere Lacordaire, the friar who was instrumental in restoring the Order to France. He wanted to build a small commemorative oratory at Prouilhe, the cradle of the Order. But as things developed, there were many providential elements bordering on the miraculous which contributed to the monastery's restoration.

Viscountess Jurien

The Lady Viscountess Jurien, a very wealthy woman, has been described as "a curious and amazing person." While in Rome, she met Camille Lemoine, who had once been a novice at the monastery in Nay. Camille spoke to her incessantly of the restoration of Prouilhe. A month later Madame Jurien attended a Mass offered by Lacordaire and afterwards spoke to Etienne Cartier, who had served the Mass. He spoke to her of Prouilhe, as he was about to go there on business regarding the commemorative chapel that Lacordaire planned to build. In Madame Jurien's account of her first visit to Prouilhe, she relates that she heard an inner voice forcing her to kneel down there in an empty field where the monastery had stood, and telling her that she was to restore it. So Madame Jurien decided to purchase the land with that inner command in mind. She gave Lacordaire the power of attorney to acquire the land in her name. The deed of sale was signed on December 27, 1855. It was the anniversary day when St. Dominic took possession of the monastery at Prouilhe in 1206. On September 4, 1856, an expiatory Mass was celebrated in reparation for the crimes and outrages of the Revolution. Mgr. de la Bouillerie, the Bishop of Carcassonne, presided.

In June 1857, the plans of the future monastery were already drawn up, and the foundation stone blessed and laid on May 31st by the parish priest of Fanjeaux. In that same year on August 4th, there was another ceremony for the blessing of the foundation stone for a large church. In November of 1858, Lacordaire wrote the prioress of Nay that "the monastery of Prouilhe is growing as you watch it." In 1863, the shell of the monastery was just about completed, but none of the interior finishing was done; the magnificent crypt was built, but there was no church above it. At this point Madame Jurien's fortune collapsed. She then decided that Prouilhe should be "a work of universal charity" and an appeal was launched.

During the 1870s, many people approached Madame Jurien and attempted to persuade her to hand the monastery at Prouilhe over to them. Mgr. de la Bouillerie, Bishop of Carcassonne, could not see it as anything other than the contemplative monastery founded by St. Dominic himself. Meanwhile, the building work grounded to a halt and the cloister became overgrown with brambles. Madame Jurien wrote in her memoir for the Bishop of Carcassonne, "The monastery is built, but not completed, and awaits God's good pleasure!" Suddenly, on August 11, 1878, Madame Jurien died at the age of sixty-six.

The Provincial and the Prouilhe Proposal

At the time of Madame Jurien's death, Fr. Hyacinthe-Marie Cormier, O.P. was the Dominican provincial of Toulouse. He had directed a number of women to the monastery of Nay in France and had been planning a foundation of nuns at Aix-en-Provence. Nay had been founded from Prouilhe and with the death of Madame Jurien, Fr. Cormier asked the prioress if she would consider making the foundation at Prouilhe instead of Aix. It would entail assuming responsibility for the buildings and the outstanding debts. Since Madame Jurien's will was far from clear, on March 9, 1879, the civil tribunal at Castelnaudary determined that the property of Madame Jurien situated at Prouilhe was to be sold at auction. A descendant of the Chabert family, who had originally sold the land to Madame Jurien twenty-five years previously, offered to help the sisters of Nay financially, to prevent this holy place from falling into the hands of strangers. The sale was fixed for July 11, 1879, and the sisters of Nay remained in suspense. They were not at the auction and did not know if the civil authorities of the Aude County would raise objections to the property being acquired by a religious community. They were represented by a young lawyer from Castelnaudary, and indeed the lot comprising the land and buildings at Prouilhe fell to the nuns for 60,000 Francs.

In March of 1880, Fr. Cormier went to Nay accompanied by Mgr. Ducellier, Bishop of Bayonne, to select the candidates for the foundation. Besides the prioress, Mother Agnes de l'Enfant Jesus, they chose six choir sisters and two lay sisters.

Work had been underway to render the buildings habitable, as they had been abandoned for the last fifteen years. Things moved quickly and ten months after the auction sale, the nine sisters from Nay were able to move in and take possession. Although no public announcement had been made, nevertheless a small crowd had gathered to welcome the nuns. Mother Agnes wrote, "There was no mistaking the joy occasioned by our return." Fr. Cormier was there as well and celebrated a Mass in the small temporary church on April 29th. The sisters organized an "open house" of the cloister. Crowds of people flocked from all sides, including ancestors of nuns who had been dispersed because of the Revolution. The first postulant was admitted to the 'new Prouilhe' on May 19, 1880, less than three weeks later. When Fr. Larroca, the Master of the Order, visited on July 27, 1886, there were twenty-six sisters in community, their numbers had tripled in six years.

Building a Basilica

When Madame Jurien had installed her domestic chapel alongside the old guest house quarters, pilgrims once again came to Prouilhe, the site of a traditional Marian shrine. When an encyclical by Pope Leo XIII came out encouraging devotion to Our Lady of the Rosary, Mgr. Billard, Bishop of Carcassonne, convened his clergy and inaugurated what was to become the Rosary Pilgrimages at Prouilhe. The crowds sometimes reached as many as fifteen thousand pilgrims and the events called for a suitable church. When in October of 1885, a Dominican expressed the desire to see a magnificent church built in honor of the Virgin Mary above the crypt that already existed, Mgr. Billard welcomed the idea and immediately launched an appeal. The Bishop blessed the foundation stone on July 22, 1886, with three thousand people in attendance. Many problems, including bad workmanship and insufficient funding, retarded progress on the building. The following year Fr. Larroca, the Master of the Order, visited Prouilhe and wrote a moving letter to all Dominicans, inviting them to contribute to the construction of the basilica. Gifts flowed in from many countries and construction was resumed in April of 1890 under a new architect, Edward Florent, who adopted a more modest plan. Available resources made it possible to build the basilica up to one third of its intended height, but its proportions were not the most harmonious. Mr. Florent explained that the limited space available between the monastery proper and the guesthouse had dictated the design, so as to maximize the space available inside for large gatherings of the faithful. By 1898 hope was waning, and questions arose as to whether it would ever be finished.

Other difficulties arose in 1901, when religious congregations were outlawed by the political situation, and the work was brought to a halt. Pilgrimages of large numbers of people were not encouraged either, and, almost as a last straw, Mgr. Billard died suddenly. Progress was stopped again in 1914, and the construction was never completed as envisaged in the architect's plans. The monastic community of Prouilhe found themselves with a half-finished basilica on their hands, and deserted by mass religious tourism.

Adaptations continued at a snail's pace, and in 1926, a temporary roof was put in place to keep the rain out. In 1968, thermal insulation of the choir and sanctuary solved some heating problems, but produced a clash of styles within the basilica. In 1986-1987, an appeal was made and the response was such that the sisters were able to have the basilica properly roofed and proper down-pipes installed.

Tragedy struck again in 1990, when a serious fire burnt down the monastery itself and made it impossible to continue with work on the basilica, which went undamaged. The monastery was uninhabitable, and for several years the heavily burdened nuns had to live as best they could in the external guesthouse.

In 2003, a project was launched to rethink the whole of the unfinished basilica area, from the crypt to the dome, in order to restore light, height and dignity. In this way pilgrims would be welcomed in a space where prayer, beauty and functionality were combined, and the basilica would be able to take on its liturgical vocation.

The reader can see the immensity of the project by visiting the website page showing restoration progress today (http://www.prouilhe.

com/travauxeng.htm). Towards the bottom of the page are links where additional pictures of the work can be seen in slideshow format. One can see the removal of false partitions (cement) and all that it involves. Eventually stained glass windows will bring in light through currently bricked up windows.[1] At this point in the writing of this book, work on the basilica has been stopped due to various circumstances. We hope that someday it will recommence and come to completion.

Due to a lack of vocations, the monastery today is an international monastery. Nuns from different parts of the world come to Prouilhe for a three year period so as to preserve Dominican life in this cradle of the Order.

The nuns are grateful to all who help in any way in the restoration of their beginnings. At Prouilhe, the Eucharist is celebrated on the first Saturday of every month for benefactors.

(Endnotes)
1   Beaumont, o.p., Sr. Barbara, Fr. Elie Pascal Epinoux, o.p. and Sr. Marie de Jesus, o.p., "Sainte-Marie de Prouilhe 1206-2006", (Germany, Editions du Signe:2006) 42-49, 56-60.

CHAPTER 28

A Closing Word of Surprise

Surely you have granted him eternal blessings and made him glad
with the joy of your presence. Ps. 21:6 (NIV®)

.

On January 8, 2008, the feast of the Epiphany of the Lord, the 800th Anniversary Jubilee Year of the Nuns came to a close and with it ended the special privilege of the plenary indulgence. There were many blessings during the celebratory year and we pray that the blessings continue. Although the plenary indulgence is no longer available, there are other means for the faithful to obtain a plenary indulgence, such as praying the litany of the Sacred Heart of Jesus for one month, together with the sacrament of reconciliation and the reception of Holy Communion as well as prayers for the Holy Father.

A Surprise Reconciliation

First go and be reconciled to your brother... Mt. 5:24 (NIV®)

Reconciliation with God and one's neighbor is a gospel precept, not an option. If we ask the Lord to help us make it happen, it will. We can experience inner peace, healing and freedom. The God of surprises will amaze us with blessings, if only we give him a chance. It was no chance happening when at one of our monthly celebrations, I am told, two individuals approached the chapel entrance from different directions. Both of them were looking downwards and unaware of the other's presence until they were practically face to face. Then both looked up and their eyes met. The two had been estranged for years and at that moment, one reached out asking for forgiveness.

Surprising Strength

> *But the Lord is faithful, and he will strengthen*
> *and protect you from the evil one. 2 Thess. 3:3 (NIV®)*

In our daily struggles and challenges, we need divine assistance to deal with those challenges. The Lord will provide for our needs. He gives us the opportunity to receive him in Holy Communion every day. Taking time to pray each day is a way of reaching out for his help. Each person needs to decide what opportunities best suit his/her situation to grow in holiness of life. If we ask the Lord to show us and help us, he will, and so will Our Lady.

A Surprise for Our Mother

Then to the disciple he (Jesus) said, "This is your mother". And from
that moment the disciple made a place for her in his home.
Jn. 19:26-27 (JB)

Speaking of Our Lady, I cannot help but mention how wonderful it is to have devotion to her. She obtains so many blessings for us from her divine Son. I am grateful to my own mother for fostering my love and devotion to Our Lady. I recall my mother showing me how to make a shrine for Our Lady for the month of May. We covered a shoe box with crepe paper, then decorated it, each year a different way. The box, transformed into a shrine, was stood on end and Our Lady's statue was placed inside. Small flowers, such as pansies, were placed in a small vase in front of the shrine. This exercise together with the example of my mother sitting in her chair and praying the rosary, influenced my devotion to Our Lady, which grew as I did.

A Surprising and Delightful Story

I cannot help but share a surprising story from one of the expectant parents, represented in proxy by the unborn baby's aunt and uncle, at our very first celebration service (See Chapter 2). The baby's parents prayed the rosary for their baby during the time of pregnancy.

ANGELA BROER:

I have a tape of the rosary, and the priest leading the rosary sings a short "Ave Maria" tune between each decade. Benjamin loves this part. He will stop whatever he is doing and look right at the TV and intently listen. On Dec 7th, he began saying "Ave Maria." It sounds so sweet. When we went to Mass on Dec 8th, he was ready to go! During the first song, "Immaculate Mary," he sang his own version of "Ave Maria!" all the way through the song. He also said "Ave Maria" several times during the Mass. It really made Chris and me smile.

Benjamin and I went to the grocery store. He was sitting in the front of the shopping cart and I was putting groceries in the trunk of the car, and he very enthusiastically said, "Sing Ave Maria!" So I sang the tune, and then he said, "Again!" His energetic "again"s have made me think about prayer. If anyone questions repetitive prayers, they just need to spend some time around children. They love saying prayers over and over again!

Our Song to Mary

A great and wondrous sign appeared in heaven:
a woman clothed with the sun, with the moon under her feet
and a crown of twelve stars on her head. Rev. 12:1 (NIV®)

We Dominicans have a special devotion to Our Lady, sparked by Mary herself. Our day closes with Compline, the liturgical night prayer. At the end of Compline we sing the antiphon *Salve Regina* (Hail, Holy Queen) as we process to Our Lady's shrine and are blessed with holy water. St. Dominic had an apparition of Mary in which he saw her in the dormitory sprinkling each of the brethren with holy water and making the sign of the cross over them. Prior to that apparition, the *Salve* was simply recited after Compline. In the apparition, Mary had identified herself saying, "I am she whom you invoke every evening, and when you say *Eia ergo advocate nostra* (turn then, our advocate), I prostrate before my Son for the preservation of this Order." Consequently, the *Salve* began to be sung and continues to this day. In this antiphon we ask this sweet and loving Mother to turn her "eyes of mercy" towards us.

Not only do we entrust ourselves to Our Lady at the end of each day, but we also have a tradition of turning to this Mother of Mercy as each brother or sister approaches the end of his/her life on this earth. The community gathers around the bed of the dying brother or sister and sings the *Salve*, entrusting our dear one to her loving care and powerful intercession.

Hail, Holy Queen, Mother of Mercy, our life our sweetness and our hope. To thee do we cry, poor banished children of Eve. To thee do we send up our sighs, mourning and weeping in this valley of tears. Turn then, most gracious advocate, thine eyes of mercy towards us. And after this our exile, show unto us the blessed Fruit of thy womb, Jesus. O clement, O loving, O sweet Virgin Mary.

Memorial Epilogue

Alexander Harshuk
September 4, 1927 - August 12, 2008

Sr. Maureen Magdalen Nelligan, O.P.
d. Nov. 14, 2008

SGT Mark Ecker II
November 7, 1985 - July 10, 2009

Ofc. Michael J. Vezzola
April 7, 1955 - November 5, 2009

Sr. Mary of the Assumption Matthews, O.P.
November 19, 1926 - October 16, 2009

Alexander "Alex" Harshuk was a faithful server at the monastery.

Sr. Maureen Magdalen was in education for many years both as a Sister of St. Joseph and a laywoman before entering the monastery. She encouraged her young student authors and had classroom publications. She was always secretive about her age and we will respect that.

Passenger **SGT Mark Ecker II** was killed in an automobile accident on July 10, 2009. His passing was a tragic loss to his family and to local residents who took him into their hearts and who supported him throughout his recovery after losing both his legs in Iraq.

After a brief illness **Ofc. Michael J. Vezzola** went to his eternal reward. He almost always had a smile on his face and was very much respected and loved by the local community. Having known him through repeated encounters during the Jubilee year, Mike was as a brother.

Sr. Mary of the Assumption Matthews, O.P. was a member of our community. She was a gracious woman from West Virginia and always had a great appreciation for things literary. She wrote poetry and on many occasions assisted sisters with articles for publication.

Please pray for these dear ones in Christ.

Eternal rest grant unto them,
O Lord, and let perpetual light shine upon them.

May they rest in peace. Amen.

U.S Monasteries of Nuns

Alabama

Monastery of St. Jude
PO Box 170
Marbury, AL 36051-0170
Ph. (205) 755-1322
Fax (205) 755-9847
Email: opstjude@aol.com

California

Monastery of the Angels
1977 Carmen Ave
Los Angeles, CA 90068-4098
Ph. (323) 466-2186
Fax (323) 466-6645
Email: monastery_angels@att.net

Corpus Christi Monastery
215 Oak Grove Ave
Menlo Park, CA 94025-3272
Ph. (650) 322-1801

Fax (650) 322-6816
Email: nunsmenlo@comcast.net

Connecticut

Monastery of Our Lady of Grace
11 Race Hill Rd
Guilford, CT 06437-1099
Ph. (203) 457-0599
Fax (203) 457-1248

Delaware

Caterina Benincasa Monastery
6 Church Dr
New Castle, DE 19720-1211
Ph. (302) 654-1206

Massachusetts

Monastery of the Mother of God
1430 Riverdale St
West Springfield, MA 01089-4698
Ph. (413) 736-3639
Fax (413) 736-0850
Email: monasteryws@comcast.net

Michigan

Monastery of the Blessed Sacrament
29575 Middlebelt Rd
Farmington Hills, MI 48334-2311
Ph. (248) 626-8321

Fax (248) 626-8724
Email: opnunsfh@sbcglobal.net

New Jersey

Monastery of the Perpetual Rosary
1500 Haddon Ave
Camden, NJ 08103-3112
Ph. (856) 342-8340
Email: sisters1500@netzero.com

Monastery of Our Lady of the Rosary
543 Springfield Ave
Summit, NJ 07901-4498
Ph. (908) 273-1228
Fax (908) 273-6511
Email: nunsopsummit@op.org

New York

Corpus Christi Monastery
1230 Lafayette Ave
Bronx, NY 10474-5399
Ph. (718) 328-6996
Fax (718) 328-1974

Monastery of Our Lady of the Rosary
335 Doat St
Buffalo, NY 14211-2199
Ph. (716) 892-0066
Fax (716) 892-8846
Email: monasteryvoc@opnuns.org

Monastery of Mary the Queen
1310 W Church St
Elmira, NY 14905-1998
Ph. (607) 734-9506
Fax (607) 734-1452
Email: maryqueenop@gmail.com

Monastery of the Perpetual Rosary
802 Court St
Syracuse, NY 13208-1766
Ph. (315) 471-6762
Email: violetbop@juno.com

Pennsylvania

Monastery of the Immaculate Heart of Mary
1834 Lititz Pike
Lancaster, PA 17601-6585
Ph. (717) 569-2104
Fax (717) 569-1598
Email: monlanc@alo.com

Texas

Monastery of the Infant Jesus
1501 Lotus Ln
Lufkin, TX 75904-2699
Ph. (936) 634-4233
Fax (936) 634-2156
Email: mijtx@suddenlink.net

Virginia

Saint Dominic's Monastery
2636 Monastery Rd
Linden, VA 22642-5371
Ph. (540) 635-3259
Fax (540) 635-5086
Email: lindenopnuns@aol.com

Other Monasteries

CANADA
Queen of Peace Monastery
9383 222ND St
Langley, BC VIM 3T7
Ph. (604) 513-3665
Fax (604) 513-3932
Email: peacenun@shaw.ca

Monastere Notre-Dame Du Rosaire*
1140 Rue Frontenac
Berthierville, QC CANADA J0K 1A0
Fax (450) 836-1850
Email: michelineop@monialesdominicaines.qc.ca
*French speaking

WEST INDIES
Rosary Monastery
St. Ann's Rd, Port of Spain
Trinidad, West Indies
Ph. (868) 624-7648
Fax (868) 631-2138
Email: rm1930@tstt.net.tt

Perpetual Rosary Monastery

WISCONSIN
Dominican Sisters of the Perpetual Rosary
217 North 68th Street
Milwaukee, Wisconsin 53213-3928
Ph. (414) 258-0579

Bibliography

Aloysius of Jesus, O.P., Mother Mary. <u>History of the Dominican Sisters of the Perpetual Rosary</u>. Patterson, NJ: n.p., 1959.

Ashley, Benedict. T*he Dominicans.* The Liturgical Press. 1990 (see http://op.org/international/english/History/preacher.htm

Assumpta, O.P., Sister Mary. "Master General's Retreat." <u>Association Sharings</u> 26.2 Fall 2006.

Drane, Augusta Theodosia. <u>The History of St. Dominic</u>. London & New York: Longmans, Green, and Co., 1891.

Fox, O.P., Sr. Mary Joseph. "One Giant Leap." <u>Conference Communications</u> Special Issue 1982: 9-12.

Mary of God, O.P., Sister. "Report on Term 1988 – 1992." <u>Conference Communications</u> 12.2 Fall 1992 33-36.

Mary of God, O.P., Sister. "The President's Message." <u>Conference Communications</u> 8.4 Dec. 1988: 1-5.

Maura, O.P., Sister. "Menlo." <u>Conference Communications</u> 8.4 Dec. 1988: 23.

"Report on Meeting of Infirmarians." <u>Conference Communications</u> 11.2 Oct. 1991: 12-13.

Nun, Menlo Park. "Menlo Park: Retreat Reflections." <u>Association Sharings</u> 26.2 (2006): 38.

Pia, O.P., Sr. Mary. "Master's Retreat, Adrian Michigan – 2006." <u>Association Sharings </u>Fall 2006: 31.

Marie of Jesus, O.P., Sister Dominic. "Some Reflections on the West Springfield Meeting." <u>Conference Communications</u> Special Issue 1982: 13-14.

The Dominican Nuns In Their Cloister, trans. The Dominican Nuns of Corpus Christi Monastery Menlo Park, California. Philadelphia: The Dolphin Press, 1936) 4.

Vicaire, O.P.,M.-H. Saint Dominic and His Times, trans. by Kathleen Pond. New York: Darton, Longman & Todd Ltd, 1964.

INDEX

List of Illustrations